Love & Marriage

IN EARLY AFRICAN AMERICA

Other titles in

THE NORTHEASTERN LIBRARY OF BLACK LITERATURE

edited by Richard Yarborough

For a complete list of books that are available in the series, visit www.upne.com.

Love & Marriage

IN EARLY AFRICAN AMERICA

FRANCES SMITH FOSTER, *Editor*

NORTHEASTERN UNIVERSITY PRESS *Boston*

Published by UNIVERSITY PRESS OF NEW ENGLAND

Hanover and London

Northeastern University Press
Published by University Press of New England,
One Court Street, Lebanon, NH 03766
www.upne.com
© 2008 by Northeastern University Press
Printed in the United States of America
5 4 3 2 1

Library of Congress Cataloging-in-Publication Data
Love and marriage in early African America / Frances Smith Foster, editor.
    p. cm. — (Northeastern library of Black literature)
An anthology of nineteenth and early twentieth century African American
writings (stories, songs, poems, sayings, sermons, etc) on love, courtship,
and family.
ISBN-13: 978-1-55553-676-3 (cloth : alk. paper)
ISBN-10: 1-55553-676-x (cloth : alk. paper)
ISBN-13: 978-1-55553-677-0 (pbk. : alk. paper)
ISBN-10: 1-55553-677-8 (pbk. : alk. paper)
1. American literature—African American authors.
2. African Americans—Literary collections. 3. Love—Literary collections.
4. Marriage—Literary collections. I. Foster, Frances Smith.
PS508.N3L68 2007
810.803543—dc22   2007014751

CONTENTS

ILLUSTRATIONS

My Cherished Hope, my Fondest Dream.

WRITTEN, COMPOSED AND ARRANGED FOR THE PIANO-FORTE,

AND MOST RESPECTFULLY DEDICATED TO

MISS SARAH MATILDA CORNISH.

By A. J. R. CONNOR.

My cherished hope, ... my fond-est dream, . . . Still, dearest, rest . . . . on thee, A blank with-out . . . . . thee, all would

INTRODUCTION

BY WAY OF AN OPEN LETTER TO MY SISTER

Dear Cle,

Here it is! This is the collection of some of the stories, songs, poems, sayings, sermons, and other writings we found during our archival expeditions. You said, "Hey, this stuff is interesting. I bet lots of people would like to read it. You ought to make a book of it." Well, here's the book. I hope it's what you had in mind. I decided to focus on love and marriage from the beginnings of our print culture until just before the Harlem Renaissance because so many people believe that slavery destroyed our interest in and abilities to sustain intimate relationships. But, that's clearly not the case. Cle, I hope you are right. I hope people hear about this book, buy it, and read it with surprise and recognition and pleasure. And most of all, I hope they'll be impressed enough to read more of the writings left by our ancestors about their ideals, their dreams, and their aspirations.

Do you remember how this project got started? I was researching the life and writings of Frances E. W. Harper for the book I edited called *A Brighter Coming Day: A Frances E. W. Harper Reader.* I discovered that Harper had published in a lot of newspapers and magazines and that many of them were papers by African Americans, for African Americans. I was surprised to learn that, long before slavery ended, we had so many periodicals; that, in fact, there were many published documents and that even before there was a United States of America, there were people of African ancestry living in North America, reading about and writing for one another. I had assumed that before the Civil War, we had only token literature. Especially in the South, where most people of African ancestry lived, few people, black, white, or red could read and write. So, it made sense to think of black authors as what June Jordan called "difficult miracles." Their writings, I thought, were basically evangelical Christian stuff or anti-slavery narratives. I took it that Phillis Wheatley's poem, "On Being Brought from Africa to America," was typical. Phillis was just a little bit sassy when she wrote:

> Remember, *Christians, Negroes,* black as *Cain,*
> May be refin'd and join th' angelic train.[1]

But, that poem, like most in her book, *Poems on Various Subjects, Religious and Moral,* seemed directed more to white people than to black people.

Then I read letters from Phillis Wheatley to Obour Tanner, an African woman enslaved in Newport, Rhode Island. I saw more of Phillis's personality and learned more of her personal life and opinions. I discovered that she was a pen pal with Native American writer Samson Occom, that her love of fashionable clothes concerned both Susanna Wheatley and John Thornton, and that she was not happy being enslaved. (You know what's kind of weird? Most anthologies still don't include Wheatley's sassy poems and letters.) But until I read her letters—especially the one to Tanner wherein, as Julian D. Mason, Jr., pointed out, she seems to be referring to John Peters, the man she later married—I had not paid much attention to the curious exchange of poems between her and two military officers in Mason's 1989 collection of her writings. Cle, Phillis Wheatley was a flirt! Wheatley wrote a poem to "Rochford," an officer of the British navy, that says

> Struck with thy song, each vain conceit resign'd
> A soft affection seiz'd my grateful mind,
> While I each golden sentiment admire
> In thee, the muse's bright celestial fire.[2]

Wheatley's letters made me realize that even though enslaved (and maybe most of it was only in her imagination), she did have a love life. Then I started to remember how often in her poems her "bosom burns," she has "intrinsic ardor," and her *"Fancy"* has "raptur'd eyes."

I just had to include this poem even though it is so very "eighteenth century" with elaborate style and multiple mythological references. Read it anyway, OK? I think it works to show how in the context of other writings we might read individual texts differently. Plus, Wheatley actually did write some poems to people of African descent (Scipio Morehead, for example—hmm, I wonder whether there was something going on there too). And she had quite a following among African Americans in the eighteenth century and long after her death. Did you know that nearly fifty years after Wheatley's death, *Freedom's Journal* was reprinting her poetry and celebrating her as a literary foremother?

Like most people, I had been told that during slavery days, it was illegal to teach black people to read. If they weren't allowed to learn to read, didn't it naturally follow that there wouldn't have been much literature published about them, for them, by them? I had forgotten two important things. First, not all people of African ancestry were enslaved. In the eighteenth century, there were schools for African Americans and census figures show that in some cities like Boston, New York, and Philadelphia, literacy rates among African Americans were as high as 92 percent. More important, how could I forget that just because something is illegal, doesn't mean it isn't done. Here in Georgia, it's illegal to sell liquor on Sunday, but when I go out to dinner on Sundays, I can buy all the drinks that my credit card will allow. Nowadays, I'm learning to think of laws as evidence that something was being done so often and by so many that it threatened or irritated others who decided "there ought to be a law against that." Laws are made by someone who wants to control someone else's behavior. But that doesn't mean they always get what they want.

I can't believe I studied African American literature for years without knowing that in the eighteenth and nineteenth centuries, we had a viable print culture. Even before Phillis Wheatley's book of poems appeared in 1773, African Americans were writing and publishing sermons and minutes of meetings, poems, essays, and autobiographies. At least by 1817, when the African Methodist Episcopal Book Concern was chartered, we had black editors and publishers, printers and marketing agents, journalists and correspondents, and enough people who could read and had money to buy books, newspapers, and magazines. Do you realize this was before there was a public school system in this country? You know what this means? It means that slaves weren't the only illiterates. In the antebellum period, most people in this country were illiterate!

I was also surprised to learn that this early print culture was often international and inextricably bound up with the Afro-Protestant Church. The earliest known newspaper, *Freedom's Journal,* was started by a consortium of African Americans who lived in several different states and cities. Many, probably half of them, were ministers. The newspaper was printed in the basement of an African Methodist Episcopal Zion Church in New York and distributed not only in the Northern free states, but in parts of the slave South and in Haiti, Canada, and England. Did I tell you that before joining Frederick Douglass in publishing the *North Star,* Martin Delaney sold his Pittsburgh paper, the *Mystery,* to the AME Church? The *Mystery* became the *Christian Herald,* then was moved in 1854 to Philadelphia and renamed the *Christian Recorder.* The *Christian Recorder* is still published today—making it the oldest African American newspaper in the world. But I digress.

Cle, this book testifies to the strength of African American families and to the many ways in which love lives in them. I'm not speaking just of its contents. I'm talking about its very existence. One reason I took on this project was that many of the archives and libraries I needed to use were within easy driving distance of Mama and Daddy's house. I could cut costs and have home-cooked meals, sleep in my old room, and hang out evenings with the family. I would fly into Dayton and you would agree to drive me to Miami, Wilberforce, and Central State Universities, to the Ohio and Indiana Historical Societies, to the Cincinnati Public Library. You were bored waiting around for me, so you began to make the photocopies, to find the microfilms, to read the newspapers, and to search the special collections folders. You got involved in this because you are my sister and because sisters help sisters even when they are a pain in the butt. But, then, like me, you got hooked on the material. You went from being my "ride" and "go-fer" to being a researcher yourself. You began to make a separate stash of copies for yourself and to share with Mama and Crystal and Giz. Soon, I could call you to go back to the libraries and archives to review and recopy or just to do some of the research for me.

Reading the writings of our ancestors gave us an unexpected but incredibly valuable gift. These writings validated some of our experiences that were not like those we saw in the media or learned in school. We found sermons and poems like those we heard in church. We discovered that the songs and rhymes we shouted on the school ground had been shouted in similar situations long before we were even thought of. They were "folklore" so that meant we were "folk." We had always thought our parents were "old-fashioned" and their rules and ideals were out of step with the times. But reading the old documents showed us where those ideas came from and we were impressed with the changing same and had a bit more respect for what they had taught us. The writings and sentiments in the Afro-Protestant Press and the minutes of the African Union Society, like the essays and poems in the *Repository of Religion and Literature,* were so like those in the *Christian Outlook* that Mama subscribed to and the minutes of my sorority. Reading this old material linked my life directly to those of our ancestors. It made me curious about our family and its history. I began to ask Mama questions. "Did you sing 'Shorten' Bread' and 'Ol' Mary Mack' when you were a kid? Did you know 'The Yellow Rose of Texas' is about a black woman? When did your mama and daddy let you go out with boys? How did you meet Daddy?"

> When I came home from work (after school, I worked at Bernice's Beauty Shoppe), he was on the front porch, sitting with a bunch of boys who had come over to visit my sisters and some of their friends. You see, Jewel lived in the East End and he was kinda liking my sister Helen. And your daddy, Quint, he had a car, a cute little blue car with bright red wheels. It was really

clean and shiny. Well, anyway, Jewel got him to drive over to the West Side
where we lived so Jewel could see Helen. And well, the others came along for
the ride cause it wasn't unusual to have a bunch of girls at our house. There
were three of us and if each had a friend come over, . . . Anyway, our porch
was a gathering place for our friends and neighbors. (Part of that was be-
cause Mama was so strict, she wouldn't let us hang out at other folks' houses.)
But, I didn't usually waste time with them and I was really tired that night,
so I just said, "hello" and went on in the house. But then later that evening,
Sarah Allen had to leave. She lived a few blocks away and she kinda liked
Quint, so she asked him to walk her home. But Sarah wasn't allowed to keep
company with boys—she was only about sixteen or seventeen so they asked
me to walk with them so her father wouldn't get upset. And I did. And then
he walked me back home and then, well it just went from there. He kept com-
ing around and then he started showing up at the beauty shop where I
worked and driving me home.

I learned from what she said. But I also heard what she didn't say. In Dayton,
Ohio, in the 1940s, most people of African ancestry lived on the West Side of
the river that divided the city. But there were one or two blocks in the East
End, near the stockyards and meat processing companies, where black people
lived. Most of those people were from the same home town, often related by
blood, or they were fictive kin in extended families. The antebellum South
may have been notorious for marrying cousins, but African Americans had
inherited an aversion to endogamy from our African ancestors that was close
to being a phobia. For folks in the East End, courtship and marriage with people who were not "part of the family" was hard. Between the East End and the
West Side was the great white way where individual black people were not
welcome. Public transportation was humiliating and dangerous. It was safest
to travel in a group by car.

In the days of slavery, African American lovers faced similar problems.
People of African descent in rural areas, in villages and towns, or on the fron-
tiers, generally lived in small groups and had little or no opportunity to meet
people who were not kin. To meet, to court, and in the cases of most enslaved
people, to maintain a marriage relationship, they generally had to cross hostile or alien territories. But this they did. Autobiographical accounts abound
with revelations of how enslaved people would sneak off for clandestine
meetings and of severe whippings when they were caught. Some reveal how
they persuaded the slave owners to permit them to go visit other African
Americans or how some African Americans forged written permissions for

themselves and others. We also read of frolics hosted or condoned by whites who understood that social mingling within African America provided outlets for anger and frustration and that romantic relationships discouraged individuals from running away or behaving obstinately. Marriages enriched the owners of female slaves, especially, because by law they owned the children.

Like with Mama and Daddy, courting rituals whether among enslaved people, between enslaved and free people, or among free people of African ancestry tended to be enacted in group gatherings under the watchful eyes of the neighbors and families. Like Sarah Allen, many girls were not allowed to keep company until they were well into their teens. Mama and her two sisters formed a nucleus around which gathered neighboring girls and boys and to which traveled boys from the East End. (I wonder what girls on the East End did?) But Grandma was inside listening and neighbors were outside watching. Courtship was conducted by conversation and letter writing more than by dating.

Hearing Mama's silences helped me realize that I had to read between the lines of the documents that we discovered. The biggest thing I had to understand is that the selections in this book demonstrate not what was, but what was expected or desired. They are the definitions and behaviors that African American wanted to represent themselves and to guide their children and to protect their unions. Another thing is that, in some ways, the depictions and opinions in documents of early African America seem quite like the values and expectations of Euro-Americans, but in many ways they are very African, very African American. Sometimes the distinctions are in the subtle details of the scenes drawn, the assumptions not verified. For example, Sarah Douglas's "Dialogue Between a Mother and her Children on the Precious Stones" begins with a mother and her four daughters ending tea time by talking about what the girls had learned in school that day. The mother uses her jewels to supplement their lesson on minerals. She asks them to identify various gems and to name those that God told Moses to use in the breastplate of priests. Before the girls go to their chambers to say prayers and go to bed, they talk of vanity and charity and truth, obedience, love and gratitude. The first time we read a story such as this, we might be inclined to think it is too bourgeois, too "white" to be truly "black." The family at tea, the science lesson turned into statements on ethics and fashion, even the box of precious stones and jewelry might seem too unrealistic. But, then, think about it. When a middle class developed in the United States, it also developed in African America. Some, like Paul Cuffee, Venture Smith, Mary Ellen Pleasant, and Frederick Douglass, were quite wealthy and pretty powerful politically. Others were college graduates and business people, politicians, morticians, doctors, ministers, and teachers. Wouldn't they have tea with their children, discuss their schoolwork, and supplement it with lessons in morals and values?

Now, think again. What is missing in this scene of domestic tranquility? There's no father in the picture. The mother shows them an agate her father gave her. But, there's no mention of the girls' father or mother's husband at all. Was he at work? Did he exist? Is it important to know? Or, does his absence make this ideal family more possible for more people of African ancestry without commenting upon the rightness or wrongness, the existence, the reasons or excuses for single parent homes?

"A Dialogue Between a Mother and her Children on the Precious Stones" was published in the *Repository of Religion and Literature and Science and Art,* a periodical published in Indianapolis, Indiana, before the Civil War by a consortium of literary societies from Indiana, Missouri, and Maryland. It resonates with Afro-Protestant values. Afro-Protestants interpret their theology, express their worship, and live their lives distinctly differently in some ways, subtly so in others, and just the same in many, maybe most, ways. For example, Afro-Protestantism conveniently ignores biblical passages that condone slavery or forbid braided hair but is generally theologically compatible with other Protestant organizations. African Americans extolled the importance of sexual morality and marriages that were monogamous and until death. But these ideals were intertwined and inextricably woven with the realities of our cultural traditions and options. The writings of early African America require us to recognize that there's more to some things than what meets the eye. Even in the earliest extant texts, such as the minutes and proceedings of the African Union Society of Newport, Rhode Island, we can practice reading between the lines and see an unshakeable determination to define and to discipline love and marriage on their own terms.

Consider this. On December 1, 1796, in Newport, Rhode Island, a group of African Americans gathered at Abraham Casey's house. It was probably night because most people wouldn't stop work to attend a meeting, even if it had been called by the eminent members of the African Union Society. Those who came must have thought the matter was serious because many had walked a fair piece to get there and they faced a long, dark walk home when they left. The people crowded into the largest room (maybe the only room) in a little house. The officers probably claimed the few chairs and stools. Everybody else hunkered down in the corners, sat on the floor, leaned against the walls, chatting.

According to the minutes of this meeting, it was first called to order. Then came the election of the presiding officer and the clerk. (The African Union

Society had its own officers, but this was not a regular meeting of the society, it was a meeting of the African American community.) Those present voted Charles Chaloner as moderator and Newport Gardner as clerk. There was only one agenda item: to hear the report of a committee formed to respond to a letter dated January 6, 1796, and addressed "To the free Africans and other free people of colour in the United States." The letter had been sent by the "Deputies from the Abolition Societies in the United States, assembled at Philadelphia." Apparently some abolition societies did more than campaign against slavery. This one had decided upon nine ways in which African Americans could improve themselves. Signing themselves as "friends and advocates," the abolitionists advised the free African Americans that accepting their recommendations would prove that they were worthy "of the rank you have as free men" and "justify . . . in the eyes of the world" the abolitionists themselves. The nine articles were, for the most part, exactly what the members of the Newport African Union Society had formed itself to do. They met regularly to worship. They promoted education, fidelity, temperance, frugality, civility, self-sufficiency, and self-respect. Only the seventh article of advice caused the African Americans to balk. In that article, their "friends and brethren" suggested that people of African descent needed to have their marriages "legally performed" and they needed to keep careful records of all marriages, births, and deaths in every African American family.

Can you read between the lines here? These people did not gather to worship or to socialize. They were probably tired and maybe they hadn't stopped for dinner. It was December and many probably would rather be preparing for Christmas. The "Africans" and "people of colour" were learning to think of themselves not as Ibo, Mandinka, Muslim, or Christian, but as "Africans" and "people of colour," in part because they were defined as such by the "whites" and that definition defined their social status more than religion, tribe, or place of birth. (And, the "whites" or "Europeans" were similarly learning to think of themselves not as Irish, English, Lutheran, Presbyterian, or Methodist but as "Americans.") Anyway, they had come to hear the report of the committee on whether to require legal marriages and official records of three milestones of life. They were hushed and expectant. Newport Gardner rose and read:

> . . . the said committee report that they have taken the said article into serious consideration and are of opinion that if the said article were executed, it would be a great benefit and blessing even to generations to come; and that it appears to be within the competency of those persons in this town

to whom the said address is directed, *and that they only are the proper persons to carry out the seventh article into execution, so far as it concerns themselves.* (emphasis added)

Nods and affirmations, "amens" and "that's right!" could have greeted this, and quickly the assembled individuals voted to purchase three books, one for births, one for deaths, and one for marriages. They voted to choose from among themselves a recorder. And, they went even farther than their "brethren" had advised. They agreed to notify "all free blacks and other people of colour" to bring existing evidence of their marriages, births, and deaths to be recorded in the new books.

Now I find this very revealing. The group consisted of members of the Newport African Union Society, a mutual aid organization with affiliations in other cities including Providence, New York, and Philadelphia. And it included other people of African ancestry who did not belong to that particular fraternity. They had been addressed collectively and they created a collective response. They agreed that they needed official communal records. By extending the call for all people of colour to bring their evidence for inclusion, they did not differentiate between "free" and "enslaved." If they were to bring their evidence, then ought we not assume that documentation of their marriages already existed? By emphasizing that African Americans were competent to keep such records, that indeed they were the "only" people who ought to do so, these Newport, Rhode Island, people affirmed their sovereignty. The call had been for "legally performed" marriages. The response was that they and they alone would determine legality. They would perform their marriages and they would keep their own vital statistics. The committee's recommendation ignored the question about what determined the legality of a ritual, but it did make plain who they thought should perform it and who should confirm that it had occurred.

My narrative of this event comes from reading the *Proceedings of the Free African Union Society and the African Benevolent Society of Newport, Rhode Island, 1780–1824,* edited by William H. Robinson and published by the Urban League of Rhode Island. Professor Robinson had published books with mainstream presses, so why not this one? Do you see the legacy here? Even today we continue to create our own texts. As with Mama's stories, there are circumstances outside of these documents that can enhance our understanding. But in this case, I want to mention a few ideas that I get when I go between the lines or look for what is hidden in plain sight. White people offered black people advice about their conduct. The black people took issue with only one of the nine topics—that was the one about love and marriage. The letter from the "Deputies" was dated January 6, 1796, and signed by their president, Theodore Foster. The committee gave its report on December 1, 1796, nearly a full year later. The community agreed that it would not suffer outsiders to interfere with their marital traditions. Its response was dated December 15, 1796, and addressed that letter to the "honourable Theodore Foster, Esq'r, Senator in Congress of the United States at Philadelphia." Those "friends and brethren" urging particular behaviors that would justify their continuing support were not a motley group of busybodies or socially marginal people. They were powerful actors on the abolitionist and other political stages. In this case, "advice" may have been a synonym for "order." But some things are too important to concede. Perhaps they took so long to respond because the African Americans thought if they simply ignored the letter the issue would go away. Maybe they were so mad, it took months to cool down enough for a politic response. It is clear, at any rate, that advice about love and marriage from outsiders was not immediately welcomed inside African America. And, the bottom line is that African Americans considered themselves competent to define and to discipline, to regularize and record for themselves the most intimate aspects of their lives.

Love and marriage were serious investments in the eighteenth century and are so in our own contemporary experiences. I now see how the rhymes and sayings, the folk stories we absorbed, were our heritage being passed down, particular values being enforced or espoused. Remember when we spotted a friend talking with a potential boyfriend or girlfriend and we would chant "First comes love, then comes marriage, then comes Mary with the baby carriage?" How much of it was teasing and how much was warning? We knew the proper sequence for heterosexual relationships. And what we expected, or were expected to believe, and do was what we tried to do. We knew that we were expected to fall in love, marry, and then have lots of babies. Sexual promiscuity would mess up the sequence. As teenagers, we spent a lot of time trying to understand "how far we could go without getting into trouble." And, if some of us crossed the line, we kept quiet about it.

The sayings and songs, the poems and stories I learned from African American print culture colored my interpretations of what I witnessed. In our neighborhood, I can remember only one family whose father didn't live with them. Miz Iron was divorced or her husband was dead—it never was quite clear. But she had four children and they were our friends. And Miz Iron had a boyfriend, "Mr. Jammie," who visited regularly, enforced good behavior among us all, and eventually married Miz Iron and moved in with her family.

Looking back, I remember that sometimes when we picked up Alma and Martha on the way to school, Mr. Jammie was sleeping on the couch. Maybe he hadn't slept on the couch all night, but what is important is that we thought he had and probably our friends did too. Sex was something that married people did in their bedrooms behind closed doors. It never occurred to me think that maybe Mr. Jammie and Miz Iron. . . . It certainly never occurred to me that maybe Miz Iron had never been married at all. Oh sure, I knew some of our schoolmates didn't live in families like ours. William lived with his grandmother. When Buckwheat, Mary Jane, and Ronnie lived with Aunt Helen and Uncle Pete, we knew they weren't our biological cousins. Some of the kids from the DeSoto Bass and the Homeview Courts and some from the Joy Apartments didn't seem to have a daddy around. Some had one around all day because he was "out of work." Others, some in our own extended family, were brothers and sisters who didn't have the same daddy or mama. But it was not a topic of conversation, and not being talked about, we tended not to have an interest in those abnormalities. When we got older, "First comes love" was replaced by "Another bride, another groom, another sunny honeymoon, that's what you get for making whoopie." But here, too, love, marriage, family were the trinity, the true and right way to be and do.

Cle, it's taken a really long time—almost twenty years since I started the Harper stuff. But, late or not, this book is a response to your call. And I see it in common with the words compiled and published in those early periodicals and memoirs and organizational documents and minutes of meetings and such that were calls for responses and/or responses to earlier calls. These publications are ways in which our African American ancestors chose to define and to discipline, to motivate and to celebrate their ideals and accomplishments about the most important and intimate aspects of our lives and culture: love, marriage, and family.

Now, let me explain how I put this book together. I want it to work for many kinds of people with many kinds of intents and purposes. So, I arranged the pieces in an order that recreates the "marriage plot" that I see in early African American print culture. I made five sections to represent what I take as the ideals and models for love and marriage. Within each section, I divided the selections by type: lyrics, letters, memoirs, stories, newspaper articles, etc. This way, a reader doesn't have to keep switching mental gears, because stories require a different investment and method of reading than do autobiographical narratives or short snappy sayings. Plus, it makes it easier to tell what is intended to be read metaphorically and what is a true story. For each type of literature, it made sense to arrange the texts chronologically.

That way, anybody who wants to have a general idea of when something was written is satisfied as much as possible. It's not possible to have actual dates for the folklore. I gathered it from various publications but their dates are not relevant. Folklore, or as some scholars say, "the vernacular," by definition has no one author or known origin. It is passed along over time to many people in many places and with many variations. Many people like to think that the recorded oral texts predate written texts, but it ain't necessarily so. Folklore is always being made up, and quiet as it's kept, some of it isn't as authentic as that which was created for publication. Think about rap or hip-hop, for example. Some of it came straight from the heart and souls of black folk. Lots of it came in response to the call of money offered by black folk and other folk. But I decided to begin with the vernacular because those are the sources of my first ideas about love and marriage, and because the rhymes and songs are usually most accessible and pretty funny. I hope they will serve as hooks to get a reader's attention, then lead that person to the less friendly or happy writings.

The collection begins with the ideal—the concept of love, the initial ideas and desires that many of us have when our attraction to others has moved from pestering or playing games to looking for love, or being "In Love—with Love." In this part, though, I split the poems and vernacular texts into two parts: the euphoric or ideal, which is usually how we start out, and the bewilderment, disappointment, and anger that almost everyone experiences at some point.

The next section shows various ruminations on "Whether to Marry—and Who?" Back in the day, whether to marry was not a very serious concern. Marriage was considered a good thing for the community and, generally, a good thing for a particular individual. "Old maids" are pitied and "confirmed bachelors" are ridiculed. The real concern in most of this literature is that one choose one's mate wisely, and the early newspapers are replete with advice on how "To Avoid a Bad Husband," how not to be "Yoked Unequally," and full of the danger of being seduced by "Young Ladies of Today." "The Two Offers" is one of the rare examples that I found that asserts that once in a while it is better to remain single.

The third section I call "Proposals and Vows." It may have the largest number of flat-out funny items. Even the unhappy stories "Miseries of an Engaged Woman" and "Miseries of an Engaged Man" make me smile. The fourth section, "Married Life," is a mixed bag. Some items are very philosophical, theological, or just plain idealistic. Others hit the nail of discord right on the head. Daniel A. Payne's two-part series on "Matrimony" is a strange hybrid. It is decidedly sermonic in its avowals that marriage is "the design of the deity" with a "high and holy" purpose. But his description of Adam and Eve in Eden is ripe with sensuality.

This book is titled *Love and Marriage in Early African America,* but I have a long section on Family because, at least in early African America, family is inextricable from both. In the early press, family inevitably means that one plus one equals three and more. And, marriage was often a communal relationship, joining not just two lovers. The final section, "Family Trees Rooted in Love," picks up on the "first comes love" and "making whoopie" ideas. Lovers reproduce but they also create families within and from and of other families. I end the collection with "family," but I think of it as also starting over and spreading out. Familial love is love. From that love or for that love, we need something akin to courtship, that is, efforts to please, to attract, and to persuade another or others to join forces and think of themselves not simply as a singular but also maybe even only as a plural. Families in early African America were extended—including generations of biological and of fictive kin. In "Charles and Clara Hayes," for example, the wife, the children, the house, the financial security were not enough. Until his sister could join him, Charles was missing something required for his happiness. His wife and children, who had never met Clara, felt they knew her and they loved her and they finally felt complete when she came to live with them.

And, finally, on the point of how I arranged this book, I have to admit one thing and warn you of another. I tried to tell a story using pieces from many places, times, and situations. I tried to make it orderly, but love, marriage, and family—and the writings about them—don't make one orderly picture. My sections are messy. Some things in "Love" are also about courtship or marriage and family. Some things written as letters are autobiographical and actually quite poetic. And, unfortunately, in some cases, the old documents were torn or smeared, making some words, sometimes even a sentence or two indecipherable. Although I used chronology or the dates of publication to arrange the materials, I am not suggesting an evolution or that each is a response to the call of the prior one. There were lots of calls, but this collection does not include responses to all of them. Some responses are to multiple calls over periods of time and across various cultures.

Finally, My Sister, my friend, my fellow researcher, this book is for you and for our children and our great-grandchildren. Though our parents are dead, it is for them too. It is for our brothers and their wives, our nieces and nephews, our cousins and our fictive kin—for Rosie and Uncle David, for Cousin Mildred and Hadassah and her baby, for Melvin, Brisa, and Daniel, for Dorothy and Tracy and Michael and Imani, India, and Autumn. It is for anyone and everyone interested or who can be made interested in *Love and Marriage in Early African America.*

Love,

Frankie

NOTES

1. Julian D. Mason, Jr. ed., *Poems on Various Subjects, Religious and Moral: The Poems of Phillis Wheatley.* (1773; Chapel Hill: University of North Carolina Press, 1989), 53.

2. Ibid., 162.

Dere's de fox an' de hare,
De badger an' de bear,
An' de birds in de greenwood tree,
An' de cunnin' little rabbits
All engagin' in deir habits,
An' dey all got a mate but me.

Lyrics—SECTION 1

WHAT'S YOU LOOKIN' AT ME FER?
Anonymous

What's you lookin' at me fer?
I didn' come here to stay.
I wants dis bug put in yo' years,
An' den I'se gwine away.

I'se got milk up in my bucket,
I'se got butter up in my bowl;
But I hain't got no Sweetheart
Fer to save my soul.

LOVE IS JES A THING O' FANCY
Anonymous

Love is jes a thing o' fancy.
Beauty's jes a blossom;
If you wants to git yo' finger bit,
Stick it at a 'possum.
Beauty, it's jes skin deep;
Ugly, it's to de bone.
Beauty, it'll jes fade 'way;
But Ugly'll hol' 'er own.

YOU LOVES YO' GAL?

Anonymous

You loves yo' gal?
Well, I loves mine.
Yo' gal hain't common?
Well, my gal's fine.

I loves my gal,
She hain't no goose—
Blacker 'an blackberries,
Sweeter 'an juice.

CREOLE CANDIO

Anonymous

One day one young Creole candio,
Mo' fineh dan sho nuf white beau,
　　　Kip all de time meckin' free—
　　　"Swithawt, meck merrie wid me."
"Naw, sah, I dawn't want meck merrie me.
Naw, sah, I dawn't want meck merrie."

I go teck walk in wood close by;
But Creole tek' sem road, and try
　　　All time, all time, to meck free—
　　　"Swithawt, meck merrie wid me."
"Naw, sah, I dawn't want meck merrie, me.
Naw, sah, I dawn't want meck merrie."

But him slide roun' an' roun' dis chile,
Tell, jis' fo' sheck 'im off lill while,
　　　Me, I was bleedze fo' say, "Shoo!
　　　If I'll meck merrie wid you?"
O, yass, I ziss leave meck merrie, me;
Yass, seh, I ziss leave meck merrie."

I wish you'd knowed dat Creole swell,
　　　Wid all 'is swit, smilin' trick'.
　　　'Pon my soul! you'd done say, quick,
"O, yass, I ziss leave meck merrie, me;
Yass, seh, I ziss leave meck merrie."

ONE SWEET KISS

Anonymous

A sleish o' bread an' butter fried,
Is good enough fer yo' sweet Bride.
Now choose yo' Lover, w'ile we sing,
An' call er' nex' onto de ring.

"Oh my Love, how I loves you!
Nothin' 's in dis worl' above you.
Dis right han', fersake it never.
Dis heart, you mus' keep forever.
One sweet kiss, I now takes from you;
Caze I'se gwine away to leave you."

ON FRIENDSHIP

Phillis Wheatley

Let amicitia in her ample reign
Extend her notes to a Celestial strain
Benevolent far more divinely Bright
Amor like me doth triumph at the sight
When my thoughts in gratitude imploy
Mental Imaginations give me Joy
Now let my thoughts in Contemplation steer
The Footsteps of the Superlative fair

1769

PHILIS'S REPLY

Phillis Wheatley

For one bright moment, heavenly goddess! shine,
Inspire my song and form the lays divine.
Rochford, attend. Beloved of Phœbus! hear,
A truer sentence never reach'd thine ear;
Struck with thy song, each vain conceit resign'd
A soft affection seiz'd my grateful mind,
While I each golden sentiment admire
In thee, the muse's bright celestial fire.
The generous plaudit 'tis not mine to claim,
A muse untutor'd, and unknown to fame.
    The heavenly sisters pour thy notes along
And crown their bard with every grace of song.
My pen, least favour'd by the tuneful nine,
Can never rival, never equal thine;
Then fix the humble Afric muse's seat
At British Homer's and Sir Isaac's feet.
Those bards whose fame in deathless strains arise
Creation's boast, and fav'rites of the skies.
    In fair description are thy powers display'd
In artless grottos, and the sylvan shade;
Charm'd with thy painting, how my bosom burns!
And pleasing Gambia on my soul returns,
With native grace in spring's luxuriant reign,
Smiles the gay mead, and Eden blooms again,
The various bower, the tuneful flowing stream,
The soft retreats, the lovers golden dream,
Her soil spontaneous, yields exhaustless stores;
For phœbus revels on her verdant shores.
Whose flowery births, a fragrant train appear,
And crown the youth throughout the smiling year,
    There, as in Britain's favour'd isle, behold
The bending harvest ripen into gold!
Just are thy views of Afric's blissful plain,
On the warm limits of the land and main.

Pleas'd with the theme, see sportive fancy play,
In realms devoted to the God of day!
Europa's bard, who the great depth explor'd,
Of nature, and thro' boundless systems soar'd,
Thro' earth, thro' heaven, and hell's profound domain,
Where night eternal holds her awful reign.
But, lo! in him Britania's prophet dies,
And whence, ah! whence, shall other *Newton's* rise?
Muse, bid thy Rochford's matchless pen display
The charms of friendship in the sprightly lay.

Queen of his song, thro' all his numbers shine,
And plausive glories, goddess! shall be thine.
With partial grace thou mak'st his verse excel,
And *his* the glory to describe so well.
Cerulean bard! to thee these strains belong,
The Muse's darling and the prince of song.

1774

BEHAVE YOURSELF

AIR — "GOOD MORROW TO YOUR NIGHT-CAP"

from Freedom's Journal

Behave yoursel' before folk,
Behave yoursel' before folk,
And dinna be sae rude to me,
As kiss me sae before folk.

It wadna gi'e me meikle pain,
Gin we were scen and heard by name,
To tak' a kiss, or grant you ane,
But, gudesake! no before folk,
Behave yoursel' before folk,
Behave yoursel' before folk,
Whate'er you do, when out o' view,
Be cautious ay before folk.

Consider, lad, how folk will crack,
And what a great affair they'll mak'
O'naething but a simple smack,
That's gain or taen before folk,
Behave yoursel' before folk,
Behave yoursel' before folk,
Nor gi'e the tongue o' auld and young
Occasion to come o'er folk.

It's no through hatred o'n kiss,
That I sae plainly tell you this;
But losh! U tak' it sair amiss,
To be sae teaz'd before folk,
Behave yoursel' before folk,
Behave yoursel' before folk,
When we'er alane ye may tak' ane,
But fient a ane before folk.

I'm sure wi'you I've been as free
As any modest lass should be;
But yes, it doesna do to see
Sic freedom used before folk,
Behave yoursel' before folk,
Behave yoursel' before folk,
I'll ne're submit again to it—
So mind you that—before folk.

Ye tell me that my face is fair;
It may be sae—I dina care—
But ne'er again gar't blush sae sair
As ye hae done before folk,
Behave yoursel' before folk,
Behave yoursel' before folk,
Nor heate my cheeks wi' your mad freaks,
But ay be douce before folk.

Ye tell me that my lips are sweet;
Sic tales, I doubt, are a' deceit;
At eny rats, it's hardly meet
To prie their sweets before folk,
Behave yoursel' before folk,
Behave yoursel' before folk,
Gin, that's the case there's time and place,
But surely not before folk.

But gin ya really do insist
That I should suffer to be kiss'd,
Gae, get a license frae the priest,
And mak' me yours before folk,
Behave yoursel' before folk,
Behave yoursel' before folk,
And when we'er ane, baith flesh and bane,
Ye may tak' ten—before folk.

1827

LINES TO MY——

George Moses Horton

I would be thine when morning breaks
    On my enraptured view;
When every star her tow'r forsakes,
And every tuneful bird awakes,
    And bids the night adieu.
I would be thine, when Phoebus speeds
    His chariot up the sky,
Or on the hell of night he treads,
And thro' the heav'n's refulgence spreads—
    Thine would I live or die.
I would be thine, thou fairest one,
    And hold thee as by boon,
When full the morning's race is run,
And half the fleeting day is gone,
    Thine let me rest at noon.
I would be thine when ev'ning's veil
    O'er mantles all the plain,
When Cynthia smiles on every dale,
And spreads like thee, her nightly sail
    To dim the starry train.
Let me be thine, altho' I take
    My exit from this world;
And when the heavens with thunder shake,
And all the wheels of time shall break,
    With globes to nothing hurl'd,
    I would be thine.

1843

COURTING IN CONNECTICUT

from Provincial Freeman

'Twas Sunday night in Podunk valley,
In clear cold wintry weather;
Josiah Perkins and his Sally
Sat by the fire together.

'Twas no new-fashioned iron case
With fancy work adorning,
But a real old-fashioned fire-place,
On purpose made for warming.

The crackling wood in cheerful blaze
Around the room was throwing
It's heat in bright and rudy rays,
And on their faces glowing.

The apples by the chimney rug
Were slowly getting warmer;
The cider in the pewter mug
Was bubbling in the corner.

A wooden settle, firm and good,
Their loving forms supporting;
'Twas made of seasoned white pine wood,
And just the time for courting.

At one end Sally stuck like pitch,
While Josiah seemed to fear her,
But after a while he gave a hitch,
And got a little nearer.

Sal caster her eyes down—looked quite tame,
Though very sweetly blushing;
While all the blood in Josh's frame
Seemed to his face a-gushing.

He hitched again and got quite near—
He could not then resist her;
He called her his own Sally dear,
Then bashfully he kissed her.

Good gracious, she gave a start from him,
Her anger did not smother—
She said if you do that again,
Now Josh, I'll tell my mother.

They soon made up, and she came back,
And calmed her agitation;
When last I saw them through the crack,
They were kissing like tarnation.

1855

TO ANNIE

from the Pacific Appeal

Ask me not *if* I love thee;
    A glance would declare,
Though the words were not spoken,
    The flame that was there.
My spirit would seek thee,
    Though severed apart,
And speak its own language
    Direct to thy heart.

Ask me not *why* I love thee:
    Why murmur the trees,
When their foliage is kissed
    By the evening breeze?
As the stream from the mountain
    E'er tends to the sea,
So my heart's devotion
    Flows only to thee.

Blame me not *that* I love thee:
    Nay, rather forgive;
Is the light of thy beauty
    Permit me to live,
a kind word or token
    Thou surely canst spare,
To one whom thy coldness
    Would plunge in despair.

1862

TO MISS W——

A. I[slay] Walden

Therefore you were not slighted,
Not in the least degree;
Although, when not a thinking,
I turned aside from thee.

I thought it was a token
That A. G. Spoke for all,
And feared myself to ask your
Permission to the hall.

Then I, with this impression,
Kind Miss, what could I do?
Could I escort you safely,
Without consent from you?

And then, too, shamed to venture
Or linger by your side,
And this explains the reason
Why thus I turned aside.

Therefore, you will excuse me,
For I have made it plain,
And sorry that I left you,
Last night within the rain.

Now, when the night grows darker,
And rain shall harder fall,
Then you shall have my presence
From prayer to Miner Hall.

Or when the moon is shining,
And stars shall fill the sky,
I will not forsake you,
Nor let you pass me by.

1873

DEDICATED TO A YOUNG LADY REPRESENTING THE INDIAN RACE AT HOWARD UNIVERSITY

A. I[slay] Walden

While sitting in my room kind Miss,
  I thought I'd sing a praise,
But now I think I'll write a word,
  To lighten up thy days.

It's true I often write on Queens,
  And those of noble fame;
But now I seek to write a line
  Upon thy honored name.

What's in thy name moves me to write,
  This little verse on thee?
Perhaps it is thy pleasant ways,
  And cheering looks to me.

How oft I think of thee, kind Miss,
  And oft admire thy grace,
Because I know that thou art of
  Another noble race!

When by the bells to meals we're called,
  Or round the table meet,
With anxious eye I look to see
  If thou are in thy seat.

And when I cast my eyes around,
  Through hall, though long and wide,
And then I quickly look to see
  Thy tea-mate by thy side.

But first of all the bell is rung,
  And each within his place,
In silence each one bows his head,
  'Till some one asks the grace.

Then each in seat with upturned plates,
    And scarce a word is said,
Until we have a full supply
    Of meats and baker's bread.

And dishes, too, are passing round
    About from you and me;
And Clara she looks up and asks—
    Pray, sir, what can it be?

It's pork, of course, or else it's beef;
    Perchance it may be ham—
Except the baker cooked a goose,
    And passed it off for lamb.

And if he has a cut will tell,
    If round about its swallow,
For surely it is not so dead,
    That it would fail to halloo.

While all of this is going on,
    There're other things in view;
For oft I catch myself, dear Miss,
    Exchanging looks with you.

But soon we're through, the bell does ring,
    We're called by duty's 'larms;
Nor can I longer sit and look
    Upon thy brilliant charms.

I'd speak of all my table mates
    Had I another pen,
For surely we're as happy guests
    As here have ever been.

1873

A NEGRO LOVE SONG

Paul Laurence Dunbar

Seen my lady home las' night,
    Jump back, honey, jump back.
Hel' huh han' an' sque'z it tight,
    Jump back, honey, jump back.
Hyeahd huh sigh a little sigh,
Seen a light gleam f'om huh eye,
An' a smile go flittin' by—
    Jump back, honey, jump back.

Hyeahd de win' blow thoo de pine,
    Jump back, honey, jump back.
Mockin'-bird was singin' fine,
    Jump back, honey, jump back.
An' my hea't was beatin' so,
When I reached my lady's do',
Dat I couldn't ba' to go—
    Jump back, honey, jump back.

Put my ahm aroun' huh wais',
    Jump back, honey, jump back.
Raised huh lips an' took a tase,
    Jump back, honey, jump back.
Love me, honey, love me true?
Love me well ez I love you?
An' she answe'd, "'Cose I do"—
    Jump back, honey, jump back.

1895

DINAH KNEADING DOUGH

Paul Laurence Dunbar

I have seen full many a sight
Born of day or drawn by night;
Sunlight on a silver stream,
Golden lilies all a-dream,
Lofty mountains, bold and proud,
Veiled beneath the lacelike cloud;
But no lovely sight I know
Equals Dinah kneading dough.

Brown arms buried elbow-deep
Their domestic rhythm keep,
As with steady sweep they go
Through the gently yielding dough.
Maids may vaunt their finer charms—
Naught to me like Dinah's arms;
Girls may draw, or paint, or sew—
I love Dinah kneading dough.

Eyes of jet and teeth of pearl,
Hair, some say, too tight a-curl;
But the dainty maid I deem
Very near perfection's dream.
Swift she works, and only flings
Me a glance—the least of things.
And I wonder, does she know
That my heart is in the dough?

1899

SHOW YOUR LOVE

James E. McGirt

Pray, if you love me show it now;
    Wait not until I've passed away,
And lying cold in yonder grave,
    I cannot hear then what you say.

And if a wreath await my death,
    Pray one green leaf now to me give,
All thy sweet sayings—say them now,
    Pray let me hear them while I live.

Ah, if the half had been made known,
    That which was said on burial day,
The many fainted would have risen,
    And bounded upward on life's way.

1901

THE PARTING KISS

Jos. D. H. Heard

We were waiting at the station,
    Soon the cars would surely start,
Hearts beat high with love's emotion,
    For we knew we soon must part.
On dark lashes seemed to glisten
    Tiny crystal tear drops shine;
To the fond voice glad I listen,
    While dear eyes look into mine.

And the last words quickly spoken,
    Darling, still to me be true,
Let your promise be unbroken,
    For I will be true to you.
Once I felt the soft hand tremble,
    And my heart throbbed with its bliss;
Lips that rose-buds did resemble,
    Met in one last loving kiss.

Sweet good-bye, do not forget me,
    Spoken in the softest tone,
In your mem'ry, precious keep me,
    For my love is all your own.
I will ever be brave-hearted—
    Nothing shall your love efface;
One last kiss and then we parted,
    One last loving, long embrace.

1901

JESSE AND I

Timothy Thomas Fortune

What time the August days were dying,
    And leadened clouds hung dense and low,
And drowsy Summer winds were sighing,
And seagulls, far away, were crying,
    And merry throngs passed to and fro,
We two, Jessie and I, together
Thought not of time or place or weather,
    But, strolling on the golden sand,
We lived in "grand old ocean," dreaming,
Mute, watching white-caps dancing, gleaming,
    Far to sea—we two, hand in hand.

1905

KISS ME AGAIN

Samuel Alfred Beadle

Oh, give me a kiss
To mate with the bliss
Of the heart I swear, love, is thine;
Let beam a smile
To cheer the while
I give thee of all that is mine.

Now, ere we part,
Let's feel your heart
In unison beat, love, with mine;
Your head at rest
Sweet on my breast,
While my arms, dear, about thee I twine.

Kiss me again,
And then again!
Turn Cupid wild tonight, sweetheart.
Thy soul and mine
By a kiss confine,
To love's wild dream, dear, ere we part.

1912

LOVE'S LAMENT

Olive Ward Bush-Banks

Ah, love, if you could only know
    The longing in this heart of mine,
You would unsay those fateful words,
    And I no longer would repine.

Your fond desire is to share
    All that you have—all that you own,
I ask of you far greater wealth,
    The priceless gift of love, alone.

Steadfast and true I still remain,
    In spite of utter loneliness,
O, let thy soul go forth with mine,
    Upon this quest of happiness.

For love is life, and life is love,
    Break not the bond 'twixt thee and me,
Then shall this precious, priceless gift,
    Be ours for all eternity.

1914

FILLED WITH YOU

Olive Ward Bush-Banks

By your fireside, close to my side,
You are sitting silently,
Eyes so tender—I surrender
To their charm and mystery:
     All the room is filled with you.

Tho' no word of hope you've spoken,
Still my faith remains unbroken:
All the room is filled with you, dear,
     Filled with you.

In the twilight, by your firelight,
I would linger yet awhile,
Waiting gladly, loving madly
You, your sweetness and your smile:
     All my world is filled with you.

Even tho' your love lies sleeping,
In the silence you are keeping:
All my world is filled with you, dear,
     Filled with you.

1920

Lyrics—Section 2

DOES YOU LAK STRAWBERRIES?

Anonymous

Miss, does you lak strawberries?
____ * ____ * ____ * ____ * ____ *
Den hang on de vine.
____ * ____ * ____ * ____ * ____ *
Miss, does you lak chicken?
____ * ____ * ____ * ____ * ____ *
Den have a wing dis time.

WHEN I WUS A "ROUSTABOUT"

Anonymous

W'en I wus a "Roustabout," wild an' young,
I co'ted my gal wid a mighty slick tongue.
I tol' her some oncommon lies dere an' den.
I tol' her dat we'd marry, but I didn' say w'en.

SHE HUG ME

Anonymous

I see'd her in de Springtime,
I see'd her in de Fall,
I see'd her in de Cotton patch,
A cameing from de Ball.

She hug me, an' she kiss me,
She wrung my han' an' cried.
She said I wus de sweetes' thing
Dat ever lived or died.

She hug me an' she kiss me.
Oh Heaben! De touch o' her han'!
She said I wus de puttiest thing
In de shape o' mortal man.

I told her dat I love her,
Dat my love wus bed-cord strong;
Den I axed her w'en she'd have me,
An' she jes say "Go long!"

A LETTER

Anonymous

She writ me a letter
As long as my eye.
An' she say in dat letter:
"My Honey!—Good-by!"

YOU NASTY DOG!

Anonymous

You nasty dog! You dirty hog!
You thinks somebody loves you,
I tells you dis to let you know
I thinks myse'f above you.

PRETTY LIDDLE PINK

Anonymous

My pretty liddle Pink,
I once did think,
Dat we-uns sho' would marry;
But I'se done give up,
Hain't got no hope,
I hain't got no time to tarry.
I'll drink coffee dat flows,
From oaks dat grows,
'Long de river dat flows wid brandy.

IS IT SO?

from Freedom's Journal

They have told me that thou art
Not what thy lips have told,
But a fickle thing, whose heart
Is as vain as it is cold.
They have told me that in turn,
Pride and envy rule thy breast;
That tomorrow thou wilt spurn,
What today thou covetest;
Tell me truly, yes or no,
Tell me, lady, is it so?

They have said those eyes of thine,
Which so fondly beam on me?
Would with equal fondness shine,
Were my rival near to thee:
That those cheeks thus overspread
With their blushes when we meet,
Would assume as deep a red
Were another at thy feet;
Tell me, lady, yes or no,
Tell me truly, is it so?

They have sworn that placid smile
Is but meant to lead astray;
That those lips are lips of guile,
And those eyes are false as they:
That thou now could'st bid farewell,
Without pain, without regret,
Such, alas! the tales they tell;
Not that I believe them—yet
Answer truly, yes or no,
Answer, lady, is it so?

1827

STANZAS

from Freedom's Journal

He told me I was fair as morn,
Mine eyes were bright as stars of even;
In fine, that I was seraph born,
Could make his lot an earthly heaven.
I lov'd him well albeit I might,
Have deem'd his praise as vainly offer'd;
I thought him true with fond delight,
And took the troth he warmly proffer'd.
Pure happiness was mine awhile,
But ah! he chang'd and vilely left me,
And now what can my woe beguile,
Since my young heart is wanton reft me.
I've this, and only this—to weep,
And know that man is e'er deceiving;
That when he smiles your breast he'd steep,
In deepest ills beyond retrieving.
Caroline

1828

TO ELIZA

George Moses Horton

Eliza, tell thy lover why
Or what induced thee to deceive me?
　　Fare thee well—away I fly—
I shun the lass who thus will grieve me.

Eliza, still thou art my song,
Although by force I may forsake thee;
　　Fare thee well, for I was wrong
To woo thee will another take thee.

Eliza, pause and think awhile—
Sweet lass! I shall forget thee never:
　　Fare thee well! although I smile,
I grieve to give thee up forever.

Eliza, I shall think of thee—
My heart shall ever twine about thee;
　　Fare thee well—but think of me,
Compell'd to live and die without thee.
　　"Fare thee well!—and if forever,
Still forever fare thee well!"

1829

FORGET ME NOT

Ann Plato

When in the morning's misty hour,
When the sun beems [*sic*] gently o'er each flower;
When thou dost cease to smile benign,
And think each heart responds with thine,
When seeking rest among divine,
        Forget me not.

When the last rays of twilight fall,
And thou are pacing yonder hall;
When mists are gathering on the hill,
Nor sound is heard save mountain rill,
When all around bids peace be still,
        Forget me not.

When the first star with brilliance bright,
Gleams lonely o'er the arch of night;
When the bright moon dispels the gloom,
And various are the stars that bloom,
And brighten as the sun at noon,
        Forget me not.

When solemn sighs the hollow wind,
And deepen'd thought enraps the mind;
If e'er thou doest in mournful tone,
E'er sigh because thou feel alone,
Or wrapt in melancholy prone,
        Forget me not.

When bird does wait thy absence long,
Nor tend unto its morning song;
While thou are searching stoic page,
Or listening to an ancient sage,
Whose spirit curbs a mournful rage,
        Forget me not.

Then when in silence thou doest walk,
Nor being round with whom to talk;
When thou art on the mighty deep,
And do in quiet action sleep;
If we no more on earth do meet,
                    Forget me not.

When brightness round thee long shall bloom,
And knelt remembering those in gloom;
And when in deep oblivion's shade,
This breathless, mouldering form is laid,
And thy terrestrial body staid,
                    Forget me not.

"Should sorrow cloud thy coming years,
And bathe thy happiness in tears,
Remember, though we're doom'd to part,
There lives one fond and faithful heart,
                    That will forget thee not."

1841

FAREWELL TO FRANCES

George Moses Horton

Farewell! If ne'er I see thee more,
 Though distant calls my flight impel,
I shall not less thy grace adore,
 So friend forever fare thee well.

Farewell forever did I say?
 What! Never more thy face to see?
Then take the last fond look to-day,
 And still to-morrow think of me.

Farewell, alas! The tragic sound,
 Has many a tender bosom torn,
While desolation spread around,
 Deserted friendship left to mourn.

Farewell, awakes the sleeping tear,
 The dormant rill from sorrow's eye,
Expressed from one by nature dear,
 Whose bosom heaves the latent sigh.

Farewell, is but departure's tale,
 When fond association ends,
And fate expands her lofty sail,
 to show the distant flight of friends.

Alas! And if we sure must part,
 Far separated long to dwell,
I leave thee with a broken heart,
 So friend forever fare thee well.

I leave thee, but forget thee never,
 Words cannot my feeling tell,
Fare thee well, and if forever,
 Still forever fare thee well.

1865

A LOVE SONG

John Willis Menard

My love has gone to roam,
  Beyond the deep blue sea;
But my kisses on his cheek
  Will bring him back to me.

Although he is away,
  Far on a distant shore;
He left his heart behind,
  With me forevermore!

I feel the lingering glow
  Of his kisses even now;
Like sunny beams of morn
  Upon my cheek and brow!

Dear darling of my heart—
  Star of my blooming life;
I've vow'd, on your return,
  To be your darling wife!

1879

A DOUBLE STANDARD

Frances E[llen] W[atkins] Harper

Do you blame me that I love him?
        If when standing all alone
I cried for bread a careless world
        Pressed to my lips a stone.

Do you blame me that I love him,
        That my heart beat glad and free,
When he told me in the sweetest tones
        He loved but only me?

Can you blame me that I did not see
        Beneath his burning kiss
The serpent's wiles, nor even hear
        The deadly adder hiss?

Can you blame me that my heart grew cold
        That the tempted, tempter turned;
When he was feted and caressed
        And I was coldly spurned?

Would you blame him, when you draw from me
        Your dainty robes aside,
If he with gilded baits should claim
        Your fairest as his bride?

Would you blame the world if it should press
        On him a civic crown;
And see me struggling in the depth
        Then harshly press me down?

Crime has no sex and yet to-day
        I wear the brand of shame;
Whilst he amid the gay and proud
        Still bears an honored name.

Can you blame me if I've learned to think
        Your hate of vice a sham,
When you so coldly crushed me down
        And then excused the man?

Would you blame me if to-morrow
    The coroner should say,
A wretched girl, outcast, forlorn,
    Has thrown her life away?

Yes, blame me for my downward course,
    But oh! remember well,
Within your homes you press the hand
    That led me down to hell.

I'm glad God's ways are not our ways,
    He does not see as man;
Within his love I know there's room
    For those whom others ban.

I think before His great white throne,
    His throne of spotless light,
That whited sepulchres shall wear
    The hue of endless night.

That I who fell, and he who sinned,
    Shall reap as we have sown;
That each the burden of his loss
    Must bear and bear alone.

No golden weights can turn the scale
    Of justice in His sight;
And what is wrong in woman's life
    In man's cannot be right.

1893

SENCE YOU WENT AWAY

James Weldon Johnson

Seems lak to me de stars don't shine so bright,
Seems lak to me de sun done loss his light,
Seems lak to me der's nothin' goin' right,
    Sence you went away.

Seems lak to me de sky ain't half so blue,
Seems lak to me dat eve'ything wants you,
Seems lak to me I don't know what to do,
    Sence you went away.

Seems lak to me dat eve'ything is wrong,
Seems lak to me de day's jes twice ez long,
Seems lak to me de bird's forgot his song,
    Sence you went away.

Seems lak to me I jes can't he'p but sigh,
Seems lak to me ma th'oat keeps gittin' dry,
Seems lak to me a tear stays in ma eye,
    Sence you went away.

1900

REGRET

Olive Ward Bush-Banks

I said a thoughtless word one day,
A loved one heard and went away;
I cried: "Forgive me, I was blind;
I would not wound or be unkind."
I waited long, but all in vain,
To win my loved one back again.
Too late, alas! to weep and pray,
Death came; my loved one passed away.
Then, what a bitter fate was mine!
No language could my grief define;
Ah! deep regret could not unsay
The thoughtless word I spoke that day.

1914

VIOLETS

Alice Dunbar Nelson

I had not thought of violets of late,
The wild, shy kind that springs beneath your feet
In wistful April days, when lovers mate
And wander through the fields in raptures sweet.
And thought of violets meant florists' shops,
And bows and pins, and perfumed paper fine;
And garish lights, and mincing little fops
And cabarets and songs, and deadening wine.

So far from sweet real things my thoughts had strayed,
I had forgot wide fields, and clear brown streams;
The perfect loveliness that God has made—
Wild violets shy and heaven-mounting dreams.
And now—unwittingly, you've made me dream
Of violets, and my soul's forgotten gleam.

1917

THE HEART OF A WOMAN

Georgia Douglas Johnson

The Heart of a woman goes forth with the dawn,
As a lone bird, soft winging, so restlessly on,
Afar o'er life's turrets and vales does it roam
In the wake of those echoes the heart calls home.

The heart of a woman falls back with the night,
And enters some alien cage in its plight,
And tries to forget it has dreamed of the stars,
While it breaks, breaks, breaks on the sheltering bars.

1918

Fiction

A CHRISTMAS SKETCH

Mrs. M. B. Lambert

> "It came upon the midnight clear,
> That glorious song of old.
> From angels bending near the earth
> To touch their harps of gold.
>
> Peace on the earth, good will to men,
> From heaven's all-gracious king.
> The world in solemn stillness lay
> To hear the angels sing."

With sweet and tender pathos the song is floating, filling every corner of a large and well attended church, in one of our most aristocratic thoroughfares. A vast concourse of fashionable people are standing spell-bound beneath the fascinating influence of that glorious voice. Their strains of worship ceased with the soaring of those melting notes and the fair young creature by the side of the massive organ is bearing to God's throne the increase of scores of hearts in the pure burden of her song.

"Peace on earth, good will to men," and the head instinctively bows itself in reverence on every breast. The Amen is reached, the instrument throbbing and trembling, and the girlish figure sinks into a seat with a radiance on her pale features that makes the great dark eyes look as if they belonged to another sphere. She is clad in deepest mourning and drawing her heavy veil over her face, its friendly shade hides from the outside world the hot tears that are falling thick and fast through her slender fingers.

Below, are the rich, the gay and the happy-hearted. Here and there she could discern well-remembered faces which she had known in happier days, but between whom and herself rose the inseparable barrier of poverty. At last the great throng was leaving the edifice, and after watching the last of the number, she threw her veil aside from the tear-stained face and seats herself at the organ. Her frail fingers meander dreamily over the keys, now in plaintive cadence, now in soft winning melody, then suddenly rising, soaring, bursting, as it were, into a grand volume of sound, the stately walls seemed to tremble with delight. She sees not a strange figure enter very near her, and sink crouching out of sight that her presence will not be observed when the young musician shall pass out.

There is a pause now, all the church within seems alive with sweetest echoes of her grand anthems, as slowly and reverently she leaves the place.

How beautiful she is. How like a young priestess as she glides along unhesitatingly and seemingly so terribly alone, yet around the lovely mouth there is a sadness that makes the heart ache and the dear eyes seem indeed like "homes of silent prayer." She reaches her home, not amid the beautiful dwellings through which she has walked, but to an unpretending, yet respectable, humble street, and before a very modest looking house, where she unceremoniously enters. No glad voices bid her welcome, and she reaches her little room in silence, almost in gloom.

Pausing on the threshold she is surprised at the unusual stillness, for her beautiful bird has always greeted her with an outburst of song. The little fellow now sat on his perch shivering when she reaches in her hand and takes him with loving caress to her warm, loving breast.

"Ah, birdie, this is cold for you and me," she murmurs, "and our Christmas is sad indeed." The little fellow is very comfortable now, and he seems to take in the loneliness of his young mistress, for such a peal of song as he sends forth from his little throat seems to tell that there will be better days bye and bye.

She now gently replaces him and laying aside her wraps, her rich, dark, wavy hair, from which her comb has fallen, rolls down and about her, enveloping her slender form most gloriously. She stands there a creature of perfect loveliness, face to face with direst poverty—of *fare* and *friend*. God pity the beautiful Ivy, with thy fond heart reading forth its sweet tendrils for love and friends recoiling again more restless and longing than before. She thinks of the past, and the beautiful hands sink lower and lower on the breast. "Oh sorrow's crown of sorrow, remembering happier things."

Ivy Varden was the only child of wealthy parents whose first care ever was to guard their potted darling from the ills of life. She was reared in such tender consideration that one would naturally ignore the idea of the lovely blossom coming in contact with the rude, unfeeling world.

But there came a change, and in the period of life so full of beauty, and of love and joy, to tender, blooming girlhood, by one rude stroke all was swept away and life was now one deep, unfathomable shade. For a while the fond parents battled with fate, but soon, under its privations and hardships, sank into death's dreamless rest, and Ivy was alone. She soon found that her fashionable friends were giving her the cold shoulder, which fact so stung her pride that she at once resolved to set their cold looks at defiance.

"I must *eat,* I must *work,* I must *love,* and may God help me to do *all* to a pure and noble end."

She rented a little room, placed within the very barest necessaries of life and managed to be, in a measure, comfortable. She met with better success than she anticipated in obtaining employment as day governess in a few families among those of her former acquaintants.

She was an accomplished girl in every sense of the word, but if she excelled in any one thing more than another, it was music. In this she stood always among her associates in happier days without a rival. She also was only too glad to accept the position as soprano in one of the largest churches, and from the first effort hundreds would throng Sabbath after Sabbath, to drink in the melody of her wonderful voice. Today so her notes rang sweet and clear over the vast congregation, telling of peace and good will to man, none dreamed that the fair young creature had scarcely where to lay her head.

"Miss Ivy, mamma wishes very much that you will come and eat dinner with us today, and I begged her so hard to let me come and bring you. Uncle Phil, came last night and brought us lots of beautiful things, and I want you to come and see them. Will you come?"

Ivy raised her pale, tear-stained face toward the little speaker, who seemed as if she would never get to the end of mamma's message. She was about to refuse, but the earnestness and anxious expectation on the sweet little face compelled her at last to accept, so again donning her wraps she was soon walking rapidly to the great warm house by the side of the little prattler. The kind-hearted lady was at the door to meet her.

"My dearest Ivy, how glad I am that you have not waited for ceremony. I intended to have gone for you myself yesterday, but my brother arrived unexpectedly and I could not get away. He knew your dear papa well and wanted I should make him my messenger to fetch you hither."

All this while she bustled about the lonely girl, removing her things and drawing her to a great easy chair before the bright fire, seated herself beside her and tenderly sought to bring out the smiles from the young heart of her friend. She had succeeded well and Ivy's clear laugh was rippling forth, bringing out her charming dimples, and the great eyes looked like imprisoned stars, when the door opened and a tall, handsome stranger entered the room.

"Oh, Uncle Phil, here is Miss Varden; she is just lovely; come and see for yourself."

"A very charming introduction, I am sure, my little chatterbox," then approaching Ivy said with exquisite grace, "If we grown up people were allowed the perfect candor of childhood, I should feel that I were not presuming too much on my privileges as an old friend of your honored father, Miss Varden, by answering her question as my observation would fully allow me. I am sure I am proud and most happy to meet you."

"Your password into my very highest favor and esteem, Mr. Gray, was spoken at mention of dear papa's name. That you knew him and loved him, makes me feel that we are friends."

"A little child came into the world ages and ages ago, and brought into it life and joy and peace, and my little Daisy yonder, through her love prattlings for her 'beautiful Miss Ivy,' has given me more joy and happiness than I have known for years."

A shade of sadness swept over the noble face, and for a moment both were quiet until aroused by the pleasant voice of their hostess.

"Well, I thought you two people were going to mope away the Christmas hours. I shall have to send out for some one to come in and entertain you."

"Pray, do not think of it, sister mine. There are enough of us here and I promise you there shall be no more moping."

What a delightful day, after all. They talked, and sang and played, until the day was lost in night shade, and the gay world was still. Phillip Grey thought there was not in the whole wide world one so beautiful a woman as Ivy Varden, while Ivy thought what a noble, good man was Phillip Grey, and felt that she had known him for years.

As may be expected the rich, handsome bachelor was the delight of admiring mammas and the centre of attraction to the adoring daughters, and, or course, Ivy must be kept in the shade; and the little sisters were severely chastised for admiring her in their outspoken candor before the rich Mr. Grey, and when it was announced that the nuptials of this happy couple would be celebrated at a very early date, indignation knew no bounds and many were the maledictions hurried upon poor Ivy's head. In Mr. Grey's presence, however, none dared breathe the name so dear to him save in most respectful terms.

One morning, after all the arrangements were completed for the wedding and departure, Ivy thought she would go over and have a parting with the grand old organ which had been such a source of comfort to her in lonely hours. How the sweet echoes stole through the silent edifice. How the great bursts of song seem to people the vast space with devout worshippers, than sinking into soft trembling melody where her glorious voice would glide in, making a most perfect harmony of sweetest sounds.

Suddenly a hand is laid upon her shoulder and Ivy is startled to find herself alone with the sad looking stranger. Her cheeks are wet, her frame trembles with her heart-sobbing.

"I know you will think me rude, young lady, but you are going away from here and I shall hear your sweet notes nevermore, but I wanted you to know how much good you have done me. Oh, if in all God's temples here on earth, such poor, sinful souls as mine are brought into his everlasting joy as you have had the power to do with me, your songs will mingle with the redeemed in the world of song."

Poor Ivy. Tears were falling with the poor creature's beside her.

For answer she turned and sang the same hymn she had sung on Christmas morn, when her life seemed so dark and alone, and when she had reached the beautiful verse.

O ye beneath life's crushing lead,
Whose forms are bending low,
Who toil along the climbing way
With painful steps and slow
Look now, for glad and golden hours
Come swiftly on the wing;
O rest beside the weary road,
And hear the angels sing."

She raised her eyes and the poor creature was gone; but Phillip Grey stood now beside her with eyes full of tender love and moisture which he does not try to hide.

"Whatever of burden has been yours, my priceless love, may they be lost in my deep affection, and ever through the storms of life may we together listen and "hear the angels sing."

1882

VIOLETS

Alice Dunbar Nelson

I.

"And she tied a bunch of violets with a tress of her pretty brown hair."

She sat in the yellow glow of the lamplight softly humming these words. It was Easter evening, and the newly risen spring world was slowly sinking to a gentle, rosy, opalescent slumber, sweetly tired of the joy which had pervaded it all day. For in the dawn of the perfect morn, it had arisen, stretched out its arms in glorious happiness to greet the Saviour and said its hallelujahs, merrily trilling out carols of bird, and organ and flower-song. But the evening had come, and rest.

There was a letter lying on the table, it read:

"Dear, I send you this little bunch of flowers as my Easter token. Perhaps you may not be able to read their meaning, so I'll tell you. Violets, you know, are my favorite flowers. Dear, little, human-faced things! They seem always as if about to whisper a love-word; and then they signify that thought which passes always between you and me. The orange blossoms—you know their meaning; the little pinks are the flowers you love; the evergreen leaf is the symbol of the endurance of our affection; the tube-roses I put in, because once when you kissed and pressed me close in your arms, I had a bunch of tube-roses on my bosom, and the heavy fragrance of their crushed loveliness has always lived in my memory. The violets and pinks are from a bunch I wore to-day, and when kneeling at the altar, during communion, did I sin, dear, when I thought of you? The tube-roses and orange-blossoms I wore Friday night; you always wished for a lock of my hair, so I'll tie these flowers with them—but there, it is not stable enough; let me wrap them with a bit of ribbon, pale blue, from that little dress I wore last winter to the dance, when we had such a long, sweet talk in that forgotten nook. You always loved that dress, it fell in such soft ruffles away from the throat and bosom,—you called me your little forget-me-not, that night. I laid the flowers away for awhile in our favorite book,—Byron—just at the poem we loved best, and now I send them to you. Keep them always in remembrance of me, and if aught should occur to separate us, press these flowers to your lips, and I will be with you in spirit, permeating your heart with unutterable love and happiness."

II.

It is Easter again. As of old, the joyous bells clang out the glad news of the resurrection. The giddy, dancing sunbeams laugh riotously in field and street; birds carol their sweet twitterings everywhere, and the heavy perfume of flowers scents the golden atmosphere with inspiring fragrance. One long, golden sunbeam steals silently into the white-curtained window of a quiet room, and lay athwart a sleeping face. Cold, pale, still, its fair, young face pressed against the satin-lined casket. Slender, white fingers, idle now, they that had never known rest; locked softly over a bunch of violets; violets and tube-roses in her soft, brown hair, violets in the bosom of her long, white gown; violets and tube-roses and orange-blossoms banked everywhere, until the air was filled with the ascending souls of the human flowers. Some whispered that a broken heart had ceased to flutter in that still, young form, and that it was a mercy for the soul to ascend on the slender sunbeam. To-day she kneels at the throne of heaven, where one year ago she had communed at an earthly altar.

III.

Far away in a distant city, a man, carelessly looking among some papers, turned over a faded bunch of flowers tied with a blue ribbon and a lock of hair. He paused meditatively awhile, then turning to the regal-looking woman lounging before the fire, he asked:

"Wife, did you ever send me these?"

She raised her great, black eyes to his with a gesture of ineffable disdain, and replied languidly:

"You know very well I can't bear flowers. How could I ever send such sentimental trash to any one? Throw them into the fire."

And the Easter bells chimed a solemn requiem as the flames slowly licked up the faded violets. Was it merely fancy on the wife's part, or did the husband really sigh,—a long, quivering breath of remembrance?

1895

"THERE WAS ONE TIME!"

A STORY OF SPRING

Jessie Fauset

I

"There was one time" began the freckled-faced boy. Miss Fetter interrupted him with emphasis—"but that is not idiomatic, our expression for *il y avait une fois* is 'once upon a time.' The value of a translation lies in its adequacy." And for the fiftieth time that term she launched into an explanation of the translation of idioms. The class listened with genial composure—the more she talked, the less they could read. She reached her peroration. "Do you understand, Master Reynolds?"

The freckled-faced boy, who had been surreptitiously consulting his vocabulary, turned deftly back to the passage. "Yes'm," he nodded. "There was one time"—he began again unabashed.

Miss Fetter sighed and passed on to another pupil. Between them all there was evolved in hopelessly unsympathetic English the story of a dainty French shepherdess who growing tired of her placid sheep left them to shift for themselves one gorgeous spring-day, donned her sky-blue dress, traversed the somber forest and came to another country. There she met the prince who, struck with her charm and naiveté, asked her to play with him. So she did until sunset when he escorted her to the edge of the forest where she pursued her way home to her little thatched cottage, with a mind much refreshed and "garlanded with pleasant memories."

The pupils read, as pupils will, with stolid indifference. The fairy-tale was merely so many pages of French to them, as indeed it was to Miss Fetter. That she must teach foreign languages—always her special detestation—seemed to her the final irony of an ironic existence.

"It's all so inadequate," she fumed to herself, pinning on her hat before the tiny mirror in the little stuffy teachers' room. She was old enough to have learned very thoroughly all the aphorisms of her day. She believed that all service performed honestly and thoroughly was helpful, but she was still too young to know that such was literally true and her helplessness irked her. See her, then, as she walked home through the ugly streets of Marytown, neither white nor black, of medium height, slim, nose neither good nor bad, mouth beautiful, teeth slightly irregular, but perfect. Altogether, when she graduated at eighteen from the Business High School in Philadelphia she was as much as any one else the typical American girl done over in brown, no fears for the future, no regrets for the past, rather glad to put her school-books down for good and decidedly glad that she was no longer to be a burden on her parents.

Getting a position after all was not so easy. Perhaps for the first time she began to realize the handicap of color. Her grade on graduation had been "meritorious." She had not shone, but neither had she been stupid. She had rarely volunteered to answer questions, being mostly occupied in dreaming, but she could answer when called on. If she had no self-assurance, neither had she a tendency to self-belittlement. Her English, if not remarkable, was at least correct; her typewriting was really irreproachable; her spelling exact; and she had the quota of useless French—or German—vocabulary which the average pupil brings out of the average High School. Perhaps it was because she had lived all her life in a small up-town street in a white neighborhood and played with most of the boys and girls there, perhaps it was because at eighteen one is still idealistic that she answered advertisement after advertisement without apprehension. The result, of course, was always the same; always the faint shock of surprise in the would-be employer's voice, the faint stare, the faint emphasis—"You! Oh, no, the position is not open to—er—you." At first she did not understand, but even when she did she kept futilely on—she *could* not, she *would* not teach—and why does one graduate from a Business High School, if one is not to be employed by a business firm?

That summer her father, a silent, black man, died and her decisions against teaching fled. She was not a normal school graduate, so she could not teach in Philadelphia. The young German drummer next door told her of positions to be had in colored schools in the South—perhaps she could teach her favorite stenography or drawing in which she really excelled. Fate at that point took on her most menacing aspect. Nothing that was not menial came her way, excepting work along lines of which she knew nothing. Her mother and she gave up the little house and the two of them went to service. Those two awful years gave Anna her first real taste of the merciless indifference of life. Her mother, a woman of nerveless and, to Anna, enviable stolidity found, as always, a refuge in inapt quotations of Scripture. But Anna lived in a fever of revolt. She spent her days as a waitress and her evenings in night school trying feverishly to learn some of those subjects which she might have taught, had she been properly prepared. At the end of two years the change came carelessly, serenely, just as though it might always have happened. The son-in-law of Mrs. Walton, for whom she worked, passed through town late one night. The family had gone out and for want of something better he had, as he ate his solitary dinner, asked the rather taciturn waitress about her history. She had told him briefly and he had promised her, with equal brevity, a position as drawing teacher in a colored seminary of which he was a trustee. Anna, stunned, went with her mother to Marytown. Just as suddenly as it started, the struggle for existence was over, though, of course, they were still poor. Mrs. Fetter found plenty of plain sewing to do and Anna was appointed. But Fate, with a last malevolence, saw to it that she was appointed to teach History and French, which were just being introduced into the seminary. She thought of this as she opened her mother's gate,—the irony of the thing made her sick. "Since my luck was going to change, why couldn't I have been allowed to teach mechanical drawing," she wondered, "or given a chance at social work? But teaching French! I suppose the reason that little shepherdess neglected her sheep that day was because *they* were French."

II

Still one cannot persist in gloom when it is April and one is twenty-six and looks, as only American girls, whether white or brown, can look, five years younger. Anna hastening down the street in her best blue serge dress, her pretty slim feet in faultless tan shoes, felt her moodiness, which had almost become habitual, vanish.

The wearing of the blue dress was accidental. She had come down to breakfast in her usual well-worn gray skirt and immaculate shirt-waist in time to hear her small cousin, Theophilus, proclaim his latest enterprise. A boy was going to give him five white mice for his pen-knife and he was going to bring them home right after school and put them in a little cage. Pretty soon there'd be more of them—"they have lots of children, Aunt Emmeline, and I'm going to sell them and buy Sidney Williams' ukulele, and"—

"Indeed you are going to do no such thing," exclaimed Anna, her high good humor vanishing. "Mother, you won't let him bring those nasty things here, I know. As for keeping them in a cage, they'd be all over the house in no time."

But Mrs. Fetter, who loved Theophilus because he was still a little boy and she could baby him, opined that foxes and birds had their nests. "Let's see the cage, Philly dear, maybe they can't get out."

The rest had followed as the night the day. Theophilus, rushing from the table, had knocked Anna's cup of cocoa out of her hand and the brown liquid had run down the front of her immaculate blouse and settled in a comfortable pool in her lap.

"Oh well," her mother had said, unmoved as usual, "run along, Anna, and put on your blue serge dress. It won't do you any harm to wear it this once and if you hurry you'll get to school in time just the same. You didn't go to do it, did you, Philly?"

Theophilus, aghast, had fled to the shelter of his banjo from which he was extracting plaintive strains. He played banjo, guitar and piano with equal and indeed amazing facility, but as his musical tastes were surprisingly eclectic, the results were at times distressing. Anna, hastening out, a real vision now in her pretty frock, an unwonted color in her smooth bronze cheeks, heard him telling his aunt again about the ukulele which Sidney Williams owned but couldn't play. "It's broke. Some folks where his father works gave it to him. Betcher I'll fix it and play it, too, when I get hold of it," his high voice was proclaiming confidently.

"I suppose he will,"—thought his cousin, "I hope that North street car won't be hung up this morning. He ought to make a fine musician, but, of course, he won't get a chance at it when he grows up." The memory of her own ironic calling stung her. "He'll probably have to be a farmer just because he'll hate it. I do wish I could walk, it's so lovely. I wish I were that little shepherdess off on a holiday. She was wearing a blue dress, I remember."

Well, her mind leaped up to the thought. Why shouldn't she take a day off? In all these six years she had never been out once, except the time Theophilus had had the measles. The street car came up at this point, waited an infinitesimal second and clanged angrily off, as if provoked at its own politeness. She looked after it with mingled dismay and amusement. "I'd be late anyway," she told herself, "now that I've lost that car. I'll get a magazine and explore the Park; no one will know."

Two hours of leisurely strolling brought her to Hertheimer Park, a small green enclosure at the end of the ugly little town. Anna picked her way past groups of nurse-maids and idlers looking in newspapers for occupation which they hoped they would never find. She came at last to the little grove in the far side of the Park where the sun was not quite so high and, seating herself near the fountain, began to feed the squirrels with some of the crackers which she had bought in one of the corner groceries.

Being alive was pretty decent after all, she reflected. Life was the main thing—teaching school, being colored, even being poor were only aspects, her mind went on. If one were just well and comfortable—not even rich or pampered—one could get along; the thing to do was to look at life in the large and not to gaze too closely at the specific interest or activity in hand. Her growing philosophy tickled her sense of humor. "You didn't feel like that when you were at Mrs. Walton's," she told herself bluntly and smiled at her own discomfiture.

"That's right, smile at me," said an oily voice, and she looked up to see one of the idlers leaning over the back of her bench. "You're a right good-looking' gal. How'd you like to take a walk with me?"

She stared into his evil face, fascinated. Where, where, where were all the people? The nurse-maids had vanished, the readers of newspapers had gone—to buy afternoon editions, perhaps. She felt herself growing icy, paralyzed. "You needn't think I mind your being a nigger," went on the hateful voice, "I ruther like 'em. I hain't what you might call prejudiced."

This was what could happen to you if you were a colored girl who felt like playing at being a French shepherdess. She looked around for help and exactly as though at a cue in a play, as though he had been waiting for that look a young colored man stepped forward, one hand courteously lifting his hat, the other resting carelessly in his hip-pocket.

"Good afternoon, Miss Walker," he said, and his whole bearing exhaled courtesy. "I couldn't be sure it was you until you turned around. I'm sorry I'm late, I hope I haven't kept you waiting. I hope you weren't annoying my friend," he addressed the tramp pleasantly.

But the latter, with one fascinated glance at that hand still immobile in that suggestive hip-pocket, was turning away.

"I was jus askin' a direction," he muttered. "I'll be going now."

III

The two young colored people stared at each other in silence. Anna spoke first—

"Of course, my name isn't Walker," she murmured inadequately.

They both laughed at that, she nervously and he weakly. The uncertain quality of his laughter made her eye him sharply. "Why, you're trembling—all over," she exclaimed, and then with the faintest curl of her lip, "you'd better sit down if you're as much afraid as all that," her mind ended.

He did sit down, still with that noticeable deference, and, removing his hat, mopped his forehead. His hair was black and curly above a very pleasant brown face, she noted subconsciously, but her conscious self was saying "He was afraid, because he's colored."

He seemed to read her thoughts. "I guess you think I'm a fine rescuer," he smiled at her ruefully. "You see, I'm just beginning to recover from an attack of malarial fever. That is why I pretended to have a gun. I'm afraid I couldn't have tackled him successfully, this plagued fever always leaves me so weak, but I'd have held him off till you had got away. I didn't want him to touch you, you seemed so nice and dainty. I'd been watching you for sometime under the trees, thinking how very American you were and all that sort of thing, and when you smiled it seemed to me such a bit of all right that you should be feeling so fit and self-confident. When I saw the expression on your face change I almost wept to think I hadn't the strength to bash his head in. That was why I waited to catch your eye, because I didn't want to startle you and I didn't have strength for anything but diplomacy."

She nodded, ashamed of her unkindness and interested already in something else. "Aren't you foreign?" she ventured, "You seem different somehow, something in the way you talk made me feel perhaps you weren't American."

"Well I am," he informed her heartily. "I was born, of all places, in Camden, New Jersey, and if that doesn't make me American I don't know what does. But I've been away a long time, I must admit, that's why my accent sounds a little odd, I suppose. My father went to British Guiana when I was ten; but I got the idea that I wanted to see some more foreign countries, so when I was fifteen I ran away to England. You couldn't imagine, a girl like you, all the things I've seen and done, and the kinds of people I've known. I had such an insatiable thirst for adventure, a sort of compelling curiosity."

He paused, plainly reminiscent.

"I've picked up all sorts of trades in England and France—I love France and it was my stay there that made me long so much to get back to America. I kept the idea before me for years. It seemed to me that to live under a republican form of government, with lots of my own people around me, would be the finest existence in the world. I remember I used to tell a crowd of American chaps I was working with in France about it, and they used to be so amused and seemed to have some sort of secret joke."

Anna thought it highly probable.

He looked at her meditating. "Yes, I suppose they had—from their point of view but not from mine. You see," he told her with an oddly boyish air of bestowing a confidence, "life as life is intensely interesting to me. I wake up every morning—except when I have malarial fever"—he interrupted himself whimsically—"wondering what I'll have to overcome during the day. And it's different things in different environments. In this country it's color, for instance, in another it might be ignorance of the native tongue.

"When I came back to New York I was a little nonplussed, I must confess, at the extraordinary complexes of prejudice. I went to a nice-looking hotel and they didn't want me a bit at first. Well, I pick up the idiom of a language very quickly and I suppose at this point my English accent and expression out-Englished most Englishmen's. After a bit the clerk asked where I hailed from and when I told him Manchester, and displayed my baggage—only I called it luggage—all covered with labels, he said 'oh, that was different,' and gave me a room just as right as you please. Well, it struck me so peculiarly idiotic to refuse your own countryman because he is brown, but to take him in, though he hasn't changed a particle, because he hails from another country. But it gave me a clue."

"Yes?" she wondered.

"You see, it made me angry that I had allowed myself to take refuge under my foreign appearance, when what I really wanted to do was to wave my hat and shout, 'I'm an American and I've come home. Aren't you glad to see me? If you only knew how proud I am to be here.' The disappointment and the sting of it kept me awake all night. And next day I went out and met up with some colored fellows—nice chaps all right—and they got me some rooms up in Harlem. Ever see Harlem?" he asked her,—"most interesting place, America done over in color. Well it was just what I wanted after Europe.

"But it struck me there was a lack of self-esteem, a lack of self-appreciation, and a tendency to measure ourselves by false ideals." He was clearly on his hobby now, his deep-set eyes glowed, his wide, pleasant mouth grew firmer.

"Your average British or French man of color and every Eastern man of color thinks no finer creature than himself ever existed. I wanted to tell our folks that there is nothing more supremely American than the colored American, nothing more made-in-America, so to speak. There is no supreme court which rules absolutely that white is the handsomest color, that straight hair is the more alluring. If we could just realize the warmth and background which we supply to America, the mellowness, the rhythm, the music. Heavens," he broke off, "where *does* one ever hear such music as some of the most ordinary colored people can bring out of a piano?"

Anna, thinking of Theophilus, smiled.

"And there's something else, too," he resumed. "The cold-bloodedness which enables a civilized people to maim and kill in the Congo and on the Putumayo, or to lynch in Georgia, isn't in it with the simple kindliness which we find in almost any civilized colored man. No people has a keener, more rollicking humor, and the music—

"Excuse my ranting," he begged, all apology, "but I get so excited about it all. Did you ever read any Pater?" he asked her abruptly.

"No," she told him shamefacedly—Pater was not included in her High School English and she had read almost no literature since.

He nodded indifferently. "Well, in 'The Child in the House,' the chap says if he had his way he wouldn't give very poor people 'the things men desire most, but the power to realize and taste at will a certain desirable, clear light in the new morning.' That's me," he concluded, too earnest to care about grammar. "I'd give us the power to realize how wonderful and beautiful and enduring we are in the world's scheme of things. I can't help but feel that finally a man is taken at his own estimate."

They were silent a moment, watching a flock of pale, yellow butterflies waver like an aura over a bed of deep golden crocuses.

"Have you told your views to many people?" Anna asked him a trifle shyly. His mood, his experiences, his whole personality seemed so remote from anything she had ever encountered.

"No," he told her dryly. "I haven't done anything. I came from New York down to this town to visit my aunt, my mother's youngest sister—she's as young as I am, by the way, isn't that funny? And I've had the malarial fever ever since. I get it every spring, darn it!" He ended in total disgust.

"You might tell me something of yourself. We'll probably never see each other again," he suggested lingeringly, with just the faintest question-mark in his voice.

But Anna didn't catch it, she was too absorbed in the prospect of having some one with whom to discuss her perplexities. She launched out without a thought for the amazing unconventionality of the whole situation. "And so," she finished, "here I am painfully teaching French. I don't make enough to allow me to go to summer school and I don't seem to make much progress by myself." He seemed so terribly competent that she hated to let him know how stupid she was. Still, it was a relief to admit it.

"I know," he comforted her. "You needn't feel so very bad, there are some things that just don't come to one. I'm a mechanical engineer and I can read any kind of plans but it worries me to death to have to draw them."

"Why, I can draw," she told him—"anything."

Their first constraint fell upon them.

He tried to break it. "If you teach," he asked her, "What are you doing here? Wednesday isn't a holiday, is it?"

She broke out laughing. "No, it's too funny! You wouldn't believe how it all happened"—and she told him the story of the little shepherdess. "And this morning my little cousin spilt cocoa all over my school clothes and I had to put on my blue dress. It made me think of the little shepherdess and here I am."

He was watching her intently. How charming she was with all that color in her face. Comely, that was the word for her and—wholesome. He was sure of it.

"How did the story end?" he wondered.

She didn't know, she told him, shamefaced anew at her stupidity. "You know it is so hard for me, every year we read a new book and I never get a chance to get used to the vocabulary. And so the night before I just get the lessons out for the next day. I teach six preparations, you see, three in history and three in French. And it takes me such a long time I never read ahead. I simply cannot get the stuff," she explained, much downcast.

"I've tried awfully hard; but you know some people have absolutely no feeling for a foreign language. I'm one of them! As for composition work"— she shook her head miserably, "I have to dig for it so. The only thing is that I *can* feel whether a translation is adequate or not, so I don't mind that part of the work. But when we got that far in this story the head language teacher— crazy thing, she's always changing about—said to lay that aside and finish up all the grammar and then go back and do all the translating. I've never looked at the story since. All I know," she ended thoughtlessly, "is that the shepherdess played and talked with the prince all day and he took her to the edge of the forest at sunset—what's the matter?" she broke off.

"You didn't tell me," he said a trifle breathless, "that she met a prince."

"Didn't I? Well she did—and it's four o'clock and I must go. My mother will be wondering where I am." She held out her ungloved hand, shapely and sizeable and very comely. It took him some time to shake hands, but perhaps that was one of his foreign ways.

She had gone and he stood staring after her. Then he settled back on the bench again, hat over his eyes, hands in his pockets, long legs stretched out in front of him.

"Of course," he was thinking, "you can't say to a girl like that, 'well, if you're playing shepherdess let me play your prince?' Wasn't she nice, though, so fine and wholesome—and colored. What's that thing Tommy was playing last night with that little Theophilus somebody? Oh yes,"—he hummed it melodiously:

"*'I'm for you, brown-skin.'*"

IV

Not until June did Anna encounter the little shepherdess again.

She settled down the night before the lesson was due to read it with a great deal of interest. Her meeting with "the prince," as she always called the strange young man, had left on her a definite impress. She wondered if ever she would meet him again, and wished ardently that she might. Her naiveté and utter lack of self-importance kept her from feeling piqued at his failure to hunt her up. She wondered often if life still seemed interesting to him, found herself borrowing a little of his high ardor. On the whole, her attitude toward "the adventure," as she loved to call it, was that of the little shepherdess and she brought back from that day only a mind "garlanded with pleasant memories."

Perhaps, she thought fancifully that Thursday evening, the shepherdess meets the prince again and he gives her a position as court artist. And she opened the little text to find out. But that lesson was never prepared, for Theophilus came in at that point with a bleeding gap in his head, caused by falling off a belated ice wagon. The sight of blood always made Mrs. Fetter sick, so Anna had the wound to clean and bind and Theophilus to soothe and get to bed.

So as it happened all she could do was to underline the new words and get their meaning from the vocabulary and trust to the gods that there would be no blind alleys in construction.

Anyone but Anna would have foreseen the end of that fairy-tale. For the prince, with the utter disregard for rank and wealth and training which so much fails to distinguish real princes, sought out the little shepherdess, who had been living most happily and unsuspectingly with her little sheep and her "so pleasant souvenirs" (so said Miss Selena Morton in translation), and besought her to marry him and live forever in his kingdom by the sea.

"'Oh, sky!'" (thus ran Miss Morton's rendition for the French of "Oh, heavens!"). "'Oh, sky!' exclaimed the shepherdess, and she told him she would accompany him all willingly, and when the prince had kissed her on both jaws they went on their way. And if you can find a happier ending of this history it is necessary that you go and tell it to the Pope at Rome." Thus, and not otherwise, did Miss Selena Morton mutilate that exquisite story!

But Miss Fetter was too amazed to care. Moreover, Tommy Reynolds and some of the other pupils had translated very well. Perhaps the work in grammar had been the best thing, after all—and perhaps she, too, was becoming a better teacher, she hoped to herself wistfully.

"I'm very much pleased with the work you've done today," she told the class. "It seems to me you've improved greatly—particularly Master Reynolds."

And Master Reynolds, who was cleaning the black-boards, smiled inscrutably.

All the way home Anna pondered on something new and sweet in her heart.

"But just think—the first part of the story had come true, why shouldn't the second? Oh, I wish, I wish—" She rushed into the "front-room," where Theophilus sat, his small broken head bandaged up, picking indefatigably at his banjo, and hugged him tumultuously.

He took her caress unmoved, having long ago decided that all women outside of aunts and mothers were crazy. "Look out, you'll break my new strings," he warned her. And she actually begged his pardon and proffered him fifteen cents towards the still visionary ukulele.

One can't go far on the similarity between one incident in one's life and the promise of a French fairy-tale. "Still things do happen," she told herself, surprised at her own tenacity. "Think of how Mr. Allen came into Mrs. Walton's that night and changed my whole life." She went to bed in a maze of rapture and anticipation.

Her mother was interested in a bazaar and dinner for the bazaar workers in the Methodist Church, but she had quarrelled with one of the sisters and she meant to go and arrange her booth and come back, so she shouldn't have to eat at the same table with that benighted Mrs. Vessels.

"I'd rather eat stalled oxen by myself all my days," she told her daughter Saturday morning, "than share the finest victuals at the same table as Pauline Vessels."

"Oh, mother," Anna had wailed, "how *can* you say such things? 'Stalled oxen' *is* the choice thing, the thing you are supposed to want to eat. You've got it upside down."

"Well, what difference does it make?" her mother had retorted, vexed for once. "I'm sure I shouldn't like the stuff, anyway. They'd probably be tough. Don't you let Philly stir out of this house till I came back, Anna. I don't want him to hurt hisself again. Do you think you can manage everything? I swept all the rooms yesterday but the kitchen. There's only that to scrub and the dusting to do."

Anna nodded. She was glad to be alone, glad to have work to do. She sent Theophilus out to clean up the side yard. She could hear him aimlessly pattering about.

"Ann," he called. She had finished scrubbing and all the dusting, too, except in the "front-room," which her mother *would* keep full of useless odds and ends—sheaves of wheat, silly bric-a-brac on what-nots. Ordinarily she hated it, but to-day—"to be alive"—her mind, not usually given to poetical flights, halted—"to be alive," no, "to be *young*," that was it, "to be young was very heaven." And he *had* said in the queerest say, "you didn't say she met a prince." If she could just find out something about him, who he was, where he lived, who *was* his mother's youngest sister. Why, what had she been thinking about to let two months go by without making any inquiry? True, she didn't know many colored people in Marytown, she had never bothered—she had been so concerned with her own affairs—but her mother knew everybody, positively, and a question here or there! Oh, if he only knew how the story ended! She became poetical again—"Would but some winged angel ere too late." She had to smile at that herself. Yet the winged angel was on the way in the person of Theophilus. He couldn't have adopted a more effective disguise.

"Ann," he called again. "C'n I go fishin' now with Tommy Reynolds? I've found all these nice worms in the garden, they'll make grand bait. Aunt (he pronounced it like the name of the humble insect) won't mind. She'd let me go 'n the air'll be good for my head," he wheedled.

Anna, dusting the big Bible, hardly turned around. "No," she told him vigorously, "you can't go, Philly. You must stay till mother comes—she'll be here pretty soon, and you wash your hands and study your lessons a bit. Your last report was dreadful. Tommy Reynolds is only one year older than you and there he is in the second year of the seminary and you still in the graded schools. He plays, but he gets his lessons, too."

And then Theo began to rustle his wings, but neither he nor his cousin heard them.

"Oh, pshaw!" he retorted in disgust. "Tommy don't get no lessons. Someone around his house's always helpin' him—he don't do nothin'. Why, his mother always does his drawin' for him."

"I don't know about his drawing," retorted his cousin, "but I know he does his French. He had a beautiful lesson yesterday. Don't laugh like that, Theophilus, it gets on my nerves."

For Theophilus was laughing shrilly, which perhaps drowned the still louder rustling of his wings.

"There you go," he jibbed, "there you go. He doesn't do his French at all, his uncle does it for him; he did it Thursday night when I was there. I heard him and I ain't tellin' any tales about it, neither," he put in, mistaking the look on her face, "for he said you'd be interested to have him do it for Tommy. He said he'd tell you about it the next time he saw you."

"Theophilus Jackson, you're crazy. I never saw Tommy Reynolds' uncle in my life. I don't even know where they live."

"Well, he's saw you," the child persisted and hesitated and looked puzzled—"though he did ask an awful lot of questions about you as if he didn't know you. Well, I don't know what he meant, but he did Tommy's French for him, I know that!" he ended in defiance.

Some faint prescience must have come to her mind, for she spoke with unwonted alertness. "He asked about me?" she insisted. "Sit down here, Theo, and tell me all about it. Who is his uncle?"

"Oh, I don't know, you needn't hold me so tight. I ain't goin' to go. Uncle Dick, Tommy calls him, Uncle Dick somethin'—oh—Winter—Mr. Richard Winter I heard Mrs. Reynolds call him. 'Now see here, Mr. Richard Winter,' she said to him—and she's his aunt, Anna, ain't that funny?—and he's bigger'n she and older, I guess, 'cause she looks awful young. I thought aunts were all old like Aunt Em."

She was sure now, and this miserable little boy had known all along. She alternately longed to shake him and hug him. She restrained both desires, knowing that the indulgence of either would dam the fount interminably.

"Go on, Philly," she begged him. "Maybe I can get Sid Williams to let you have the ukulele right away and you can pay him on the installment plan."

"Well, ain't I tellin' you? Tommy and me, we wanted to go to the movies and his mother said, 'No,' he'd got to get all his lessons first, and Tom winked at me and said he had 'em all, and his mother said, 'Not your French,' and Tommy said, 'Well, Uncle Dick's well again now, c'n I ask him tonight?' And just then his uncle walked in and said, 'Hullo, what's it all about?'—he talks so funny, Anna, and Tommy said, 'Please do my translation!' His mother said, 'Not till he's reviewed the first part; then, he hasn't seen the part for two months, because he's been studying something else.' And his uncle said, 'All right, hurry up, kid, because I must pack, I've got to go away again to-morrow.' And that was when Tommy's mother said, 'Well, Mr. Richard Winter, do you own the railway? Why don't you stay in one place? You've been here and gone again four times in the last two months!' and he said, 'Oh, Nora, I'm looking for something and I can't find it.' And she said, 'Did you lose it here?'—and he answered, awful sad, 'I think I did.' Why doesn't he buy another one, whatever it is, Cousin Anna?"

"I don't know, dear. Go on—did he say anything else?"

"Uh, huh—my but your face is red! And he said, 'Hit it up, Thomas-kid,' and Tommy opened the book and began to read all the silliest stuff about a lady in a park tending goats in a blue dress, and he said, his uncle did, 'What's that? What's that?' and he snatched the book away and looked at it, and he said in the funniest voice, 'I thought you said you were studyin' German all along. I never realized till this minute. Who's your teacher, Thomas?' And Tommy said *you* was. And he said, 'What does she look like?' Tommy said, 'She's awful cute, I must give her that, but she is too darn strict about her old crazy French,' and I said you was my cousin, and I told him not to get gay when he talked about you and if you was strict he needed it. And Mr. Winter said, 'Right-oh!' and asked me a lot of questions, and I said, no, you weren't pretty, but you were awful nice looking and had pretty skin and little feet, and he asked me did I ever spill a cup of cocoa in your lap."

She was on the floor now, her arms around him. "And what else, Philly. Oh, Philly, what else?"

"Lemme go, Ann, ain't I tellin' you?" He wriggled himself free. "Oh, yes, and then he said, 'Where does she live?' I said, 'With me, of course,' and he said, 'Here, in Marytown?' and I said, 'Yes, 37 Fortner street, near North,' and he said—oh, he swore, Ann—he said, 'My God, to think she's been here all this time. Here, boy, gimme that book,' and he sat down and started to read the old silly stuff to Tommy, and I ran out and jumped on the ice wagon and got my head busted. And will you get me the ukulele, Anna?"

She would, she assured him, get him anything, and he could go fishing and she would explain to Aunt Emmeline. "And here, take my apron upstairs with you. Why didn't you tell me before, Philly?"

"Well, what was there to tell, Anna?" he asked her, bewildered.

V

As soon as her mother should come in she'd bathe and dress and go out—but where? After all she was a girl, she must stand still, she didn't even know Mrs. Reynolds. But she could go by the house—yes, but he was to go away Friday, Theo said—why he *had* gone. Well, he would come back.

The gate clicked. At least, she could tell her mother. But she was crazy—she had only seen him once—well, so had the shepherdess seen the prince only once. Her mother would *have* to understand. What an age she was talking to one of those old Dorcas society sisters! She ran to the door and, of course, it was he on the steps, his hand just raised to knock.

Together they entered the room, silent, a little breathless. Even *he* was frightened. As for Anna—

"You knew I was coming," he told her. "I didn't find out until Thursday. Somehow I thought you lived in another town. You know you said the shepherdess had come such a long, long way, and I thought that meant you had too, and I was afraid to ask you. Oh, I've hunted and hunted, and Tommy, the rascal, told me he was crazy about German because he wanted some illustrated German books he saw in my trunk, and I thought he was studying it," he rushed on breathlessly. "And Thursday night I had to go right away to New York to be sure about something, before I dared to talk to you. And I'm to be a social settlement worker, and I can talk and talk and tell people about all those things," he ended lamely.

Anna stood silent.

"Anna, I thought, I hoped, I wondered"—he stammered. "Oh, do you think you could go with me—I want you so. And don't say you don't know me, we've always known each other, you lovely, brown child." His eyes entreated her.

But she still hung back. "*You* could talk to people about those wonderful things, but I, what could I do?"

"After the war," he explained to her, "we could go back to Europe and I could build bridges and you could draw the plans, and after we had made enough money we could come back and I could preach my gospel—for nothing."

"But, till then?"

"Till then," he whispered, "you could help me live that wonderful fairy-tale. Dear, I love you so"—and he kissed her tenderly, first on one cheek and then on the other.

"On both jaws," she whispered, a bit hysterically.

So then he kissed her on her perfect mouth.

Just then her mother, bidding Sister Pauline Vessels an amicable good-bye at the gate, came up the walk. So, hand in hand, they went to tell her about the happy ending.

1917

Letters

FROM PHILLIS WHEATLEY TO OBOUR TANNER

Boston Oct. 30, 1773

Dear Obour

I rec'd your most kind Epistles of Augt. 27th, & Oct 13th by a young man of your Acquaintance, for which I am obligd to you. I hear of your welfare with pleasure; but this acquaints you that I am at present indisposed by a cold. & Since my arrival have been visited by the asthma.—

Your observations on our dependence on the Deity, & your hopes that my wants will be supply'd from his fulness which is in Christ Jesus, is truely worthy of your self.—I can't say but my voyage to England has conduced to the recovery (in a great measure) of my Health. The Friends I found there among the Nobility and Gentry. Their Benevolent conduct towards me, the unexpected, and unmerited civility and Complaisance with which I was treated by all, fills me with astonishment, I can scarcely Realize it.—This I humbly hope has the happy Effect of lessning me in my own Esteem. Your Reflections on the sufferings of the Son of God, & the inestimable price of our immortal Souls, Plainly dem[on]strate the sensations of a Soul united to Jesus. What you observe of Esau is true of all mankind, who (left to themselves) would sell their heavenly Birth Rights for a few moments of sensual pleasure whose wages at last (dreadful wages!) is eternal condemnation. Dear Obour let us not sell our Birth right for a thousand worlds, which indeed would be as dust upon the Ballance.—The God of the Seas and dry Land, has graciously Brought me home in safety. Join with me in thanks to him for so great a mercy, & that it may excite me to praise him with chearfulness, to Persevere in Grace & Faith, & in the Knowledge of our Creator and Redeemer,— that my heart may be filld with gratitude. I should have been pleasd greatly to see Miss West, as I imagine she knew you. I have been very Busy ever since my arrival or should have, now wrote a more particular account of my voyage, But must submit that satisfaction to some other Opportunity, I am Dear friend, most affectionately ever yours.

Phillis Wheatley

my mistress has been very sick above 14 weeks & confind to her Bed the whole time. but is I hope s[om]e what Better, now

The young man by whom this is handed you seems to me to be a very clever man knows you very well & is very Complaisant and agreable.—

P.W.

I enclose Proposals for my Book, and beg youd use your interest to get Subscriptions as it is for my Benefit.

MR. OBSERVER, —

I am a young girl, not out of my teens, and with a decent share (if I may believe people) of personal charms. I have had several beaus (my grandfather a short time ago left me a small legacy,) but have seen none who have made an impression on my heart. You must not from this infer that mine is made of stone, for I assure you, I am very tender hearted. But the fact is, my mother is a very particular old lady, and has made me, unwillingly, I confess, turn a deaf ear to all my suitors. She says all they want is the money my grandfather left me. If this is to be always so, I wish I had no money at all; for to tell you the truth, Mr. Observer, I am dying to get married. All my young acquaintances are married, or are engaged to be married, and I am sure I would not die an old maid for all the world. My object in writing to you is to ask your advice. Mother always speaks very highly of you, and says you have at heart the interests of all of us females. You must know there is a young man, who wants to pay his addresses to me. He is well to do in the world, and I don't know as I would have any objection to him. But mother says I must not think of him, for he is faithless and inconstant, and more than all, he is a male coquette. This last word I don't understand, for how can a man be a coquette? But my mother said he is, and I suppose she must know, for she had a great many beaux in her youth. She says he will never make a good husband, because he has courted every thing that's courtable, from sixteen to twenty-five. Now, for my part, Mr. Observer, I can't see the great harm of all this. A man must seek until he finds, for I suppose men have as much abhorrence to be old bachelors, as we girls have to be old maids. But do give me your opinion, whether you think I had better encourage him, for if you think with me, I know mother will consent, for she pays a great deference to any thing you say.

Your humble servant,

HARRIET

The case of our correspondent Harriet, is one that requires consideration. And we could wish that all mothers would think with her mother. From the bottom of our hearts we despise the man who flits about from house to house, trying to engage the affections of your girls, for no other purpose than to boast of his conquests to the base hearted of his sex. We ourselves know several such fellows, having the appearance of men, who make no secret of their conduct. If young women would show their displeasure of such behaviour, by keeping them at a distance, there would be less complaints on this head. But we too often find the contrary to be the case. And men, who are notorious for inconstancy, are always most encouraged. We think a young woman of Harriet's mind, will be convinced that her mother's opinion is both for her interest and happiness.

1827

FROM AMELIA TO *FREEDOM'S JOURNAL*

MR. OBSERVER,

You will greatly oblige a subscriber, by inserting the following. I am a church-going lady, and occupy a pew in the middle aisle of St. Philip's; but lately myself, and several others, have been so annoyed by a party of male-starers, who make a practice of turning their backs on the minister, and staring every woman out of countenance; that we shall be compelled to remove our seats, if persisted in. And now, Mr. Observer, as you have proffered to take the welfare of us poor females at heart, I beseech you, in the name of one and all, to use your influence in removing the evil; by so doing, you will confer a favor on, Sir, your well-wisher.

AMELIA

The above letter was handed us a few days ago; and to one who subscribed herself our well-wisher, we cannot do less than give it publicity. She may rest assured, that as far as our influence extends, it shall be exerted to lessen the grievance she complains of. By the way we would remark, that it would be well for Amelia to use her influence among the female starers.

1827

MR. EDITOR—

While I am always desirous to acquiesce with the superior opinions of the female sex; and never wish to offend them, by word or deed, I am constrained to disagree with the learned and modest Amelia's illiberal, and uncourtly attack upon certain (as she terms them) base, and unprincipled male-starers; who have become such an intolerable grievance, to several young ladies who occupy seats in the middle aisle of St. Phillip's church, that they will be compelled to resign their seats. This appears to be a new, and novel mode of punishing offences; first, by publicly assailing, and exposing the offenders; and secondly, by depriving the more courteous part of the congregation, of the company of several of the most amiable and fashionable ladies, who grace the pews of the abovementioned church; who strive to surpass each other in applauding, or censuring the deportment and apparel of newly married couples, upon their first appearance at church; in prescribing the most suitable improvements that can be made upon any new, or fashionable dress, and in detecting the trifling errors, or misdemeanors of the thoughtless and undesigning. These, I think, are very unworthy subjects to occupy the thoughts of those emblems of perfection, while sitting in the house of God. It occurs to men, that if those unnecessary superfluities of fashion and unnatural combinations of adornments about the heads, &c. of those fashionable and amiable young ladies were gradually dispensed with, and they appear in such habiliments as become them, as pure and chaste beings, they would not be so grossly annoyed by the rude gaze of impertinent male starers.

Respectfully, yours,

CRITICUS

N.B. It may not be amiss to inform the "OLD MAN," that those troublesome machines, called Bolivars, will soon be laid aside, as the approaching season renders them very uncomfortable, even to the wearer. C.

My Dear Observer,

I read your Numbers as fast as they appear, and with much pleasure. But, my dear Observer, it is almost the only pleasure I have this side the grave. I am fond of society, and delight much to join the circle, where woman's smiles impart joy and happiness to all. Yet amid the enjoyment of such a scene, when voices are in high glee, and the laughter of maidens is heard, I am the most miserable puppy on earth. Yes, I Tom Little, with a soul trembling alive to every tender feeling, and with a deep devotion to the cause of the daughters of Adam, am tittered at and laughed at by them! And why, my dear Observer, you are ready to ask? Forsooth, I happen to be five or six inches below the common standard in height. I know you will think with me, that it is unfair to undervalue a man on account of his size; for they well know, at least they ought to know, that I had no agency in the matter. I think, my dear Observer, if you publish this letter, they will see their injustice in ridiculing a man, for that in which he had no part nor lot.

Yours, ever,

TOM LITTLE

For our friend Little, we who are little ourselves (being some five feet three,) feel no small consideration. A wise man has said, ladies are perverse things, and there is no forcing them to love against their will. The utmost we can do, is to intreat him to bear his misfortunes like a man, to show them that, if the "compound of bone and muscle," which compose his bodily frame is somewhat less than the portion assigned to other men; he has a heart equal to that possessed of yore by Goliah himself. Let him recollect for his inward satisfaction, that the Emperor of all the French, who made both lords and ladies bow at his feet,—was a little man. John Peter Boyer, President of Hayti, and possessor of the hearts of all the Haytien ladies, is a little man. Alexander Pope, the child of song, was a little man. It was this same Pope who said,

An honest man's the noblest work of God.

Which, according to the rules of interpretation, adopted by Divines of the present day, signifies,

A little man's the noblest work of God.

Lastly, we ourselves, who are welcome in every house, honoured by old maidens and loved by young virgins—are a little man!

1827

FROM HENRY H. GARNET TO "DEAR FRIEND"

New York, May 13, 1837

Dear Friend:

The ladies would not admit any males [to the Convention] therefore I can tell you nothing about them more than that Miss Julia Williams of Boston was one of the delegates and I had the pleasure of waiting upon her six or seven times, and dined, and supped with her. What a lovely being she is! Modest, susceptible and chaste. She seems to have everything which beautifies a female, a good Christian and a scholar. I don't want you to think that I am in love, yet I shall keep a correspondence with her. I have received a polite invitation from Miss Hannah Lewis to call and see her. Of course I am going. I am quite popular among the people, and were I not so well acquainted with the honesty of the world there would be some danger of being puffed up. I [am] called the poet, and often solicited to write in albums and so on. I never saw so much fashion in all my life as now is.

Your father is very much altered as well as my poor unfortunate Sire. I have not yet seen your mother though I have called several times. Your sister looks well. Very hard times in New York. I am in great haste.

Henry H. Garnet

Alexander Crummell Papers, Manuscripts, Archives and Rare Books Division, Schomburg Center for Research in Black Culture, The New York Public Library, Astor, Lenox and Tilden Foundations

FROM WILLIAM H. WORMLEY TO CATTO

Washington, September 11, 1860

My Dear Old Friend:

You don't know what pleasure it gave me to read that some fair young lady had won the gallant heart of our most noble Catto. I tell you, old boy, you may say what you will about that young lady, but old Wormley is in the picture yet and has made up his mind not to run except when I see in the distance a Catto striding toward me. Is there any danger?

I suppose you have heard of the wedding, have you? Jim Johnson–Liz Dogans has been tied together in hymenal tie, to love through all ages and live till they die. Do you think they will, old boy?

Ha! more news yet. Did you know James and Robert Hays? They have put their foot into the noose also. What is the matter with the boys? I think the disease is contagious.

Miss Pet Jones has come home from Oberlin, and I am going out in the spring to stay two years. I wrote to Miss Susie Goines yesterday. Miss Jennie Browne asked me to give her best love to you. The Georgetown ladies are all well and send their love. Mrs. Johnson—alias Dogans—sends her very best love and says she would like very much to see you. Will you come, won't you come, and bring "Blue Dress" with you?

Dear Cat, it is time for me to go to the President's and I must close with great respect,

William H. Wormley

N.B. I heard your father lecture last night in the Presbyterian Church. It was on the "Condition of Our Race" in the United States. It was excellent. Three cheers for Mr. Catto—hip-hip-hip.

Jacob C. White Collection, Moorland-Spingarn Research Center, Howard University

Waterbury Aug. 30 1859

My ever Dear Friend

I no doubt you will be surprise to received a letter so soon I think it will be received with just as much pleasure this week as you will nexe my <u>Dearest Dearest Rebecca</u> my heart is allmost broke I don't know that I ever spent such hours as I have my loving friend it goes harder with me now then it ever did I am more acquainted with you it seem to me this very moments if I only had the wings of a <u>dove</u> I would not remain long in Waterbury although we cant allway be together O it tis hard

O Dear I am so lonesome I barelly know how to contain myself if I was only near you and having one of those <u>sweet</u> kisses. Man appoint and God disappoints. There is not much news here worthy to attention there is going to be a picnic tomorry the Childrens temperance Jubilee. The hand of hope will be celebrated to it will be a grand affair. Mr. Pete Sinclair the well known apostle of temperance will address the Gathering I suppose it tis quit gay in Hartford [...]

O my <u>Dear</u> Friend how I did miss you last night I did not have any one to hug me and to kiss. Rebecca dont you think I am very foolish I don't want anyone to kiss me now I turn Mr Games away this morning no <u>kisses</u> is like yours [...]

You are the first Girl that I ever <u>love</u> so it you are the <u>last</u> one Dear Rebecca do not say anything against me <u>loving</u> you so for I mean just what I say O Rebecca it seem I can see you now casting those loving eyes at me if you was a man what would things come to they would after come to something very quick what do you think the matter don't laugh at me [...] I must say I don't know that I every injoyed myself any better than I did when I was at your parents house. I was treated so rich by all the Family I hope I may have the extreme pleasure returning the same pleasure to you all each will remember the visit as for your self Dear H[enrietta] there is no one like her if you was to travel all over united states [...]

Affectionate Friend Addie

PS give my love to all the Family and kiss also to

your Mo.   Addie

please to write soon

Hartford Aug. 31 1861

My Dear Friend

Im now going to comply to your request you would like to know my feelings toward you when I come here it seems strange that you should ask such a question did you think that I did not <u>love</u> you as much as I profess or what was it? it was not that my <u>love</u> you remember the day I come up on the P.M. I come over to your house or in the eve you come home with me you know the conversations we had I felt hurt about it I did not expected it I try to forget it as you ask me to do but ever time I come near you I thought of it and thought perhaps you did and that make me feel as I did you spoke in the manner that you could not trust me out of your site for this I would do most anything if I did not think you would hear of it my Darling that not so for I'm not ashamed to do anything that un proper in your site or out of your site Dear Rebecca the love I have you I will commit that I was rather in a hurry in everything you know my love you are better offense to young man and you know you don't care to have any one as go with me and course I don't feel that fear now to come to you I tell you how I feel towards you that is this like a Child would feel toward a Mother how has forbidden Gentlemen to go with her Daughter and she <u>loves</u> her <u>Mother</u> to that extent that you don't want to displease and still she would like to have her say in that line and sometimes when I think of it all most here for my hearts. Dear Rebecca no ones know the love I have for you I have tried to tell you but have not Rebecca there is one thing no <u>one</u> on the face of this earth that love any more than I do and you are the only that I love or ever try to love nobody will come between us in love if they do anything else the one thing that I do truly wish from the bottom of my <u>heart</u> that you could to talk free with me in everything I must close this

hoping to see you
soon from you Dearest
and Devoted Addie

New York Sept. 29 1861

My Darling Friend

Ive just come from downstairs from a harghty laugh I will tell what occur this P.M. I went to church when it was out Mr. Jacobs escorted me home when I got to the door I ask him if he would could come in he said no that he would call in the eve. The folk say that he comes to see me I tell them to the contrary. Selina she did not expected her Lover so she went to her room to write to him. I came up to put the Children to bed then I went to reveling I got tired then threw myself on the bed thinking of my beloved Friend wondering what was she doing at that present moments while in that deep reverie I fell a sleep. I got up in a little while and found that I was in the dark so I went downstairs and found Mr. Jacobs there Mother call me in the parlo. Mo left. I had to entertain the Gent, while in deep conversation there came a ring at the door so I went to who should it be but Selina Lover then the four of us. I did not feel like seeing company for I did not feel very well I dreadful cold in my head. After Mr. M come in Mr. J would not talk any you know I'm no great talker so there we to set so when it got 9 o'clock that he would go Selina was provoke about it half past nine he sit and ten he still. I threw out as many hints as I could and still he never took them. I got up went out of the room and staid out quite a while. Grandma went in to bid them good night so about half past ten he start off. I was so glad so Selina come in the room and was telling Mother what I said to him. My Darling Friend have you been there so if you have then you can feel for me.

How I wish to be in Hartford this P.M. coming from Church remind me of when I was there when you and me would be returning from Church having you whisper in my ears sweet words or asking what is the matter with you my Dear girl I have no one to day that I'm called by sweet and Affectionate words but they not you all day yesterday and even last night I wishing that I was in your loving arms and you would be imprinting sweat kisses [. . .] I must bring this to a close for it tis 11 o'clock I must soon retire for the night prepare to get up tomorrow A.M. early so good night my sweet Friend and except one fond kiss

Believed me to be your most Dear and Near Friend   Addie

Farmington Oct 6, 1867

My Dear Sister Rebecca:

A week ago today I was in Philadelphia having a delightful time and now where am I now. Here in my lonely room thinking of my two absent friends. I am sorry I did not rec your first letter in Phila. So thoughtful and kindly to send it to me. Mrs. Tines sent on to Joseph. He forwarded it on to Farmington.

I shall tell you how I spend the Sunday in Phila. I accompany Mrs. Micks and Mrs. Scaden to the Episcople church. I return home with them and dine with Mr. Parnell family. Amelia father. Mr. Tines called for me and we attend the Central Church where Rev. Mr. Reaves is the Pastor. He had an excellent sermon. Church was well attended and very good singing. I did not see but one or two that I was acquainted with in my childhood and they had forgotten me. Mr. T had a friend of his to stay to tea. We did not attend church in the eve but made several calls and then took a little walk and then return home and spent the rest of the evening in talking about the future. We have postpone our marriage again. I was thinking it all over. I cannot afford to get anything for winter as I would like to have and the Spring will suit me best. Don't you agree with me my Sister?

His father is going to have another room built on for us. They was talking about it in the presence of me Sunday evening. I am very much pleased with his family and they seems to be likewise with me. Mrs. Tines desired my picture I promised I would send it on I had some taken the same day I arrive home. That was on Tuesday. I shall send you one on and also one to Josie. He ask me for one. I would not promise. I shall surprise him. Further we left Philadelphia Monday 8 A.M. and arrived in NY a few moments after 12 and then he got me a lunch to the house he has a room and then went on to see the Albany boat called the Dew. It is superb. I only wish that you was with us. I then took the City Hartford. I had quite a pleasant time. All the Chamber Maids was very kind to me. Mrs. Seymes gave me a state room. Little Mary Asher came up the same time as usual. The City got a ground at Pratt Ferry so the passengers took a tun boat and arrive at Hartford 15 minutes.

Thursday I came out to Farmington. Mrs. Jefferson was married at 11 AM at the church. She look very nice indeed. A blue silk and white shawl and purple stripe and a white bonnet and veil. Not as many out as I expected to see Mr. R Mitchell and Mr. Douglass stood up with them. They all look very well considering being young folks.

Now I must lay aside my pen a few moments I am writing down in the kitchen—too cold in my room. I tell you a good fire feel comfortable. Miss Porter has 14 young ladies and I believe not all come yet. She is getting her winter provision. Her brother sent on from Washington three barrells of sweet potato we are going to have nearly a bushell for dinner. Two barrels of Cranberries and apples. Mr. Sands made ice cream for tea last evening. Very good. Young ladies had a dance last night. Miss Porter allow them two evening in the week. Now I must tell you a little Farmington news. Going to be two weddings this month. One party's be courting 15 years. I think they ought to know each other well and the other the gent was waiting on the mother and she get all ready to be married and left and court the daughter and now she ready to be married the 16th of this month. What do you think of that. It rather dangerous to place your affection on anyone nowadays.

A white woman married a colored man here sometime ago we received introduction to her at Mrs. Tyler and since I have been gone she has invited Mr. Sands and his wife out to see her. A party to be given at her husband family in Plumville so she extended invitation to Mr. Sands and his Lady. Cook Miss Brown I gave one of those smiles when he told me.

Now I shall return to your letters. One that was write in Bath you will not have any one offer an objection now perhaps not in the future I am sorry you had to cross the bay alone at night too. I see disappointment still follow you. I think you felt the low spiritness sometime before you left home. I hope you will have spirits ever up. [. . .] Rebecca I would inform you how long I should stay in Philadelphia if I had of known it depend on Josie and his family I would have staid until Wednesday if Mrs. Brown had not been sick. They did not have anyone and it was too much for Mr. Tines to do so I thought it best to shorten my visit. I presume you having grand time in Royal Oak today. I should like to be there to the dedication

Now it time for me to part for dinner. Mr. Sands send his love. Mr. T wish to be remember to you and wish you to direct your letters to 101 Lawrence Street New York. Except my love,

From Your Affectionate Sister
Addie

Courtesy of Farah Jasmine Griffin

Autobiographical Accounts

WILLIAM GRIMES

from Life of William Grimes

There is a holiday which our master gave us, called Easter Sunday or Monday. On one of those days I asked my young master, Stuart Thornton, to let me go and see Miss Jourdine, a mulatto girl who was brought up with me and sold by Doct. Steward to Mr. Glassel. It was eight years before that when I saw her last. She was then a beautiful girl. I cannot describe the emotions of pleasure with which her presence filled my bosom, nor forget the hour when fate parted us forever. I presume the heart and the feelings of an illiterate peasant or an ignorant slave, are as susceptible and as ardent as those of men more enlightened, at least when warmed and excited by the influence of female attractions. The last look of a woman whom you know loves you, which is given through tears and with a consciousness that you are leaving her forever, troubles my heart beyond any thing I have since experienced. My young master did not like me to go, but I did. On the way my bosom burned and my heart almost leaped from me, as I thought on this girl. I felt as though I could, unarmed, have flogged half a dozen lions if they had crossed my path. I did not find her at Mr. Glassel's, she having been sold to Mr. Jourdine, who had bought her and kept her for his wife; but I did not return without seeing her. One of the Miss Glassels sent a book to my young mistress, to whom I presented it on my return. She asked me where I had been: I told her I had been to see Miss Jourdine. And because I called the girl Miss instead of Betty, my young mistress was extremely angry with me, and said she would have me whipped in the morning. In the morning Burrows, the overseer, came after me to Aaron's cabin, where I staid. As I came towards the house, my master came out. The little rascal, says he, had the impertinence to call that wench Miss Jourdine to his mistress; take him and give it to him. So they took me and tied me on a bench, and as soon as they began to whip, I would slip out from the rope, until my master told the overseer to horse me upon another's back, and after he had whipped me a while to stop and let me rest; for he said he wanted to whip me about a month. They began to whip again in a few minutes, though not so hard, and kept it up three or four hours; I begging all the while to be forgiven, and promising to offend no more. I was so weak after this, I could hardly stand, but they would not have got me to whip if it had not snowed, and prevented me from running away to the mountain.

1855

JAMES WILLIAMS

from Life and Adventures of James Williams

Early in 1850 I returned back to Philadelphia, and went into the ice-cream and fruit business. One night I went out to have a little fun at a swing-yard that was kept by a Mr. Dennis; got into company with a couple of ladies, and there came a Mr. Brown, weighing about 190 pounds, forbidding me keeping company with those ladies. We had a great deal of controversy about it, and at last we came to blows; but he was no more than an Indian rubber ball in my hands. After a few rounds the watchman sprung his rattle, and we all commenced running. I jumped a fence six feet high, out into an alley, in which happened to be living a family that I was acquainted with. Having lost my hat, I stood in their doorway bare-headed; the watchman came running by, looking for the man that jumped the fence, and he asked me if I had seen a man jump the fence. I told him yes, and that he had just run down the street. . . .

Whilst laying at Brooklyn, New York, there came an Irishman on board of the vessel and said to me: "Cook, come up to my house to-night; we are going to have a dance." So I went up to dance with the Irish girls, and danced until my feet got in a perspiration, and then I took my boots off and took it barefooted, as I saw the girls doing the same. On the next day my feet were so swollen that I was not able to attend to my business for a week, and that put an end to my dancing. Thus I came to the conclusion that I would be a better man.

1893

FANNIE BERRY

from Federal Writers Project

Used to go over to de Saunders place fo' dancin'. Musta been hundred slaves over thar, an' they always had de bes' dances. Mos' times fo' de dance dey had Dennis to play de banjer. Dennis had a twisted arm, an' he couldn't do much work, but he sho' could pick dat banjer. Gals would put on dey spare dress ef dey had one, an' men would put a clean shirt on. Gals always tried to fix up fo' partyin', even ef dey ain't got nothin' but a piece of ribbon to tie in dey hair. Mos' times wear yo' shoes to de dance an' den take 'em off. Dem ole hard shoes make too much noise, an' hurt yo' feet. Couldn't do no steppin' in dem field shoes.

Wasn't none of this sinful dancin' where yo' partner off wid man an woman squeezed up close to one another. Danced 'spectable, de slaves did, shiftin' 'round fum one partner to 'nother an' holdin' one 'nother out at arm's length.

What kind of dances? Well, dey wasn't no special name to 'em. Dere was cuttin' de pigeons wings—dat was flippin' yo' arms an' legs roun' an' holdin' yo' neck stiff like a bird do. Den dere was gwine to de east, an' gwine to de west—dat was wid partners an' sometimes dey got to kiss each other, but dey stan' back an' kiss widout wrappin' no arms roun' like de young folks do today. An' dere was callin' de figgers an' dat meant dat de fiddler would call de number an' all de couples got to cut dat number.

Set de flo'? Dat was—well de couples would do dat in turn. Dey come up an' bend over toward each other at de waist, an' de woman put her hands on her hips an' de man roll his eyes all roun' an' grin an' dey pat de flo' wid dey feet jus' like day was puttin' it in place. Used to do dat bes' on dirt flo' so de feet could slap down hard against it. Sometimes dey would set de flo' alone—either a man or a woman. Den dey would set a glass of water on dey haid an' see how many kinds of steps dey could make widout spillin' de water.

Dancin' on de spot was de same thing as set de flo'—almos'. Jus' mean you got to stay in de circle. De fiddler would take a charred corn-cob an' draw a circle on de flo', den call one arter de odder up an' dance in de circle. Effen yo' feet tetch de edge you is out. Dat was jus' like a cake-walk, 'cause sometime dey bake a cake an' give it to de one dat did de mos' steps on de spot. No, I never did win no cake, but I was purty good at it jus' de same, I reckon.

ca. 1937

PART TWO Whether to Marry—and Who?

CHAPTER III

SPECIAL ADVICES.

I. Marriage.

¶ **34.** We do not prohibit our members from marrying persons who are not of our Church, provided such persons have the form, and are seeking the power of godliness; yet we feel it our duty to discourage their marrying persons who do not come up to this description. Many of our members have married unawakened persons. This has produced a bad effect; they have either been hindered for life, or have turned back to perdition.

¶ **35.** In order to discourage such marriages, 1. Let every Preacher publicly enforce the Apostle's caution, "Be ye not unequally yoked together with unbelievers." (II. Cor. 6:14.) 2. Let all be exhorted to take no step in so weighty a matter without advising with their most serious brethren.

II. Divorce.

¶ **36.** Our Ministers shall discourage the procurement of divorce except on Scriptural grounds. All

36

Lyrics

AURORE PRADÈRE

Anonymous

Cho.: || Aurore Pradère, pretty maid, || (*ter*)
           She's just what I want and her I'll have.
Solo: Some folks say she's too pretty, quite;
           Some folks they say she's not polite;
           All this they say—Psha-a-ah!
           More fool am I!
           For she's what I want and her I'll have.

Cho.: || Aurore Pradère, pretty maid, || (*ter*)
           She's just what I want and her I'll have.
Solo: Some say she's going to the bad;
           Some say that her mamma went mad;
           All this they say—Psha-a-ah!
           More fool am I!
           For she's what I want and her I'll have.

Solo: A muslin gown she doesn't choose,
           She doesn't ask for broidered hose,
           She doesn't want prunella shoes,
           O she's what I want and her I'll have.

Cho.: || Aurore Pradère, etc.

W'EN I GOES TO MARRY

Anonymous

W'en I goes to marry,
I wants a gal wid money.
I wants a pretty black-eyed gal
To kiss an' call me "Honey."

Well, w'en I goes to marry,
I don't wanter git no riches.
I wants a man 'bout four foot high,
So's I can w'ar de britches.

LINES, WRITTEN ON HEARING A BEAUTIFUL YOUNG LADY EXPRESS A DETERMINATION TO LIVE AN OLD MAID

from Freedom's Journal

WHAT! live an old maid! the idea is distressing,
Be banish'd for ever the thought—'tis unkind;
Remember great Natur's design, you're transgressing,
By leaving the pleasures of marriage behind.

WHY live an old maid?—have Love's arrows lost power
To wound—to infix their soft sting in thy heart?
Why offer celibacy's shrine a fair flower,
Whose fragrance such ecstatic thrills can impart.

THOU, live an old maid! nay, I cannot believe thee,
Thou wilt not connubial pleasure forego;
Hymeneal bliss is a balm will relieve thee
From every sorrow;—'tis Heaven below.

'Tis a gleam which in beautiful radiance shineth,
Vain are words, its dear rapturous transports to tell;
'Tis a flame which terrestrial comfort refineth,
A source of pure pleasure—A Heavenly spell.

THEN, avaunt with the thought—be no longer forsaken,
The soul-cheering prospect of conjugal bliss;
Call fancy to aid—it will soon re-awaken,
The thrilling delight of a chaste nuptial kiss.

WHAT, live an old maid!—thou art now in youth's morning
Be call'ed an "OLD MAID" to the close of thy life!—
More sweetly endearing—nay, far more adorning,
Are the titles of "faithful, affectionate WIFE."
    E.

1828

A YOUNG LADY'S SOLILOQUY

from the Christian Recorder

Uselessly, aimlessly, drifting through life,
What was I born for? "For somebody's wife,"
I am told by my mother. Well, that being true,
"Somebody" keeps himself strangely from view;
And if naught but marriage will settle my fate,
I believe I shall die in an unsettled state.
For, though I'm not ugly—pray, what woman is?—
You might easily find a more beautiful phiz;
And then, as for temper and manners, 'tis plain,
He who seeks for perfection will seek *here* in vain.
Nay, in spite of these drawbacks, my heart is perverse,
And I should not feel grateful "for better or worse,"
To take the first booby that graciously came
And offered those treasures—his home and his name.
I think, then, my chances of marriage are small;
But why should I think of such chances at all?
My brothers are all of them younger than I,
Yet they thrive in the world, why not let me try?
I know that in business I'm not an adept,
Because from such matters most strictly I'm kept.
But—this is the question that puzzles my mind—
Why *am* I not trained up to work of some kind?
Uselessly, aimlessly drifting through life,
Why should I wait to be "somebody's wife?"

1864

THE CHEERLESS CONDITION OF BACHELORSHIP

George Moses Horton

When Adam dwelt in Eden's shades alone,
He breathed to heaven a sad and piteous tone;
For nothing pleasing yet the world displayed,
Though he the blooming garden well surveyed.

Throughout the place no pleasing sound he heard,
No lovely scene unto his eye appeared;
Lone man was then a hermit, quite retired,
Whose flowery cot no cupid had inspired.

His maker said, he is not well alone,
Hence from his side I will extract a bone;
By an etheral opiate, sound and deep,
Man on his side was prostrate laid asleep.

Fresh to his view the smiling vision rose,
The queen of pleasure in his calm repose;
He woke in wonder from his pleasing dream,
To sing and tell it to the limpid stream.

When lo! he saw the bridal vision rise,
On whom he gazed with rapture and surprise;
Her charm was heaven, her visage glowed with love,
Whose smiles reflected grace thro' all the grove;
Thus did her glory crown the martial [marital] bower,
The rosy maid and queen of every flower.

The birds of Hymen struck the wondrous song,
And fragrant breezes flowed with peace along;
Myriads of beasts flocked round their festive place,
Which pranced and bellowed round the scene of grace.

1865

REPORT

Frances E[llen] W[atkins] Harper

I heard, my young friend,
    You were seeking a wife,
A woman to make
    Your companion for life.

Now, if you are seeking
    A wife for your youth,
Let this be your aim, then—
    Seek a woman of truth.

She may not have talents,
    With greatness combined,
Her gifts may be humble,
    Of person and mind:

But if she be constant,
    And gentle, and true,
Believe me my friend,
    She's the woman for you!

Oh! wed not for beauty,
    Though fair is the prize;
It may pall when you grasp it,
    And fade in your eyes.

Let gold not allure you,
    Let wealth not attract;
With a house full of treasure,
    A woman may lack.

Let her habits be frugal,
    Her hands not afraid
To work in her household
    Or follow her trade.

Let her language be modest,
    Her actions discreet;
Her manners refined,
    And free from deceit.

Now if such you should find,
  In your journey through life,
Just open your mind,
  And make her your wife.

             1867

ADVICE TO GIRLS

Frances E[llen] W[atkins] Harper

Nay, do not blush! I only heard
　　You had a mind to marry;
I thought I'd speak a friendly word,
　　So just one moment tarry.

Wed not a man whose merit lies
　　In things of outward show,
In raven hair or flashing eyes,
　　That please your fancy so.

But marry one who's good and kind,
　　And free from all pretence;
Who, if without a gifted mind,
　　At least has common sense.

1868

THE YOUNG MAN'S COMFORTER

A. I[slay] Walden

There is not one that can be found
More happy than the man unbound,
If he will not himself engage
To any one of any age.

He then can live a single life;
When free from wed and free from wife
There'd be no one that could control
Nor disregard him when he's old.

According to the lines above
There is no one that he should love;
But if he thinks this is not right,
Then let him seek his heart's delight.

1873

ONE TO LOVE

A. I[slay] Walden

Oh, where's the maid that I can love,
   With love which I have never told?
Where is the one that I would like
   To comfort me when I am old?

Do I not see before my face,
   A mate prepared for every one?
Then sure there's one prepared for me,
   Nor need I trudge the road alone.

Now who is he that speaks to me
   Of Mormons and of Mormonhood?
While this you know, the Lord has said,
   They twain shall be one flesh, one blood!

Come listen, then, to what I say
   Before this evening's work is done,
That you can do as you may please,
   But I'd be satisfied with one.

1873

Fiction

A WOMAN AND AN ANGEL

from Provincial Freeman

'Is my cashmere vest ironed? I want it and my white duck pantaloons this evening.' This interrogatory was addressed by a very fashionable-dressed young man to his sister, who was not so fashionably dressed; in fact, had on only a neat calico. She was putting the band to a beautifully made shirt, which was for the aforesaid fashionably dressed individual.

'No, Harry, it is not. You know this is washing-day, and it is hardly dry.'

'There is time enough to dry it by the stove, and I must have it, for I am going to wait on Miss — to the concert tonight. So don't forget,' and he took his hat and walked out.

His sister, for it *was* to her he was speaking, flushed, and it must be told, looked angry; but soon laying aside her work, went out, got the things off the line, sprinkled and folded them; then making a fire in the stove, she put her irons in, and sat down to take a few stitches while they were heating. And while she is doing so, I will tell you something about her.

The young man, her brother, belonged to rather a numerous class. He was a clerk, getting a fair salary. He lived at home, paying no regular board, helping with the expenses of the family. He dressed, as most clerks do, quite fashionably; wore the neatest made shirts, and nicest smoothed clothes, all of which was done for him by his sister. She took great pride in the appearance of her brother, and bestowed more physical labor in keeping him looking so nice than he did in return for his good salary. But lately he had become quite exacting, and ordered her in rather a peremptory manner, and at inconvenient times, to do such things as he had just asked her. She had a great deal to do in assisting her mother with the family, besides attending to his wants; and his demand at times appeared arbitrary. Yet she never refused him. He is not the only one whom a sister's toil has enabled to make a better appearance in the world at less expense than otherwise could have been done. These extra calls on her labor, and want of appreciation of them, had only been made since his acquaintance with a certain Miss M—. He was continually praising her as one of the most angelic beings in existence, perfectly beautiful, with the sweetest little hand, not broader than three of his fingers, and so white and soft: and he would glance involuntarily at his sister's hand, which was not so very small and white; and how could it be when she had to stand for hours at the ironing-table, besides sweeping, dusting and making beds, in fact, leading an active and useful life? Yet the comparison would hurt her feelings, and she often wished he would not talk to her of Miss M—, for she knew if she had done her duty, her hands would not be so very soft and white, for she had seen her mother scrubbing the steps and washing in the yard, although Harry had told her Miss M— said her "Ma had delicate health."

The more the young man thought of Miss M—, the less he seemed to care for Lizzie, and the more he asked her to do for him. And no matter how much she toiled, he never had time to do the slightest favor for her, so occupied was he with his courtship to his angel.

Now, to let you into the secret, Miss M— had something to do with this. She had learned the character of this devoted sister, and fancied her lover would expect something like it from his wife. So she had weaned him from her purposely; and from the very cause that should have made him think more of her, he actually thought less. He had unconsciously imbibed the very common idea, that soft hands and fine airs are indispensible in making a lady. His sister not having either, he felt a little ashamed for her; notwithstanding his knowledge of her sound sense and true heart. He was too much in love with a pretty face to reflect if she performed the duties called for by their circumstances, it would be impossible for his lady love to be so. They were very well performed, however, by her mother, *who was somewhat ailing, it is true.*

When at last the young man married his angel, though Lizzie shed tears at their separation, her labors certainly were considerably lightened, and her hands had a better chance of becoming soft. She loved her brother, and like a true woman, hoped he would be very happy, and that his wife would keep him *nice.* This had been her especial pride; and every wife ought to consider it a duty. But when in a very little time she saw him wearing soiled vests and crumpled bosoms she very easily knew to whom the blame belonged. He began to look frowning, and speak cross and complaining, and at length was taken very sick. When Lizzie went to see him, he begged her so hard to stay and give him real "old time nursing." She now learned that angels got very tired waiting on 'fretful sick people' who have been 'spoiled' by too much attention at home. They were enough to 'kill any with fatigue.' And how many cross looks the sister got while attending quietly but constantly to her brother's wants. The other brother-look came back to his face, and he got so much better in one day, that Lizzie offered to stay all night with him. And the angel determined to sit up with her, only lying down to take a short nap—which lasted all night.

With this experience, Lizzie thought that *woman* [*sic*] make considerably better wives than *angels*. Their proper place seems to be where there is no care or trouble. Young men, be careful of catching an angel. *They are quite numerous.*

1855

THE TWO OFFERS

Frances Ellen Watkins [Harper]

"What is the matter with you, Laura, this morning? I have been watching you this hour, and in that time you have commenced a half dozen letters and torn them all up. What matter of such grave moment is puzzling your little head, that you do not know how to decide?"

"Well, it is an important matter: I have two offers for marriage, and I do not know which to choose."

"I should accept neither, or to say the least, not at present."

"Why not?"

"Because I think a woman who is undecided between two offers, has not love enough for either to make a choice; and in that very hesitation, indecision, she has a reason to pause and seriously reflect, lest her marriage, instead of being an affinity of souls or a union of hearts, should only be a mere matter of bargain and sale, or an affair of convenience and selfish interest."

"But I consider them both very good ones, just such as many a girl would gladly receive. But to tell you the truth, I do not think that I regard either as a woman should the man she chooses for her husband. But then if I refuse, there is the risk of being an old maid, and that is not to be thought of."

"Well, suppose there is, is that the most dreadful fate that can befall a woman? Is there not more intense wretchedness in an ill-assorted marriage—more utter loneliness in a loveless home, than in the lot of the old maid who accepts her earthly mission as a gift from God, and strives to walk the path of life with earnest and unfaltering steps?"

"Oh! what a little preacher you are. I really believe that you were cut out for an old maid; that when nature formed you, she put in a double portion of intellect to make up for a deficiency of love; and yet you are kind and affectionate. But I do not think that you know anything of the grand, over-mastering passion, or the deep necessity of woman's heart for loving."

"Do you think so?" resumed the first speaker; and bending over her work she quietly applied herself to the knitting that had lain neglected by her side, during this brief conversation; but as she did so, a shadow flitted over her pale and intellectual brow, a mist gathered in her eyes, and a slight quivering of the lips, revealed a depth of feeling to which her companion was a stranger.

But before I proceed with my story, let me give you a slight history of the speakers. They were cousins, who had met life under different auspices. Laura Lagrange, was the only daughter of rich and indulgent parents, who had spared no pains to make her an accomplished lady. Her cousin, Janette Alston, was the child of parents, rich only in goodness and affection. Her father had been unfortunate in business, and dying before he could retrieve his fortunes, left his business in an embarrassed state. His widow was unacquainted with his business affairs, and when the estate was settled, hungry creditors had brought their claims and the lawyers had received their fees, she found herself homeless and almost penniless, and she who had been sheltered in the warm clasp of loving arms, found them too powerless to shield her from the pitiless pelting storms of adversity. Year after year she struggled with poverty and wrestled with want, till her toil-worn hands became too feeble to hold the shattered chords of existence, and her tear-dimmed eyes grew heavy with the slumber of death. Her daughter had watched over her with untiring devotion, had closed her eyes in death, and gone out into the busy restless world, missing a precious tone from the voices of earth, a beloved step from the paths of life. Too self reliant to depend on the charity of relations, she endeavored to support herself by her own exertions, and she had succeeded. Her path for a while was marked with struggle and trial, but instead of uselessly repining, she met them bravely, and her life became not a thing of ease and indulgence, but of conquest, victory, and accomplishments. At the time when this conversation took place, the deep trials of her life had passed away. The achievements of her genius had won her a position in the literary world, where she shone as one of its bright particular stars. And with her fame came a competence of worldly means, which gave her leisure for improvement, and the riper development of her rare talents. And she, that pale intellectual woman, whose genius gave life and vivacity to the social circle, and whose presence threw a halo of beauty and grace around the charmed atmosphere in which she moved, had at one period of her life, known the mystic and solemn strength of an all-absorbing love. Years faded into the misty past, had seen the kindling of her eye, the quick flushing of her cheek, and the wild throbbing of her heart, at tones of a voice long since hushed to the stillness of death. Deeply, wildly, passionately, she had loved. Her whole life seemed like the pouring out of rich, warm and gushing affections. This love quickened her talents, inspired her genius, and threw over her life a tender and spiritual earnestness. And then came a fearful shock, a mournful waking from that "dream of beauty and delight." A shadow fell around her path; it came between her and the object of her heart's worship; first a few cold words, estrangement, and then a painful separation; the old story of woman's pride — digging the sepulchre of her happiness, and then a new-made grave, and her path over it to the spirit world; and thus faded out from that young heart her bright, brief and saddened dream of life. Faint and spirit-broken, she turned from the scenes associated with the memory of the loved and lost. She tried to break the chain of sad associations that bound her to the mournful past; and so, pressing back the bitter sobs from her almost breaking heart, like the dying dolphin, whose beauty is born of its death anguish, her genius gathered strength from suffering and wondrous power and brilliancy from the agony she hid within the desolate chambers of her soul. Men hailed her as one of earth's strangely gifted children, and wreathed the garlands of fame for her brow, when it was throbbing with a wild and fearful unrest. They breathed her name with applause, when through the lonely halls of her stricken spirit, was an earnest cry for peace, a deep yearning for sympathy and heart-support.

But life, with its stern realities, met her; its solemn responsibilities confronted her, and turning, with an earnest and shattered spirit, to life's duties and trials, she found a calmness and strength that she had only imagined in her dreams of poetry and song. We will now pass over a period of ten years, and the cousins have met again. In that calm and lovely woman, in whose eyes is a depth of tenderness, tempering the flashes of her genius, whose looks and tones are full of sympathy and love, we recognize the once smitten and stricken Janette Alston. The bloom of her girlhood had given way to a higher type of spiritual beauty, as if some unseen hand had been polishing and refining the temple in which her lovely spirit found its habitation; and this had been the fact. Her inner life had grown beautiful, and it was this that was constantly developing the outer. Never, in the early flush of womanhood, when an absorbing love had lit up her eyes and glowed in her life, had she appeared so interesting as when, with a countenance which seemed overshadowed with a spiritual light, she bent over the death-bed of a young woman, just lingering at the shadowy gates of the unseen land.

"Has he come?" faintly but eagerly exclaimed the dying woman. "Oh! how I have longed for his coming, and even in death he forgets me."

"Oh, do not say so, dear Laura, some accident may have detained him," said Janette to her cousin; for on that bed, from whence she will never rise, lies the once-beautiful and light-hearted Laura Lagrange, the brightness of whose eyes has long since been dimmed with tears, and whose voice had become like a harp whose every chord is tuned to sadness—whose faintest thrill and loudest vibrations are but the variations of agony. A heavy hand was laid upon her once warm and bounding heart, and a voice came whispering through her soul, that she must die. But, to her, the tidings was a message of deliverance— a voice, hushing her wild sorrows to the calmness of resignation and hope. Life had grown so weary upon her head—the future looked so hopeless—she had no wish to tread again the track where thorns had pierced her feet, and clouds overcast her sky; and she hailed the coming of death's angel as the footsteps of a welcome friend. And yet, earth had one object so very dear to her weary heart. It was her absent and recreant husband; for, since that conversation, she had accepted one of her offers, and become a wife. But, before she married, she learned that great lesson of human experience and woman's life, to love the man who bowed at her shrine, a willing worshipper. He had a pleasing address, raven hair, flashing eyes, a voice of thrilling sweetness, and lips of persuasive eloquence; and being well versed in the ways of the world, he won his way to her heart, and she became his bride, and he was proud of his prize. Vain and superficial in his character, he looked upon marriage not as a divine sacrament for the soul's development and human progression, but as the title-deed that gave him possession of the woman he thought he loved. But alas for her, the laxity of his principles had rendered him unworthy of the deep and undying devotion of a pure-hearted woman; but, for awhile, he hid from her his true character, and she blindly loved him, and for a short period was happy in the consciousness of being beloved; though sometimes a vague unrest would fill her soul, when, overflowing with a sense of the good, the beautiful, and the true, she would turn to him, but find no response to the deep yearnings of her soul—no appreciation of life's highest realities—its solemn grandeur and significant importance. Their souls never met, and soon she found a void in her bosom, that his earth-born love could not fill. He did not satisfy the wants of her mental and moral nature—between him and her there was no affinity of minds, no intercommunion of souls.

Talk as you will of woman's deep capacity for loving, of the strength of her affectional nature. I do not deny it; but will the mere possession of any human love, fully satisfy all the demands of her whole being? You may paint her in poetry or fiction, as a frail vine, clinging to her brother man for support, and dying when deprived of it; and all this may sound well enough to please the imaginations of school-girls, or love-lorn maidens. But woman— the true woman—if you would render her happy, it needs more than the mere development of her affectional nature. Her conscience should be enlightened, her faith in the true and right established, and scope given to her Heaven-endowed and God-given faculties. The true aim of female education should be, not a development of one or two, but all the faculties of the human soul, because no perfect womanhood is developed by imperfect culture. Intense love is often akin to intense suffering, and to trust the whole wealth of a woman's nature on the frail bark of human love, may often be like trusting a cargo of gold and precious gems, to a bark that has never battled with the storm, or buffetted the waves. Is it any wonder, then, that so many life-barks go down, paving the ocean of time with precious hearts and wasted hopes? that so many float around us, shattered and dismasted wrecks? that so many are stranded on the shoals of existence, mournful beacons and solemn warnings for the thoughtless, to whom marriage is a careless and hasty rushing together of the affections? Alas that an institution so fraught with good for humanity should be so perverted, and that state of life, which should be filled with happiness, become so replete with misery. And this was the fate of Laura Lagrange. For a brief period after marriage her life seemed like a bright and beautiful dream, full of hope and radiant with joy. And then there came a change—he found other attractions that lay beyond the pale of home influences. The gambling saloon had power to win him from her side, he had lived in an element of unhealthy and unhallowed excitements, and the society of a loving wife, the pleasures of a well-regulated home, were enjoyments too tame for one who had vitiated his tastes by the pleasures of sin. There were charmed houses of vice, built upon dead men's loves, where, amid a flow of song, laughter, wine, and careless mirth, he would spend hour after hour, forgetting the cheek that was paling through his neglect, heedless of the tear-dimmed eyes, peering anxiously into the darkness, waiting, or watching his return.

The influence of old associations was upon him. In early life, home had been to him a place of ceilings and walls, not a true home, built upon goodness, love and truth. It was a place where velvet carpets hushed his tread, where images of loveliness and beauty invoked into being by painter's art and sculptor's skill, pleased the eye and gratified the taste, where magnificence surrounded his way and costly clothing adorned his person; but it was not the place for the true culture and right development of his soul. His father had been too much engrossed in making money, and his mother in spending it, in striving to maintain a fashionable position in society, and shining in the eyes of the world, to give the proper direction to the character of their wayward and impulsive son. His mother put beautiful robes upon his body, but left ugly scars upon his soul; she pampered his appetite, but starved his spirit. Every mother should be a true artist, who knows how to weave into her child's life images of grace and beauty, the true poet capable of writing on the soul of childhood the harmony of love and truth, and teaching it how to produce the grandest of all poems—the poetry of a true and noble life. But in his home, a love for the good, the true and right, had been sacrificed at the shrine of frivolity and fashion. That parental authority which should have been preserved as a string of precious pearls, unbroken and unscattered, was simply the administration of chance. At one time obedience was enforced by authority, at another time by flattery and promises, and just as often it was not enforced at all. His early associations were formed as chance directed, and from his want of home-training, his character received a bias, his life a shade, which ran through every avenue of his existence, and darkened all his future hours. Oh, if we would trace the history of all the crimes that have o'ershadowed this sin-shrouded and sorrow-darkened world of ours, how many might be seen arising from the wrong home influences, or the weakening of the home ties. Home should always be the best school for the affections, the birthplace of high resolves, and the altar upon which lofty aspirations are kindled, from whence the soul may go forth strengthened, to act its part aright in the great drama of life, with conscience enlightened, affections cultivated, and reason and judgment dominant. But alas for the young wife. Her husband had not been blessed with such a home. When he entered the arena of life, the voices from home did not linger around his path as angels of guidance about his steps; they were not like so many messages to invite him to deeds of high and holy worth. The memory of no sainted mother arose between him and deeds of darkness; the earnest prayers of no father arrested him in his downward course; and before a year of his married life had waned, his young wife had learned to wait and mourn his frequent and uncalled-for absence. More than once had she seen him come home from his midnight haunts, the bright intelligence of his eye displaced by the drunkard's stare, and his manly gait changed to the inebriate's stagger; and she was beginning to know the bitter agony that is compressed in the mournful words, a drunkard's wife. And then there came a bright but brief episode in her experience; the angel of life gave to her existence a deeper meaning and loftier significance: she sheltered in the warm clasp of her loving arms, a dear babe, a precious child, whose love filled every chamber of her heart, and felt the fount of maternal love gushing to new within her soul. That child was hers. How overshadowing was the love with which she bent over its helplessness, how much it helped to fill the void and chasms in her soul. How many lonely hours were beguiled by its winsome ways, its answering smiles and fond caresses. How exquisite and solemn was the feeling that thrilled her heart when she clasped the tiny hands together and taught her dear child to call God "Our Father."

What a blessing was that child. The father paused in his headlong career, awed by the strange beauty and precocious intellect of his child; and the mother's life had a better expression through her ministrations of love. And then there came hours of bitter anguish, shading the sunlight of her home and hushing the music of her heart. The angel of death bent over the couch of her child and beaconed it away. Closer and closer the mother strained her child to her wildly heaving breast, and struggled with the heavy hand that lay upon its heart. Love and agony contended with death, and the language of the mother's heart was,

> "Oh, Death, away! that innocent is mine;
>> I cannot spare him from my arms
> To lay him, Death, in thine.
>> I am a mother, Death; I gave that darling birth
> I could not bear his lifeless limbs
>> Should moulder in the earth."

But death was stronger than love and mightier than agony and won the child for the land of crystal founts and deathless flowers, and the poor, stricken mother sat down beneath the shadow of her mighty grief, feeling as if a great light had gone out from her soul, and that the sunshine had suddenly faded around her path. She turned in her deep anguish to the father of her child, the loved and cherished dead. For awhile his words were kind and tender, his heart seemed subdued, and his tenderness fell upon her worn and weary heart like rain on perishing flowers, or cooling waters to lips all parched with thirst and scorched with fever; but the change was evanescent, the influence of unhallowed associations and evil habits had vitiated and poisoned the springs of his existence. They had bound him in their meshes, and he lacked the moral strength to break his fetters, and stand erect in all the strength and dignity of a true manhood, making life's highest excellence his ideal, and striving to gain it.

And yet moments of deep contrition would sweep over him, when he would resolve to abandon the wine-cup forever, when he was ready to forswear the handling of another card, and he would try to break away from the associations that he felt were working his ruin; but when the hour of temptation came his strength was weakness, his earnest purposes were cobwebs, his well-meant resolutions ropes of sand, and thus passed year after year of the married life of Laura Lagrange. She tried to hide her agony from the public gaze, to smile when her heart was almost breaking. But year after year her voice grew fainter and sadder, her once light and bounding step grew slower and faltering. Year after year she wrestled with agony, and strove with despair, till the quick eyes of her brother read, in the paling of her cheek and the dimming eye, the secret anguish of her worn and weary spirit. On that wan, sad face, he saw the death-tokens, and he knew the dark wing of the mystic angel swept coldly around her path. "Laura," said her brother to her one day, "you are not well, and I think you need our mother's tender care and nursing. You are daily losing strength, and if you will go I will accompany you." At first, she hesitated, she shrank almost instinctively from presenting that pale sad face to the loved ones at home. That face was such a tell-tale; it told of heart-sickness, of hope deferred, and the mournful story of unrequited love. But then a deep yearning for home sympathy woke within her a passionate longing for love's kind words, for tenderness and heart-support, and she resolved to seek the home of her childhood, and lay her weary head upon her mother's bosom, to be folded again in her loving arms, to lay that poor, bruised and aching heart where it might beat and throb closely to the loved ones at home. A kind welcome awaited her. All that love and tenderness could devise was done to bring the bloom to her cheek and the light to her eye; but it was all in vain; hers was a disease that no medicine could cure, no earthly balm would heal. It was a slow wasting of the vital forces, the sickness of the soul. The unkindness and neglect of her husband, lay like a leaden weight upon her heart, and slowly oozed away its life-drops. And where was he that had won her love, and then cast it aside as a useless thing, who rifled her heart of its wealth and spread bitter ashes upon its broken altars? He was lingering away from her when the death-damps were gathering on her brow, when his name was trembling on her lips! lingering away! when she was watching his coming, though the death films were gathering before her eyes, and earthly things were fading from her vision. "I think I hear him now," said the dying woman, "surely that is his step;" but the sound died away in the distance. Again she started from an uneasy slumber, "That is his voice! I am so glad he has come." Tears gathered in the eyes of the sad watchers by that dying bed, for they knew that she was deceived. He had not returned. For her sake they wished his coming. Slowly the hours waned away, and then came the sad, soul-sickening thought that she was forgotten, forgotten in the last hour of human need, forgotten when the spirit, about to be dissolved, paused for the last time on the threshold of existence, a weary watcher at the gates of death. "He has forgotten me," again she faintly murmured, and the last tears she would ever shed on earth sprung to her mournful eyes, and clasping her hands together in silent anguish, a few broken sentences issued from her pale and quivering lips. They were prayers for strength and earnest pleading for him who had desolated her young life, by turning its sunshine to shadows, its smiles to tears. "He has forgotten me," she murmured again, "but I can bear it, the bitterness of death is passed, and soon I hope to exchange the shadows of death for the brightness of eternity, the rugged paths of life for the golden streets of glory, and the care and turmoils of earth for the peace and rest of heaven." Her voice grew fainter and fainter, they saw the shadows that never deceive flit over her pale and faded face, and knew that the death angel waited to soothe their weary one to rest, to calm the throbbing of her bosom and cool the fever of her brain. And amid the silent hush of their grief the freed spirit, refined through suffering, and brought into divine harmony through the spirit of the living Christ, passed over the dark waters of death as on a bridge of light, over whose radiant arches hovering angels bent. They parted the dark locks from her marble brow, closed the waxen lids over the once bright and laughing eye, and left her to the dreamless slumber of the grave. Her cousin turned from that death-bed a sadder and wiser woman. She resolved more earnestly than ever to make the world better by her example, gladder by her presence, and to kindle the fires of her genius on the altars of universal love and truth. She had a higher and better object in all her writings than the mere acquisition of gold, or acquirement of fame. She felt that she had a high and holy mission on the battle-field of existence, that life was not given her to be frittered away in nonsense, or wasted away in trifling pursuits. She would willingly espouse an unpopular cause but not an unrighteous one. In her the down-trodden slave found an earnest advocate; the flying fugitive remembered her kindness as he stepped cautiously through our Republic, to gain his freedom in a monarchial land, having broken the chains on which the rust of centuries had gathered. Little children learned to name her with affection, the poor called her blessed, as she broke her bread to the pale lips of hunger. Her life was like a beautiful story, only it was clothed with the dignity of reality and invested with the sublimity of truth. True, she was an old maid, no husband brightened her life with his love, or shaded it with his neglect. No children nestling lovingly in her arms called her mother. No one appended Mrs. to her name; she was indeed an old maid, not vainly striving to keep up an appearance of girlishness, when departed was written on her youth. Not vainly pining at her loneliness and isolation: the world was full of warm, loving hearts, and her own beat in unison with them. Neither was she always sentimentally sighing for something to love, objects of affection were all around her, and the world was not so wealthy in love that it had no use for her's; in blessing others she made a life and benediction, and as old age descended peacefully and gently upon her, she had learned one of life's most precious lessons, that true happiness consists not so much in the fruition of our wishes as in the regulation of desires and the full development and right culture of our whole natures.

1859

Nonfiction

ON MARRIAGE

from The Doctrines and Discipline of
the African Methodist Episcopal Church

Quest. 1. Do we observe any evil which has prevailed among our societies with respect to marriage?

Answ. Many of our members have married with *unawakened* persons. This has produced bad effects: they have been either hindered for life, or have turned back to perdition.

Quest. 2. What can be done to discourage this?

Answ. 1. Let every preacher publicly enforce the apostle's caution, "Be ye not unequally yoked together with unbelievers." 2 *Cor.* vi. 14.

2. Let him declare, whoever does this, will be put back on trial six months.

3. When any such is put back on trial, let a suitable exhortation be subjoined.

4. Let all be exhorted to take no step in so weighty a matter, without advising with the most serious of their brethren.

Quest. 3. Ought any woman to marry without the consent of her parents?

Answ. In general she ought not. Yet there may be exceptions. For if, 1. A woman believe it to be her duty to marry: If, 2. Her parents absolutely refuse to let her marry any Christian: then she may, nay, ought to marry without their consent. Yet even then a Methodist preacher ought not to be married to her.

We do not prohibit our people from marrying persons who are not of our society, provided such persons have the form, and are seeking the power of godliness; but we are determined to discourage their marrying persons who do not come up to this description. And even in a doubtful case, the member shall be put back on trial.

1817

A BACHELOR'S THERMOMETER

from Freedom's Journal

Years

16. Incipient palpitations towards the young ladies.
17. Blushing and confusion in conversing with them.
18. Confidence in conversing with them much increased.
19. Angry if treated by them as a boy.
20. Very conscious of his own charms and manliness.
21. A looking glass indispensable in his room to admire himself.
22. Insufferable puppyism.
23. Thinks no woman good enough for him.
24. Caught unawares by the snares of Cupid.
25. The connexion broken off, from self-conceit on his part.
26. Conducts himself with much superiority towards her.
27. Pays his addresses to another lady, not without hope of mortifying the first.
28. Mortified and frantic at being refused.
29. Rails against the fair sex in general.
30. Morose and out of humor in all conversations on matrimony.
31. Contemplates matrimony more under the influence of interest than formerly.
32. Considers personal beauty in a wife not so indispensable as formerly.
33. Still retains a high opinion of his attractions as a husband.
34. Consequently has no idea but he may still marry a chicken.
35. Falls deeply and violently in love with one of seventeen.
36. Au darnier desepoir another refusal.
37. Indulges in every kind of dissipation.
38. Shuns the best part of the female sex.
39. Suffers much remorse and mortification in so doing.
40. A fresh budding of matrimonial ideas, but no spring shoots.
41. A nice young widow perplexes him.
42. Ventures to address her with mixed sensations of love and interest.
43. Interest prevails, which causes much cautious reflection.
44. The widow jilts him, being as cautious as himself.
45. Becomes every day more averse to the fair sex.
46. Gouty and nervous symptoms begin to appear.
47. Fears what may become of him when old and infirm.

48. Thinks living alone quite irksome.
49. Resolves to have a prudent young woman as house keeper and companion.
50. A nervous affection about him, and frequent stocks of the gout.
51. Much pleased with his new housekeeper as nurse.
52. Begins to feel some attachment to her.
53. His pride revolts at the idea of marrying her.
54. Is in great distress how to act.
55. Completely under her influence and very miserable.
56. Many painful thoughts about parting with her.
57. She refuses to live any longer with him solo.
58. Gouty, nervous, and bilious to excess.
59. Feels very ill, sends for her to his bedside, and intends espousing her.
60. Grows rapidly worse, has his will made in her favour, and makes his exit.

1827

THE OLD MAID'S DIARY

from Freedom's Journal

Years

15. Anxious for coming out and the attention of the men.
16. Begins to have some idea of the tender passion.
17. Talks of love in a cottage, and disinterested affection.
18. Fancies herself in love with some handsome man, who has flattered her.
19. Is a little more difficult, in consequence of being noticed.
20. Commences fashionable, and dashes.
21. Still more confidence in her own attractions, and expects a brilliant establishment.
22. Refuses a good offer, because he is not a man of fashion.
23. Flirts with every young man she meets.
24. Wonders she is not married.
25. Rather more circumspect in her conduct.
26. Begins to think a large fortune not quite so indispensable.
27. Prefers the company of rational men to flirting.
28. Wishes to be married in a quiet way, with a comfortable income.
29. Almost despairs of entering the married state.
30. Rather fearful of being called an old maid.
31. An additional love of dress.
32. Professes to dislike balls, finding it difficult to get good partners.
33. Wonders how men can leave the society of sensible men to flirt with chits.
34. Affects good humor in her conversation with men.
35. Jealous of the praises of women.
36. Quarrels with her friend, who is lately married.
37. Thinks herself slighted in society.
38. Likes talking of her acquaintance who are married unfortunately, and finds consolation in their misfortune.
39. Ill nature increases.
40. Very meddling and officious. —N.B. A growing penchant.
41. If rich, as a dernier resort makes love to a young man without fortune.
42. Not succeeding, rails against the sex.
43. Partiality for cards and scandal commences.
44. Severe against the manners of the age.
45. Strong predilection for a Methodist parson.

46. Enraged at his desertion.
47. Becomes descending, and takes snuff.
48. Turns all her sensibility to cats and dogs.
49. Adopts a dependent relation to attend on dogs.
50. Becomes disgusted with the world, and vents all her ill humour on this unfortunate relation.

1827

"SIC A WIFE"

from Freedom's Journal

> *Sic a wife as Willie had, I wad na gie a button for her.*
> —Robert Burns

It is about three years since Charles Parker was married to his present wife. Charley was what you may call a right down clever fellow, and was remarkable for thinking himself in love with every pretty girl that passed him. He became acquainted with Louisa Smith, and he found no difficulty in persuading her to take the additional name of Parker. The sun came and went, the Honey Moon was well nigh passed, and Charley was beginning to think his wife was—not an Angel. But whatever were his thoughts, they were locked up in the recess of his own breast. We were often at the house, for Charles and ourself had been intimately connected, and we as often saw that things did not run so smoothly as might be wished. Sometimes we met a cloudy face, and sullen looks would greet us on entering the abode of our friend. We said nothing, for we knew curtain lectures were a part of the daily economy of married people. We had not been to Charley's for a week (an unusual absence) & we thought we would just step in to see how he and his wife did. It was a lovely night, a refreshing shower had imparted a pleasant coolness to the heated air of the city, and we sallied forth thinking no evil, and of course fearing none. What happened on that night, we shall never forget. It seems as if it occurred but yesterday, and the impression it has left on our mind, is as firm and lasting as time itself. No, no, sooner may Major Noah forget the occurrences of the 20th of June, than we forget what happened on that night. We had reached the house and were about turning the latch of the parlor door, we hesitated a moment, for there was something we thought like high words within, but our evil destiny hurried us on. We opened the door, and instead of receiving the friendly grasp of our friends' hand, a glass pitcher whirled with tremendous power from the hands of his wife, intended no doubt for himself, came in contact with our forehead just above the right eye, and floored us in an instant. It may have been that in falling to the earth in search of the centre of gravity, our head struck against the latch of the parlor door, and caused the terrible gash in the face. But that point is immaterial, for we know that our face was cut, and that it was done by our friends wife, whether by means of the door or pitcher we care not. We left the house you may be sure with certain feelings towards the lady, and it is from the bottom of hearts we speak, when we say

"We wad na gie a button for her."

Much rather had we remain in our present state of bachelorship with no one to discompose the serenity of our minds than run the risk of experiencing the like "connubial devilries."

1828

AN UNMARRIED WOMAN

from Freedom's Journal

An unmarried woman, negligent of her person, has no occasion to look out for a husband—few gentlemen will select ladies for wives, who are not attentive to their graces.

1828

A GOLD REPEATER RETURNED TO THE WATCHMAKER

from Freedom's Journal

Sir.—This Young Lady, although adorned with a fair and handsome face, and delicate hands, I have too much reason to believe has a bad heart. The traits of her character are, disregard for truth, yea, she is guilty of downright lying; and this too in the presence of her betters. If she speaks audibly, it is falsehood, and her very whispers are deception. Her obstinacy is provoking, for you know very well, how oft she has been reproved and corrected. I fear also that she had seen out her 'teens' long before I had the misfortune of being introduced to her acquaintance. I would part with her, yes, affecting as it may seem, I would willing part with her for what she has cost me. May be you can find a companion for her of more patience than I possess, if so, do let the perverse, deceitful, though pretty creature go, and she shall not be regretted by
   Yours & c,
   A.

1828

LEWIS WHITE ADVERTISES

from Freedom's Journal

Lewis White, a man of colour in Buffalo advertises for a wife among "the fair sex of colour—" He adopts this mode to save time, as the search would interfere, with his business that of wheel & chair maker—Lewis may find to his cost, that a good wife is not to be obtained through the newspapers; for those qualities which make a wife desirable, be she black or white cause her to shun public notoriety.

1829

TWO SCHOOL GIRLS

Ann Plato

I heard two girls as they conversed. "Good morning," said one, "where are you walking, and don't you calculate to attend school any more?" The answer was, "I am going to visit our Natural History Room; and do not think of attending school at present."

With these two girls I was well acquainted. Afterwards, as I reflected, I could not help saying to myself, "I think by her appearance in school, that she does not gain as much useful knowledge, as the one who was about to visit the Natural History Room."

In school, she does not pay that attention to studies as does her friend. She hastily runs over them, and pursues the lessons that require the least labor. Gives a short recitation of poetry and dialogue. She undertakes mathematics, and thinks them too dull for her—at length they are dropped. Her writing is ill performed. Her rapid and confused elocution, if not attended to, will be found adhesive through life. On this account her teacher is often obliged to speak to her, while at recitation.

Her friend is an industrious and careful girl while in school. She seeks knowledge from the most difficult and useful studies, as well as those which are less so. She collects her mind and thoughts upon the lesson which may be marked for her.

Although not in school as much as the other, still she has gained more useful knowledge, and is more prepared to encounter the world's troubles. She who is not willing to contend with difficulties, is not fitted for this world. "The being who best knows for what end we were placed here, has scattered in our path something beside roses."

Although she was not altogether distinguished for fine talents, yet she was a thorough scholar. Her answers were with entire correctness and precision. When not in school, she employed herself in that which would give her the most useful and solid instruction. She visited scenes which would help to deepen that knowledge.

She felt strongly, that strength of intellect is acquired by conquering hard studies, and strength of character by overcoming obstacles. She knew that knowledge painfully gained was not easily lost.

Look at them, after their course of scholastic training! One, with her family, considering it her ambition to make a showy appearance. No rational economy—no patience to study, nor self-control to practice. By her wasteful expenditure of dress, and servants, their affairs became seriously embarrassed; and she too helpless to do anything in their distress.

The fortune of the husband of her friend was not large; but by constant economy, she was able to secure every comfort, and to remember the poor. Her family was well regulated, and taught order, industry, and perseverance which she herself had learned. In observing these families, it was clear whose was the seat of the greatest order, comfort and happiness.

Time was, when the temple of science was barred against the foot of woman. Heathen tyranny held her in vassalage, and Mahometan prejudice pronounced her without a soul. Now, from the sanctuary which knowledge and wisdom have consecrated, and from whence she was so long excluded, the interdict is taken away. How does she prize the gift? Does she press to gain a stand at the temple of knowledge, or will she clothe her brow in vanity, and be satisfied with ignorance. May we improve the influence which is now given us, and seek for "glory and immortality beyond the grave."

1841

A BACHELOR ADVERTISES

from Provincial Freeman

A bachelor advertised for a "help-mate," one who would prove "a companion for his heart, his hand, and his lot." A fair one replying, asked very earnestly, "how big is your lot?"

1855

MATRIMONY

from Repository of Religion and Literature

Do you see that woman there? Her head is full of the most pleasing thoughts about the day when she will be led, leaning on the arm of her beloved to Hymen's altar, and there with fluttering heart and faltering lips whispers her vows to love and to cherish till life itself shall cease.

Do you know what are the preparations she is making for the momentous day—that joyous hour? Why she is shopping, buying, and also making all the articles necessary for the handsome wardrobe of a bride.

Now she is consulting her dear mother, then her bride's maid, and then her mantua-maker about the color, quality, and style of her wedding dress. Nor does she forget to commune with her beloved about the house in which they shall live, the furniture that shall decorate it, and the minister, who shall have the honor to pronounce them husband and wife.

Again she is busy in making out the list of the names of those who shall be invited to the marriage feast, and of the delicious viands, with which they shall be entertained; nor is she less concerned about the graceful manner in which she will conduct herself on that occasion.

Well the day is come, and the hour also, when her maiden name is to be changed; she enters her chamber, goes to the wardrobe, and takes out her bridal dress—she goes to the casket, and takes out her bridal jewels—she is now at the toilet, oiling, combing, curling, pressing her hair—dressing herself.

The last pin is stuck, the last string is tied—the handkerchief perfumed— the glove placed upon her hands—she is done—she looks like a full bloom rose, and is as sweet. She is now ready to be led by her espoused to the place where the sacred knot is to be tied. The groom enters the chamber, and with majestic strides leads her to the altar.

Behold! while the minister of the sanctuary invokes the blessings of God upon her, she tremblingly takes the vows, and becomes a wife.

May-hap, every thought has passed through her mind, but one thought; every feeling through her heart, but one feeling. That unknown thought is God's *design* in matrimony—that unfelt emotion, the obligations of a mother.

Young woman, wilt thou be wise? Hear me then; sister, daughter, listen while I whisper in your ears the teachings of our holy religion. In so doing, you may be saved from the deceptions of a villain, and the embraces of a murderer.

But let me set thee to thinking. Let me stir up in thy minds thoughts which will never sleep nor slumber,—emotions which, swelling up from the heart's deep fountains, shall impel thee to such a course of action, as will result in good to earth, and glory to heaven.

Do you know who instituted matrimony? When and where he instituted it? And what was his design in its institution?

Think, sweet one, think of these questions till we meet again. Mind, I tell you there is a mystery in matrimony, which none can read but the initiated; which none can fully understand but the soul which is taught of heaven.

And there is beauty also, beauty as angels love to gaze upon, and God delights to cherish. The rose, full blown, with a dozen rose-buds smiling round it, is not more beauteous—nor more fragrant.

Well, who among the ladies have thought upon our questions, and is now prepared to answer them? Do you hesitate, and do you ask me to give back the reply?

1st. Who instituted matrimony? Our respect for an institution is always more or less increased by the greatness of the character of its founder. And if it be well adapted to promote the happiness of the community in which it exists, we never fail to cherish it the more; at the same time that our respect is raised to that height of feeling which we call veneration.

Now, the author of matrimony is God, the great, the good, the just, the wise, the holy God. This fact alone, is sufficient to make us look at matrimony with other than wanton eyes, and to study it with other than a careless mind.

2d. Where was it instituted? Eden, in its pristine beauty and purity was the place of its birth. A garden filled with luscious fruits, and decked with flowers as beautiful as they were fragrant, gay with the perching, the flying, and singing of birds, whose plumage vied with the hues of the rainbow—the seat of happiness and immortality.

Then, we say, it was not stained by sin. The footsteps of the "evil one" had not polluted it, nor any unseemly object marred its loveliness. How becoming the place, for so holy an institution!

It was consummated when Adam rapturously exclaimed, "This is bone of my bone, and flesh of my flesh, she shall be called *woman*, because she was *taken out of man.*"

God had finished the formation of the earth, and decked it with herbs, plants, trees and flowers—poured out fountains, rivers, and oceans, and formed all the inferior animals with that degree of elegance and strength, which was best suited to their respective natures. But there was one wanting, the mind, the power to subdue and rule them.

Then said the Creator, "Let us make man in our own image, after our own likeness." It was done. Formed out of the dust of the earth, man stood erect, growing in the image of his Maker.

Looking up to heaven, he saw it robed with magnificence, and sublimity; looking down upon earth, he beheld it teeming with life and loveliness. But neither in heaven above nor the earth beneath did he see a creature like unto himself. To the man such a creature was a felt need, and the benevolent deity was at hand to supply it. Causing a deep sleep to fall upon Adam; he took one of his ribs and formed a woman—formed her like the man in his own image after his own likeness.

Blooming in grace and beauty he brought her to the man for his help-mate, and gave them this command: "Be faithful, multiply and replenish the earth."

To understand the scope of this mandate, let us glance at the intellectual and moral character of the newly wedded pair. In intellect they were as clear as the sun-beam, knowing God, and comprehending their relations to him.

In morals, they were as pure as the breath of heaven, loving God with all their heart, with all their soul, and with all their might. The breathing of their lips was praise; the pulsations of their hearts were adoration. Ask we now, in what were they to be fruitful? In holy beings like themselves, full of intellect, and full of love. With these they were to replenish the earth—to be fruitful, multiply and replenish it.

They were by this command unalterable and just, by this command, we maintain, they were to be the progenitors of a race as intelligent, righteous, and holy as the angels of heaven—a race who after perfecting themselves in virtue here on earth, should like Enoch be carried to heaven in the bosom of God—or like Elijah, ascend in a chariot of fire, to engage in the higher and nobler occupations of an endless life.

Such was the design of the deity in the institution of matrimony.

O, matrimony! thou glorious offspring of the skies. How high and holy was thine origin! How beneficent thy design! Thy ministering priest, was the eternal! Thy attendants, rejoicing angels! Thy temple, the green earth; thy bridal chamber, roseate Eden—thine offspring, countless millions of holy, and happy worshippers, loving, praising, adoring their Creator.

Young ladies, young gentlemen, I have made known to you the design of the Almighty in this sacred institution. Did ever the idea enter your bosoms? The great majority of mankind never spend a thought upon it. A desire to comply with it never forms a part of their motives to marry.

Some marry to increase their respectability and power: some for beauty, some for gold, others for the gratification of unholy lust. But few are they, who marry to fulfill the holy behests of the Almighty.

Hence, we see some of the reasons why there are so many strifes, heart burnings, jealousies, abandonments, divorces, and murders, that have made, and still make so many homesteads the very pictures of hell.

Not long since a young lady told me that she had not been married a week, before she wished again and again that she had never been married.

I once asked a young married woman her reasons for marrying. She said, "I thought I ought to be married, and therefore I got married."

More than three-fourths of all the married people I have ever met and conversed with on this subject, had no conception of the design of God in this institution.

In the summer of 1846, a young lady of uncommon intellect and wide information, said to me in a very playful manner, "O you gentlemen of the black coat, can tie us, but you cannot untie us." Three years after she was suing for a divorce; I then asked her why did she marry; her answer was, "I don't know why."

In 1850, Rhode Island, the smallest State of the union, granted more than three hundred divorces. How many were granted by the others I know not, nor the number of sighs, tears, broken hearts, and other domestic miseries known to any mind but the infinite.

Do you ask, if this statement be true? How can it be otherwise? There is no law of the universe which can be violated with impunity. If men and women will marry in a manner, in a spirit, and from motives that contraverne the laws of heaven, can any other consequence follow than misery?

Let none expect sweet waters to flow from a bitter fountain. Nay, rather let them look for nothing but the curses of an indignant God to descend upon them like a crushing avalanche, burying all their hopes of domestic happiness in a grave that shall never see a resurrection.

Young women, you have been to a marriage feast: there you have seen a young couple joined in holy wedlock; you have witnessed the beautiful and the gay in the giddy dance; you have heard the sound of the tamborine and the violin, the loud laugh and the witty joke. This has made you believe that matrimony is the greatest good of human life. You have therefore resolved to accept the first offer.—Beware! What you have seen is all outside, mere show. 'Tis not happiness; 'tis not so much as its shadow!

Remember Psyche; she thought that the beauty of Proserpine was shut up in the box which she bore in her hands, but when she opened it, nothing issued from it but a black exhalation, which struck her to the ground as one that was dead!

Think then, I beseech you, think frequently, and prayerfully upon the heavenly design of matrimony; think of its unspeakable results—beginning in time, ending only with eternity—think till your thoughts kindle into a flame of holy feeling, and these feelings into an unchangable purpose to accomplish the will of Heaven, in this great particular of your life. Then may you reasonably hope for happiness in that blessed estate.

O! woman, remember thy dignity. Thou art not a mere thing, to minister to man's unholy pleasures, nor a toy for him to play with, neither an idol for him to worship. Thou wast made to be a vessel of honor, promotive of the glory of God—a mother, to train immortal spirits to love, serve and adore the King of the Universe.

Arise then, my sister! arise from the dust of degradation into which man has cast thee—yea, rather, into which thou hast thrown thyself.—Arise! for thou mayest yet be the mother of children who will distinguish themselves on earth by their knowledge, goodness and usefulness.

D(ANIEL) A. P(AYNE)

1859

TO AVOID A BAD HUSBAND

from the Christian Recorder

1. Never marry for wealth. A woman's life consisteth not in the things she possesseth.
2. Never marry a fop, or one who struts about dandy-like, in his silk gloves and ruffles, with a silver cane, and rings on his fingers. Beware! There is a trap.
3. Never marry a niggard, a closed-fisted, sordid wretch, who saves every penny, or spends it grudgingly. Take care lest he stint you to death.
4. Never marry a stranger whose character is not known or tested. Some females jump right into the fire with their eyes wide open.
5. Never marry a mope or a drone, one who drawls and draggles through life, one foot after another, and lets things take their own course.
6. Never marry a man who treats his mother or sister unkindly or indifferently. Such treatment is a sure indication of a mean and wicked man.
7. Never on any account marry a gambler or a profane person, one who in the least speaks lightly of God or religion. Such a man can never make a good husband.
8. Never marry a sloven, a man who is negligent of his person or his dress, and is filthy in his habits. The external appearance is an index to the heart.
9. Shun the rake as the snake, a viper, a very demon.
10. Finally, never marry a man who is addicted to the use of ardent spirits. Depend upon it, you are better off alone than you would be were you tied to a man whose breath is polluted, and whose vitals are being gnawed out by alcohol.

In the choice of a wife, take the obedient daughter of a good mother.

1861

THE PLEASURES OF SINGLE LIFE

from the Pacific Appeal

Charles Threewill was endowed by nature with a healthy physical organism. He was good natured, generous and benevolent. He had enjoyed the advantages of a liberal education, under the fostering care of indulgent parents. At the age of sixteen he entered upon the social pleasures of life, being surrounded by friends and admirers among the youth of both sexes. His modest and unassuming deportment were household words. His studious habits and enlightened education, blended with a prepossessing disposition, excited emotions of pleasure in many a fond heart, which in secret meditation indulged in the hope that some kind fairy would convey the enchantment to their anxious and confiding spirit. The dear mothers also claimed the young man as a favorite. They saw much in Charles that was amiable, and they cautiously intimated that it would be a fortunate epoch if Cupid would send his barbed arrow, quivering into the heart of their own dear daughter. To have so worthy a son, whose heart and mind was laid out and planted in the beautiful flowers of life, so luxuriant in growth, would be the height of their felicity.

In private and in public gatherings it was amusing to witness the aspirants for special favor vie with each other, in their efforts to please. Charles was very fond of reading the newspapers, and the young ladies soon discovered the importance he attached to this department of literature.

On one occasion, while a group of ladies were attentive listeners, he told Laura Patience that by devoting a little time and attention to reading the papers it had qualified her to understand the current events of the day, and to discuss their merits in an intelligent manner. He said the ladies should form an opinion and be able to sustain an intelligent conversation concerning the mental, moral and political improvement of our times.

This was a happy moment for Laura. She felt elated, and the overpowering impression flashed through her mind when she said mentally, how glad am I that reading the newspapers has been a portion of my education.

A few ladies that were present suffered an agony that tongue cannot express. They had spent much of the time in frivolity, and in reading fictitious books, which did not add to their fund of knowledge, and in the presence of Charles they felt a painful imperfection, being unable to excite his admiration or to win his heart. They expected to make a favorable impression on his mind, because of their graceful deportment and beautiful appearance. Laura, however, was never considered beautiful, but her comeliness was proverbial.

Charles was not unmindful of the influence and esteem which his favored position in society exerted, and in due time he expected to select the most valuable gem in the cluster. He felt confident of success, because his character and motives were pure and exalted. The task was difficult, as he was surrounded by a galaxy of attractions. He was finally relieved from the dilemma, after repeating the following lines:

> "What is the blooming tincture of the skin,
>   To peace of mind and harmony within?
> What the bright sparkling of the finest eye
>   To the soft soothing of a calm reply?
> Can comeliness of form, or shape, or air,
> With comeliness of words or deeds compare?
> No: those at first the unwary heart may gain.
> But these, these only can the heart retain."

Charles decided to offer his hand and heart to the highly cultivated and devoted Laura, whose life reflected the refulgent rays of virtue, industry and benevolence. He believed that, in so doing, his happiness would be increased, and that he would find Laura a comfort and support in time of adversity; and whenever prosperity smiled on him, Laura, too, would thank God in her morning and evening prayer.

1862

YOUNG LADIES OF TO-DAY

From the Christian Recorder

Did you ever think what a contrast there is between the young lady of to-day, and the one of fifty or even a score of years ago? Then, a lady was one who could take care of herself—could sing in plain musical English, wash, bake and cook all kinds of food, milk a cow if necessary, and make herself generally useful. If she didn't she was called lazy—that was all there was about it. But now, we have no lazy women, they are all delicate. The modern young lady is a strange compound of dress and nerves—by which we mean those "exquisite susceptibilities" which cause her to shudder when she sees a washtub, and scream at the sight of a cow. She is a living image made to be waited upon. She sings "divinely" and plays the piano "exquisitely," but neither one of these affects you as much as the "jabbering of a North American Indian," for it is not half as intelligible. She lounges about in the morning, crochets or embroiders a little, then dresses herself up and promenades for the benefit of some "genteel exquisite." Thus passes her days. Now you needn't tell me that old bachelors are continually harping on women's faults—that we do not find any such ladies—that they are the same they always were. It is no such thing. It is an uncommon thing, indeed, to find a young lady now-a-days who half pays for the food she eats. She is nothing but a bill of expense to her father, and a larger one to her husband, for he has not only her to support, but one or two hired girls to wait upon her also. My advice to every young man is to beware of a fashionable young lady. Never marry the girl who sits in the parlor while her mother stands in the kitchen. It won't pay.

1864

HOW TO MAKE BEAN SOUP

from the Christian Recorder

An "old bachelor" of thirty years' standing, advertises in one of our agricultural exchanges for a receipt to make bean soup. A fair correspondent thus answers his request: "Get a wife that knows how to make."

Sensible advice.

1865

YOKED UNEQUALLY

from the Christian Recorder

> *"Be ye not unequally yoked with unbelievers."*
> —2 Cor. Vi., 14

As wisdom in the choice of companions is thus important, still more important is the exercise of Christian wisdom in the choice of a companion for life. There is no subject on which many professors of religion seem so inattentive to the rules of duty as on this, and most deplorable are the consequences of their sin and folly. If you have already entered that union which death only must dissolve and have formed it with one who is a stranger to the paths of peace, the advice contained in this chapter can be of little service to you. The die is cast, and cast for life. Your duty is to watch and pray that you may not be drawn into the paths of the destroyer. Endeavor to act the Christian's part. Labor and pray for the eternal welfare of him or her who may be as dear to you as your own life; but who you are aware is not dear to God, but perishing in sin; with what melting pity should you behold the friend of your bosom, the partner of your heart, no sharer with you in even one spiritual blessing, dear to you through nature's ties, but an enemy to your God; with what sorrow should you think that the friend who was traveling with you the journey of life sharing its cares and its comforts, has no inheritance in your home, but when the journey of his ends must be separated from you to meet no more through all eternity; how fervent should be your prayers. How watched your conduct, that if possible you may lead this dear but perishing friend to your Saviour for life and peace and pardon. But if you have not entered into the marriage union, then as you love your soul, as you regard your peace, as you value the favor of your God never form that connection with any one however amiable, however moral, however endowed, with the gifts of fortune or nature, who is not a decided follower of the Lord Jesus Christ.

This advice may be enforced by reasons the most weighty and momentous. Marriage between those who partake of divine grace and those who are strangers to religion is represented in the Scriptures as the unequal source of the greatest evils, and such matches are abundantly condemned, according to the sense usually attributed to several verses in the sixth chapter of Genesis. Unhallowed marriages are represented as the cause of that dreadful wickedness which occasioned the destruction of mankind by the general deluge. It was when the sons of God chose for their wives the fair but impious daughters of men, that the iniquity of man became so great as to call down that dreadful judgment from a patient and merciful God. These wicked connections matured human depravity, filled up the measure of man's iniquity, ripened a world for impending vengeance, banished the last lingering traces of piety from almost every heart, made this earth a scene of dreadful desolation and hurried multitudes to the pit of eternal night.

REV. A. J. KERSHAW

1876

BIGAMY

from Life and Adventures of James Williams

Let me give the reader a few items on Bigamy. They say bigamy is a wrong and a curse to the land. So say I, but I noticed, during my visit to Salt Lake, that it is one of the handsomest cities in the United States, with beautiful streams of clear water running through the streets. And Brigham allowed a man to have as many wives as he was able to take care of, but he must be able to take care of them. There were no whisky-mills, no dance-houses, and no gambling-houses, and no houses of ill-repute. Let us see the difference. Since Americans have been there, there are dance-houses, whiskey-mills, gambling-houses, and houses of ill-repute. Let me ask the reader a question: How is it that in the United States men run away with other men's wives, married men keeping three or four different women, outside of the family circle, and no notice taken of that? Which is the best law, to allow a man to marry a number of women and be able to take care of them, or allow a man to marry one and be not able to take care of her, and running away with several, and no notice of it? Then I am not an advocate of these doctrines, but I only say that we, some of the colored people, who are possessed of little learning, take notice of these matters. Look at Salt Lake four years ago, and look at it to-day, and you will see the difference. I say Brigham is an old man, and I say that we should let him alone during his lifetime.

1893

MARRIAGE LICENSE.

Bureau of Refugees, Freedmen and Abandoned Lands,
State of Kentucky, *Pendleton* County, *Oct 19th* 186 *6*

TO ALL WHOM IT MAY CONCERN:

The RITES OF MATRIMONY are permitted to be solmenized between *James L. Warner*, a free man of color, and *Cloa Coal* a free woman of color, the requirements of the law having been complied with.

Witness my signature as Superintendent of Freedmen, Refugees, &c.

A. S. V. Bloor

Sup't. Freedmen and Refugees, ▬ District.

Lyrics

WEDDING COLORS

Anonymous

Marry in green, your husband will be mean.
Marry in red, you will wish yourself dead.
Marry in brown, you will live in town.
Marry in blue, your husband will be true.
Marry in black, you will wish yourself back.
Marry in gray, you will stray away.
Marry in pink, your love will sink,
Marry in white, you have chose all right.

SLAVE MARRIAGE

Anonymous

Dark an' stormy may come de wedder;
I jines dis he-male an' dis she-male togedder.
Let none, but Him dat makes de thunder,
Put dis he-male an' dis she-male asunder.
I darfore 'nounce you bofe de same.
Be good, go'long, an' keep up yo' name.
De broomstick's jumped, de worl's not wide.
She's now yo' own. Salute yo' bride!

Illustration on page 131: Marriage license issued to James L. Warner and Cloa Coal (National Archives)

WRITTEN IN A BRIDE'S ALBUM

A[lfred] G[ibbs] Campbell

On the stream of wedded life
Hath your bark begun to glide;
Oh! may no sad breath of strife
Ever ruffle its smooth tide.

May your skies be ever bright,
And your heart forever free
From the sorrows which can blight
Hopes that now thrill joyously.

May each happy, youthful dream
Yours in full fruition be,
As you float adown the stream
To the broad, eternal sea.

O'er that broad sea may you find
Haven of delightful rest,
Where love still your souls shall bind,
And you be forever blest!

1883

MARRIAGE

Mary Weston Fordham

The die is cast, come weal, come woe,
    Two lives are joined together,
For better or for worse, the link
    Which naught but death can sever.
The die is cast, come grief, come joy.
    Come richer, or come poorer,
If love but binds the mystic tie,
    Blest is the bridal hour.

1897

Fiction

CONVERSATION

from Southern Workman

This is a conversation between a young lady and a gentleman. The girl's father wants her to marry a man with an education, so she consults with her father about the young man who is coming to see her.

SCENE I.

The first call.

HE. — "Good evening, kind miss."

SHE. — "Good evening, sir."

HE. — "Large circumstances (circles) round the moon."

SHE. — "Sir?"

HE. — "Kind miss, your eyes look like terriable dog eyes," (turtle dove eyes).

SHE. — "Oh, no sir."

HE. — "Oh, kind lady, you have gained my heart."

SHE. — "Yes, sir."

HE. — "Lady, may I have the pleasure of coming from my residence to your happy home to gain your heart and mind?"

SHE. — "Oh, sir, you will have to ask my father."

HE. — "Do your father allow you to keep company, lady?"

SHE. — "Yes, sir, with a gentleman of education."

HE. — "I shall call some other evening, lady, to see you again. Good bye."

He goes away to get some one to teach him some large words and how to use them, when he calls on the young lady another time.

SCENE II.

The girl is consulting with her father.

SHE. — "Father, have you any objections to my getting married?"

FATHER. — "To whom, daughter?"

SHE. — "To the milkman on Mars George plantation."

FATHER. — "Is he got any learning?"

SHE. — "Yes, father, you just ought to hear him split dick," (dictionary.)

FATHER. — "Yes, daughter, when will he be here?"

SHE. — "This evening, I think. He was here last night."

SCENE III.

(*Daughter alone. Father in next room where he can hear the conversation. Young man raps at the door and enters.*)

SHE. — "Good evening, sir."

HE. — "Good evening, kind miss. Seems as if I have seen you several times during the past, and your bewildering countenance has taken such impression on my heart, till necessity compels me to ask you one question."

SHE. — "Oh, kind sir, have you come from the plantation to-night?"

HE. — "Yes, miss, all the way by the marl spring."

SHE. — "It is no use for you to come from your residence to my home to gain my heart and mind, because the chunk is gone out and you can't kindle it, the road is grown up and you can't clear it, the spring is gone dry and you can't get any water out of it."

(*Then she turns and goes out to supper, leaving her caller in the room. While at supper she and her father converse together.*)

FATHER. — "Help yourself, daughter."

SHE. — "I have eaten sufficiently. Any more would be conbunctious to my system."

FATHER. — (*Not understanding the large words*) "Have you been out fishing?"

SHE. — "No, eaten a plenty."

FATHER. — "Caught twenty? Why, we had better have some for breakfast."

(*The girl now goes back into the room and the conversation between her and her visitor begins again.*)

HE. — "For several times I have attempted, my heart failing me each time. Now with the greatest and last resolution that ever human was endowed with, I again ask you for your heart, your hand and your all."

SHE. — "Wait until I see my father. (*Goes out.*) Father, the young man wants my heart, my hand and my all."

FATHER. — "What does he want? Wait a minute, and I will go and get them for him."

(Father goes and gets his brass rasp (meaning the heart) a turkey wing (for the hand) and the shoe awl. These he gives to his daughter.)

SHE. — "Oh, father, he means me."
FATHER. — "You are too young to marry, daughter send him away."

(She goes out and tells the young man all the conversation between her father and herself. Then she recites to him these lines.)

> When I become of age
>   I promise to marry thee,
> If father won't consent
>   I'll run away with you.

(After this the young man goes off to sea and stays a long while or until the girl becomes of age. Then he writes her the following letter.)

DEAR POLLIE:
I will now write you a few notes, and if your heart is willing, some day I will be at your house.

> You ask your dear old father,
>   The sad and story tell
> That I am the one that loves you,
>   Oh, yes, I love you well.
> And if he says you can marry
>   The man he turned away,
>
> If not too young to marry
>   Will you write the wedding day?
> Still land and sea divides us,
>   Your face I can not see,
> Still I am the man that loves you.
>   Pollie, do you love me?
> I love you as I foresaid,
>   Morning, mid-day and night:
> You are the rainbow on my port bow
>   And the light-house on my right.
> Pollie, my dear, good night.
>   J.

1895

Nonfiction

MISERIES OF AN ENGAGED MAN

from Freedom's Journal

> *"Trifles such as these*
> *To serious mischiefs lead."*

Were you ever engaged, Mr. Editor? tied down to the apron strings of a woman to laugh when she laughs, frown when she frowns, and what is worse than ten thousand furies, to spend your cash when she commands, nay, even hints. "He that steals my name steals trash." "A breath can give it as a breath has made" But, "he that filches from me, my good purse robs me of that which makes me poor indeed." And so I am likely to continue unless I can prevail upon my "kind dearie" to be married as soon as possible. It's the only way to retrieve my ruined fortunes, and unless it is done at once, I stand a good chance of losing even that comfort. It is no small addition to my mortification in the midst of all my misery, to be called a happy fellow! "Oh! happiness, our beings end and aim." So says the poet, but then he was never engaged. The end and aim of the luckless youth who happens to be engaged is to render himself miserable, in order to make the intended of his heart happy. His sole purpose is to study various means for his own discomfort, by yielding to and pampering the extravagancies and fancies of his "lady-love." What cares he for "sordid dust" when his maiden's wishes are to be supplied. Swift as the wind flies his rhino, and he not unfrequently has the pleasing satisfaction of knowing that he has spent his last penny in her service. Wo be unto the man's soul that shows the least unwillingness to expend his all, yea, even his little all. Epithet after epithet is heaped upon his devoted head; spiritless wretch and miserable puppy, is uttered from every lip; his reputation is forever gone, and his only refuge is a long cheerless sojourn in the dreary abodes allotted to all old bachelors. Happy is the man, who, as soon as he has heard the "sweet confession," can find a parson who will straightway make them twain one flesh. Let him not encounter a long courtship, for he may rest assured no blood-sucker will gorge itself more freely, more fully, than she with whom he is thus situated. I know something about these matters, quorum nars magna fui; that is to say, I have been engaged three years! years of trouble and of toil. I was getting a weekly pay of ten dollars. I did think by prudence and economy to lay up something at the end of the year. Vain hope! I fell in love, and was engaged to be married! and thereby hangs my tale. A visit to the theatre every now and then was indispensable. I should not have cared so much about this, but then there were always some three or four young ladies in her train, who did, so like to go to the theatre, only they had no gentleman to take them. Of course as I thought my self a gentleman, I was obliged to take the hint. Then came a walk on the battery every fine evening, with its attendant curses of ice-cream, lemonade, soda-water, &c. &c. &c. for herself and half a dozen very particular friends. I will not tire your patience—I will only say that I have been unable to save a cent. I have also heard, but I cannot believe it, that my sweetheart has said once or twice, I am too poor for her. I am determined to bring the matter to a point. If she still loves me, she must marry me next week, or not at all. I will not be bamboozled any longer. My motive in giving you this was with a hope of benefiting those of your readers who have never been engaged. E. E.

1828

MISERIES OF AN ENGAGED WOMAN

from Freedom's Journal

"Sad I am! nor small is my cause of wo!"

I saw in a late number of your paper, Mr. Editor the 'miseries of an engaged man,' depicted in somewhat glowing colours, "Miseries of an engaged man!" I exclaimed in the bitterness of my heart, what are they? Nothing! a cloud that will disperse with one beam from the eye of his 'lady-love'; but the sorrows, the heart-burnings, and anguish of myself, me an engaged woman? yes, and after two years standing, are worth commiserating. To commence then, I am a respectable female of twenty-two, as pretty as you would wish to cast your eyes on, possessing the true embon point: but to convey to you in a word a correct idea of myself, I am what you men are sometimes obliged to acknowledge, 'an elegant woman.' I have sung till my listeners melted into tears. An envious old maid once assured me, however, that it was from other cause than the melody I breathed. I silenced her with one look. My fortune (I mention all) is small. I shall be the heiress of perhaps a lone thousand, when my doting old mother is gone. It is to be expected, of course, that a female possessing the charms I have above described, would have beaus fluttering round her, eager for the partial smile of beauty, and the melting tones of her siren voice. These I had, in all their endless variety, bucks of taste and fashion, but heartless as a miser. Now you must know that I have had my dreams of love and bliss, and that their theme was some young Endymon, all feeling and sensibility, who could pour over the pages of the last novel, and melt into tenderness at the sight of a sympathetic paragraph, or glow with anger in the detestation of an act of meanness. Such a one I finally saw in the person of Edward B.; with a pleasing form he united much suavity of manners and urbanity of conduct. If I had foibles, he must have flattered them, for I became insensibly prepossessed in his favour, and the insinuating fellow so far discovered it as to declare that he loved me with the ardour of a Petrarch, and had even dared to hope he was not wholly indifferent to me? Shall I say that I swooned, or that my throbbing heart came well nigh bursting its fair casement, when he begged the oracular monosyllabic word that was to settle his destiny, and make him the most envied of human beings, or the most abject? No; I think I conducted very properly. I assured him, if he nurtured a partiality for me, he could depend upon the coalescence of my good feelings—in short, that if his love was pure, it was honestly and warmly reciprocated! This put the seal on his hopes, and he was in raptures, or told me so, which I did not doubt, as I was half so myself. Six months had passed away like a dream, a blissful one, and Edward was daily in my presence;—at the expiration of this period I began to think he would fix a definite time for the consummation of those rites that were to make me so much happier. But no, he was happy enough, or did not care to prove an untried state. Six months, I said, had elapsed; yes, and six more followed their course, and I was still Miss Elenora Clotilda Angelina. He now would be displeased if I joined in any amusements in which he had no share, as it would subject him to the pain of having those attentions paid by some one else. Here was the rub, he was jealous of any civilities bestowed on me, except they came from himself. I am fond of the drama, and once visited the Park Theatre with my friend Electa Sophia Fudge, in company with her enamoured swain; but I had to rue it dearly, for Edward was incessant in his sarcastic and illiberal remarks for at least a fortnight. This was truly insupportable, that I must not enjoy the festivities of an evening without my eternal Mentor was by. Eighteen months had now actually expired, and I was daily bored with the society of my intended at tea. There was no relief; it was constant. A thousand times have I been on the point of telling him that he might as well take board with us regularly, as to forment me with his unwished for and meddling assiduties half the time. The presence of friends is agreeable, but not their eternal shadow in sight. My dress had to always undergo the ordeal of his scrutiny—just think! a female obliged to suit the cramped fancy of but one man and his taste! Oh, it was intolerable, much like Diogenes who wanted nothing but his tub and plenty of sunshine. A cousin of mine of the fifteenth degree of consanguinity, once called on us from the country. Edward was as uneasy as a choleric Frenchman, and once gave me to understand that my sociability with my cousin was of too friendly a nature; he did not expect me to give hopes to any aspirant when I was 'engaged' to him. Yes my dear Neddy, said I, and that engagement is not likely to be soon cancelled, if I may judge the future from the past. If you wish to limit the attentions of my masculine friends, and that none should divide the smiles and pleasantries of your fair, why you have but to name the time, and I am yours at the altar; but until then, know, that I am mistress of my own actions. Now, thought I, you are brought to the point; you will either make me indissolubly yours, or let my fancies and friendships alone. Two years have wheeled their silent course since I was 'engaged' to Edward B., and never has he breathed a word of nuptials. As it is the first principle in the creed of a woman to get married, and I have hung two years on the tender hook of expectation, I now begin to feel outrageous. The stream of my affections is dammed up, my pleasures are curtailed, and I am not married! Now, Mr. Editor, I claim your advice: firstly answer me a few questions: would you wait another week for his lingering determination? Secondly, would you not disown all affection and engagement for and with him, and be free, free as the mountain breeze? Latterly I am induced to think that his affairs are not in the most favourable train—your particular attention here. A rich Carolinian waits but one word of endearing assurance, and he is at my feet at once. My love for Edward begins to evaporate; possibly it never was strong. What then shall I do? I will tell you—I shall want three weeks, and if nothing transpires to favour my first impressions, if I am not the bride of Edward B., then I am yours, my Southron, and we'll over the hills and far away.

ELENORA CLOTILDA ANGELINA.

1828

GETTING MARRIED WITHOUT KNOWING
HOW IT WAS TO BE DONE

from the Christian Recorder

A few days since a rather verdant couple presented themselves at one of the up-town churches just before the service commenced, and requested the minister to tie the mystic knot that should unite two hearts in one. The clergyman was nowise loth, and the smiling and blushing couple were marshalled up to the desk. Just as the minister was about to commence, the bridegroom grasped the sleeve of his coat with one hand whilst with the other he extracted a handful of loose change from his pantaloons pocket, and putting his mouth to the clergyman's ear, whispered, "How much is to pay, I can't afford a great deal." Quietly intimating that the pay would be received after the work was done, the minister proceeded with his duties, and the twain were soon made one. Waving the happy pair aside, the Reverend gentleman mounted the pulpit to proceed with the regular services. The new-made wife understood the wave of the hand to be an intimation for her to follow for some purpose, and after a brief whispered colloquy with the bridegroom, mounted the pulpit, and stood meekly with blushing countenance by the side of the minister. The effect of this apparition upon the nerves of all in the church "may be more easily imagined than described." Before many seconds there was a hasty exit from the church of a couple with downcast heads and very red faces, whilst the congregation—imitating the celebrated leather-stocking—indulged in "silent laughter." The lady afterwards apologized for their mistakes by saying that "it was the first time they ever got married, and they didn't know how it was to be done."

1861

MARRIAGE OF REV. JOHN BECKETT TO
MISS KATE CAMPBELL
from the Christian Recorder

MR. EDITOR: — On Thursday morning at 1.28 A.M., the residence of our venerable Bishop Campbell, was the place of an agreeable scene, in the marriage of his amiable and accomplished daughter, Miss Kate Campbell, to Rev. John Beckett of the Hagerstown Station Baltimore Conference. The ceremony was performed by our worthy Financial Secretary, Rev. J. H. W. Burley of Washington, D.C. It was solemn and impressive. The occasion was a brilliant one. Quite a number of distinguished guests were present to witness the interesting event. The Bride was tastefully attired in a beautiful dove colored silk poplin made in the latest style; white satin slippers and white kid gloves. She appeared calm, wearing an air of perfect satisfaction. The groom was attired in a full suit of black with white kid gloves, presenting quite a noble appearance; looking to be pleased with the thought that he was about to come in possession of so precious and bright a gem. The spacious parlors of the Bride's parents were filled with the numerous friends of the Bishop; likewise with the young ladies. One feature about the affair, the father and mother of the Bride would now and then look sad, at the thought of being left alone. But it was "too late," as the lamented Woodlin used to say.

The occasion was enlivened by Mrs. Thomas Boling rendering (in her unimitable style) some fine music from the Gospel Songs. A very agreeable time was spent by all present. It is needless to say that a sumptuous table was spread with delicacies of the season, from which all feasted. The clock soon informed the guests the hour had come for the parting. Some were sad and others glad. The hacks drove up; the Groom and Bride entered and were driven off to take the 12 m. [*sic*] train for Washington, at which place they will spend a few days at the home of the Groom's father: thence they will proceed to their own home at Hagerstown Maryland. The following guests were present:

Bishop D. A. Payne, D.D., Rev. B. T. Tanner, D.D., Hans Shadd Esq., and lady, Wm. Still and daughter, Mrs. Wiley, Rev. W. B. Derrick and lady, Mr. and Mrs. Thos. Boling, Rev. H. H. Lewis and lady, Rev. R. Wayman, Rev. Fells, Rev. J. H. Thomas, Mrs. Beckett and daughter, Mr. Jones and daughter, Rev. T. Gould and lady, Rev. Darkes and lady, Mr. Joseph Shire and lady, and a large number of others whose names your correspondent could not ascertain. The ladies present presented a handsome appearance in the style they were attired. The bridal presents were numerous, likewise some were valuable; these were tokens of the high esteem the bride was held by the community. We wish all the peace and prosperity that attend life's pathway to the pair who have forsaken all to cleave one to the other for better or worse. May heaven's blessings smile upon them.

W. B. D.

1876

Autobiographical Accounts

THOMAS TOMPKINS
from Freedom's Journal

My marriage was to take place on Thursday. She whom I had chosen to be the wife of my bosom, the companion of my pleasures and sweet soother of my cares, was endowed with every requisite and seemed peculiarly qualified to render the too often sad and dreary voyage of life, calm and delightful. Graced with every virtue that can grace a woman, and apparently far above the petty foibles of her sex, blame me not that I fell down and worshipped at the shrine of this lovely image. Woman, even when devoid of virtue, finds it no hard task to make us submissive to her will; but when she stands above us clothed in all its native loveliness, away with all resistance to her charms, it is rebellion foul and unnatural, and we bow in humble adoration at her feet.

Sweet are the thoughts, and pleasant the dreams of the youth who is soon to be united to the girl of his heart. Life has for him a thousand charms. He looks not upon the world with the cold feelings of philosophy, his heart has not yet had its fill of the bitter realities, that is so soon to poison the cup of his happiness. The world is to him a garden strewed with beautiful and various flowers which he may cull and collect at his pleasure. Infatuated fool! he knows not that under those of fairest dye may lurk a sting to pierce him to the heart.

I have said my marriage was to take place on Thursday. I too had sweet thoughts and pleasant dreams. Imagination rioted in forming visionary plans of enjoyment. My bark was to float smoothly down the stream with not a breath, not a wave, no not a ripple to disturb its course.

Thursday came—I had spent the preceding evening with Sarah. Need I tell the delights of a few brief moments of sweet converse. Again, and again did I rise to leave the charming girl, and as often did my unwilling footsteps linger on the way, till at last the audible yawns of the inmates of the house spoke in terms too plain to be further unheeded, and I tore myself away.—The Sun rose but not with his usual splendor. I am not apt to be superstitious, and yet I could not resist the feeling of sadness that came over me as I looked up and beheld the face of the 'god of day' obscured by clouds. My mind had so teemed with fair images, that I had not deemed it possible a cloudy morning would usher in my wedding day. It was my first lesson, and another followed.—My melancholy was of short continuance, for soon the clouds were scattered, and the Heavens presented an extended sheet of blue. The day wore heavily on. The minutes seemed hours that kept me from my love. At length it came—the hour that was to unite two fond hearts together. The coach was at the door. I sprang into it. My mind was in a perfect whirl, and I knew nothing until I found myself in the house that contained the idol of my heart. The company had assembled and there was a call for the bride and bridegroom. With a full heart I entered the room. All eyes were turned towards the door in anxious expectation of the bride. At length the door opened—she came not. There was whispering among the women, and serious looks with the men. Unable longer to endure suspense, I demanded explanation. I had it. She had eloped with another, for whom none suspected she had the least partiality and I was a fool!

1828

WILLIAM GRIMES

from Life of William Grimes

As I have spoken of a wife, it may seem strange that I have not related the tale of love which must have preceded matrimony. It would be indelicate to relate many things, necessary to a full understanding of a courtship, from beginning to end. One might tell how he got acquainted; whether he was welcomed or repulsed at first. Praise his wife's beauty, or comment her temper before the die is cast. Somehow I did not like, did not know how to tell it. I got married. Though before I went to Litchfield to live, and shortly after I returned to New Haven from Taunton, as is mentioned before, I used to hear students say something about taking Yankee girls for wives, and I thought I would look round and see if I could not find one. I had a great many clothes from the students, and I could rig myself up mighty well. And I have always seen that the girls seemed to like those best who dressed the finest. Yet I do reckon the generality of girls are sluttish, though my wife is not. When a servant, and since too, I have seen so much behind the curtain, that I don't want told. I recollect one student telling a story of this sort, when I was in the room. An acquaintance of his had been courting a lady some time, and I forget how it was exactly, but after he married her, come to see her in the morning, with all the curls, ribbons, combs, caps, earrings, wreaths, &c. &. stripped off, he did not knew her. While I was looking round, I found a plain looking girl in New Haven, and I found she was the very one Providence had provided for me; though her beauty, before it faded, and her figure before it was spoiled, as it always must be soon, were such as a fine Virginian like myself, might be proud to embrace. I paid my attention to her. I loved her into an engagement. After a while I got one of the students to write a publishment, and sent it to the Rev. Mr. M.; he did not read it the next Sabbath, as was customary, and I went to see him. He said he would read it next Sunday, though he thought it was a hoax. So next Sunday he made proclamation. I was then married in the Episcopal manner.

1855

HARRIET JACOBS
from Incidents in the Life

THE LOVER

Why does the slave ever love? Why allow the tendrils of the heart to twine around objects which may at any moment be wrenched away by the hand of violence? When separations come by the hand of death, the pious soul can bow in resignation, and say, "Not my will, but thine be done, O Lord!" But when the ruthless hand of man strikes the blow, regardless of the misery he causes, it is hard to be submissive. I did not reason thus when I was a young girl. Youth will be youth. I loved, and I indulged the hope that the dark clouds around me would turn out a bright lining. I forgot that in the land of my birth the shadows are too dense for light to penetrate. A land

> "Where laughter is not mirth; nor thought the mind;
> Nor words a language; nor e'en men mankind.
> Where cries reply to curses, shrieks to blows,
> And each is tortured in his separate hell."

There was in the neighborhood a young coloured carpenter; a free born man. We had been well acquainted in childhood, and frequently met together afterwards. We became mutually attached, and he proposed to marry me. I loved him with all the ardor of a young girl's first love. But when I reflected that I was a slave, and that the laws gave no sanction to the marriage of such, my heart sank within me. My lover wanted to buy me; but I knew that Dr. Flint was too wilful and arbitrary a man to consent to that arrangement. From him, I was sure of experiencing all sorts of opposition, and I had nothing to hope from my mistress. She would have been delighted to have got rid of me, but not in that way. It would have relieved her mind of a burden if she could have seen me sold to some distant state, but if I was married near home I should be just as much in her husband's power as I had previously been,—for the husband of a slave has no power to protect her. Moreover, my mistress, like many others, seemed to think that slaves had no right to any family ties of their own; that they were created merely to wait upon the family of the mistress. I once heard her abuse a young slave girl, who told her that a colored man wanted to make her his wife. "I will have you peeled and pickled, my lady," said she, "if I ever hear you mention that subject again. Do you suppose that I will have you tending *my* children with the children of that nigger?" The girl to whom she said this had a mulatto child, of course not acknowledged by its father. The poor black man who loved her would have been proud to acknowledge his helpless offspring.

Many and anxious were the thoughts I revolved in my mind. I was at a loss what to do. Above all things, I was desirous to spare my lover the insults that had cut so deeply into my own soul. I talked with my grandmother about it, and partly told her my fears. I did not dare to tell her the worst. She had long suspected all was not right, and if I confirmed her suspicions I knew a storm would rise that would prove the overthrow of all my hopes.

This love-dream had been my support through many trials: and I could not bear to run the risk of having it suddenly dissipated. There was a lady in the neighborhood, a particular friend of Dr. Flint's, who often visited the house. I had a great respect for her, and she had always manifested a friendly interest in me. Grandmother thought she would have great influence with the doctor. I went to this lady, and told her my story. I told her I was aware that my lover's being a free-born man would prove a great objection; but he wanted to buy me; and if Dr. Flint would consent to that arrangement, I felt sure he would be willing to pay any reasonable price. She knew that Mrs. Flint disliked me; therefore, I ventured to suggest that perhaps my mistress would approve of my being sold, as that would rid her of me. The lady listened with kindly sympathy, and promised to do her utmost to promote my wishes. She had an interview with the doctor, and I believe she pleaded my cause earnestly; but it was all to no purpose.

How I dreaded my master now! Every minute I expected to be summoned to his presence; but the day passed, and I heard nothing from him. The next morning, a message was brought to me: "Master wants you in his study." I found the door ajar, and I stood a moment gazing at the hateful man who claimed a right to rule me, body and soul. I entered, and tried to appear calm. I did not want him to know how my heart was bleeding. He looked fixedly at me, with an expression which seemed to say, "I have half a mind to kill you on the spot." At last he broke the silence, and that was a relief to both of us.

"So you want to be married, do you?" said he, "and to a free nigger."

"Yes, sir."

"Well, I'll soon convince you whether I am your master, or the nigger fellow you honor so highly. If you *must* have a husband, you may take up with one of my slaves."

What a situation I should be in, as the wife of one of *his* slaves, even if my heart had been interested!

I replied, "Don't you suppose, sir, that a slave can have some preference about marrying? Do you suppose that all men are alike to her?"

"Do you love this nigger?" said he, abruptly.

"Yes, sir."

"How dare you tell me so!" he exclaimed, in great wrath. After a slight pause, he added, "I supposed you thought more of yourself; that you felt above the insults of such puppies."

I replied, "If he is a puppy I am a puppy, for we are both of the negro race. It is right and honorable for us to love each other. The man you call a puppy never insulted me, sir: and he would not love me if he did not believe me to be a virtuous woman."

He sprang upon me like a tiger, and gave me a stunning blow. It was the first time he had ever struck me; and fear did not enable me to control my anger. When I had recovered a little from the effects, I exclaimed, "You have struck me for answering you honestly. How I despise you!"

There was silence for some minutes. Perhaps he was deciding what should be my punishment; or, perhaps, he wanted to give me time to reflect on what I had said, and to whom I had said it. Finally, he asked, "Do you know what you have said?"

"Yes, sir; but your treatment drove me to it."

"Do you know that I have a right to do as I like with you,—that I can kill you, if I please?"

"You have tried to kill me, and I wish you had; but you have no right to do as you like with me."

"Silence!" he exclaimed, in a thundering voice. "By heavens, girl, you forget yourself too far! Are you mad? If you are, I will soon bring you to your senses. Do you think any other master would bear what I have borne from you this morning? Many masters would have killed you on the spot. How would you like to be sent to jail for your insolence?"

"I know I have been disrespectful, sir," I replied; "but you drove me to it; I couldn't help it. As for the jail, there would be more peace for me there than there is here."

"You deserve to go there," said he, "and to be under such treatment, that you would forget the meaning of the word *peace*. It would do you good. It would take some of your high notions out of you. But I am not ready to send you there yet, notwithstanding your ingratitude for all my kindness and forbearance. You have been the plague of my life. I have wanted to make you happy, and I have been repaid with the basest ingratitude; but though you have proved yourself incapable of appreciating my kindness, I will be lenient towards you, Linda. I will give you one more chance to redeem your character. If you behave yourself and do as I require, I will forgive you and treat you as I always have done; but if you disobey me, I will punish you as I would the meanest slave on my plantation. Never let me hear that fellow's name mentioned again. If I ever know of your speaking to him, I will cowhide you both; and if I catch him lurking about my premises, I will shoot him as soon as I would a dog. Do you hear what I say? I'll teach you a lesson about marriage and free niggers! Now go, and let this be the last time I have occasion to speak to you on this subject."

Reader, did you ever hate? I hope not. I never did but once; and I trust I never shall again. Somebody has called it "the atmosphere of hell"; and I believe it is so.

For a fortnight the doctor did not speak to me. He thought to mortify me; to make me feel that I had disgraced myself by receiving the honorable addresses of a respectable colored man, in preference to the base proposals of a white man. But though his lips disdained to address me, his eyes were very loquacious. No animal ever watched its prey more narrowly than he watched me. He knew that I could write though he had failed to make me read his letters; and he was now troubled lest I should exchange letters with another man. After a while he became weary of silence; and I was sorry for it. One morning, as he passed through the hall, to leave the house, he contrived to thrust a note into my hand. I thought I had better read it, and spare myself the vexation of having him read it to me. It expressed regret for the blow he had given me, and reminded me that I myself was wholly to blame for it. He hoped I had become convinced of the injury I was doing myself by incurring his displeasure. He wrote that he had made up his mind to go to Louisiana; that he should take several slaves with him, and intended I should be one of the number. My mistress would remain where she was; therefore I should have nothing to fear from that quarter. If I merited kindness from him, he assured me that it would be lavishly bestowed. He begged me to think over the matter, and answer the following day.

The next morning I was called to carry a pair of scissors to his room. I laid them on the table, with the letter beside them. He thought it was my answer, and did not call me back. I went as usual to attend my young mistress to and from school. He met me in the street, and ordered me to stop at his office on my way back. When I entered, he showed me his letter, and asked me why I had not answered it. I replied, "I am your daughter's property, and it is in your power to send me, or take me, wherever you please." He said he was very glad to find me so willing to go, and that we should start early in the autumn. He had a large practice in the town, and I rather thought he had made up the story merely to frighten me. However that might be, I was determined that I would never go to Louisiana with him.

Summer passed away, and early in the autumn Dr. Flint's eldest son was sent to Louisiana to examine the country, with a view to emigrating. That news did not disturb me. I knew very well that I should not be sent with *him*. That I had not been taken to the plantation before this time, was owing to the fact that his son was there. He was jealous of his son; and jealousy of the overseer had kept him from punishing me by sending me into the fields to work. Is it strange that I was not proud of these protectors? As for the overseer, he was a man for whom I had less respect that I had for a bloodhound.

Young Mr. Flint did not bring back a favorable report of Louisiana, and I heard no more of that scheme. Soon after this, my lover met me at the corner of the street, and I stopped to speak to him. Looking up, I saw my master watching us from his window. I hurried home, trembling with fear. I was sent for, immediately, to go to his room. He met me with a blow. "When is mistress to be married?" said he, in a sneering tone. A shower of oaths and imprecations followed. How thankful I was that my lover was a free man! that my tyrant had no power to flog him for speaking to me in the street!

Again and again I revolved in my mind how all this would end. There was no hope that the doctor would consent to sell me on my terms. He had an iron will, and was determined to keep me, and to conquer me. My lover was an intelligent and religious man. Even if he could have obtained permission to marry me while I was a slave, the marriage would give him no power to protect me from my master. It would have made him miserable to witness the insults I should have been subjected to. And then, if we had children, I knew they must "follow the condition of the mother." What a terrible blight that would be on the heart of a free, intelligent father! For *his* sake, I felt that I ought not to link his fate with my own unhappy destiny. He was going to Savannah to see about a little property left him by an uncle; and hard as it was to bring my feelings to it, I earnestly entreated him not to come back. I advised him to go to the Free States, where his tongue would not be tied, and where his intelligence would be of more avail to him. He left me, still hoping the day would come when I could be bought. With me the lamp of hope had gone out. The dream of my girlhood was over. I felt lonely and desolate.

Still I was not stripped of all. I still had my good grandmother, and my affectionate brother. When he put his arms round my neck, and looked into my eyes, as if to read there the troubles I dared not tell, I felt that I still had something to love. But even that pleasant emotion was chilled by the reflection that he might be torn from me at any moment, by some sudden freak of my master. If he had known how we loved each other, I think he would have exulted in separating us. We often planned together how we could get to the north.

But, as William remarked, such things are easier said than done. My move-ments were very closely watched, and we had no means of getting any money to defray our expenses. As for grandmother, she was strongly opposed to her children's undertaking any such project. She had not forgotten poor Benjamin's sufferings, and she was afraid that if another child tried to escape, he would have a similar or a worse fate. To me, nothing seemed more dreadful than my present life. I said to myself, "William *must* be free. He shall go to the north, and I will follow him." Many a slave sister has formed the same plans.

1861

WHEN TWO OF THE SLAVES

Harriet McFarlin Payne, from Rawick, American Slave:

A Composite Autobiography

When two of the slaves wanted to get married, they'd dress up nice as they could and go up to the big house, and the master would marry them. They'd stand up before him, and he'd read out of a book called *The Discipline* and say, "Thou shalt love the Lord thy God with all thy heart, all thy strength, with all thy might and thy neighbor as thyself." Then he'd say they were man and wife and tell them to live right and be honest and kind to each other. All the slaves would be there too, seeing the wedding.

ca. 1937

THE WAR WENT ON

from Ophelia Settle Egypt, Unwritten History of Slavery

The War went on four years, and I stayed single, and I was 'gaged to marry the man I did. I never went out with anybody else, for I didn't think it was right since I was 'gaged to him. We got married after he come back. They courted then just like they do now. Only they wasn't fast like they are now. I never in all my born days went out at night by myself and stayed out like these young folks do now. When I went out I always had company.

Whenever a girl had a baby in slavery they never paid no 'tention to it, 'cause they knowed they would have more slaves the more babies they got. Sam Patton come driving up one day with two women in his carriage, and they had veils over they face, and master thought they was white, and he went out to help them and found out they was colored. He run them niggers away from there. Sam Patton was really married to them. We had a girl on the place running out all times of night. I knowed something bad was gonna follow her. You could hear the soldiers after her, and you could hear her scream. . . . When they wanted to marry they just asked old master, and the squire would marry them. Sometimes they would slip and sleep with the women and wouldn't marry at all. They would slip just like they do now. They would let us have company, but they couldn't stay no longer than ten o'clock. They couldn't stay until one and two o'clock like they do now.

IFFEN ANY OF THE SLAVES

Aunt Virginia Bell, from Rawick, American Slave:
A Composite Autobiography

"Iffen any of the slave hands wanted to git married, Massa Lewis would git them up to the house after supper time, have the man and woman jine hands and then read to them outen a book. I guess it was the Scriptures. Then he'd tell 'em they was married but to be ready for work in the mornin'. Massa Lewis married us 'cordin' to Gospel."

ca. 1937

I HAD A NICE WEDDIN'

Sarah Allen, from Rawick, American Slave: A Composite Autobiography

"I had a nice weddin'. My dress was white and trimmed with blue ribbon. My second day dress was white with red dots. I had a beautiful veil and a wreath and 'bout two, three waiters for table dat day.

"My mother was nearly white. Brighter than me. We lef' my father in Virginia. I was jus' as white as de chillen I played with."

ca. 1937

DA WAY DEY DONE

Jeff Calhoun, from Rawick, American Slave: A Composite Autobiography

"Da way dey done at weddings dem days, you picks out a girl and tell your boss. If she was from another plantation you had to git her bosses 'mission and den dey tells you to come up dat night and get hitched up. They says to de girl, 'You's love dis man?' Dey says to de man, 'You loves dis girl?' If you say you don't know, it's all off, but if you say yes, dey brings in de broom and holds it 'bout a foot off de flor and say to you, to jump over. Den he says you's married.

"If either of you stumps you toe on de broom, dat mean you got trouble comin' 'tween you, so you sho' jumps high."

ca. 1937

PART FOUR

Married Life

OH, SU-ZANN!

Oh, Su - zann, Fare you well! And ain't you mighty sorry . . . To

think I married you just last night, And gwine away in the morning?

REFRAIN.

Oh, Su- zan- na, fare you well!

Lyrics

THREE MONTHS MARRIED

Anonymous

First Mont':   "Set down in my cabin, Honey!"
Nex' Mont':   "Stan' up, my Pie."
Third Mont': "You go to wuk, you Wench!
                    You well to wuk as I!"

TO A LADY ON THE DEATH OF HER HUSBAND

Phillis Wheatley

Grim monarch! see, depriv'd of vital breath,
A young physician in the dust of death:
Dost thou go on incessant to destroy,
Our griefs to double, and lay waste our joy?
Enough thou never yet wast known to say,
Though millions die, the vassals of thy sway:
Nor youth, nor science, nor the ties of love,
Nor aught on earth thy flinty heart can move.
The friend, the spouse from his dire dart to save,
In vain we ask the sovereign of the grave.
Fair mourner, there see thy lov'd *Leonard* laid,
And o'er him spread the deep impervious shade;
Clos'd are his eyes, and heavy fetters keep
His senses bound in never-waking sleep,
Till time shall cease, till many a starry world
Shall fall from heav'n, in dire confusion hurl'd,
Till nature in her final wreck shall lie,
And her last groan shall rend the azure sky:
Not, not till then his active soul shall claim
His body, a divine immortal frame.

But see the softly-stealing tears apace
Pursue each other down the mourner's face;
But cease thy tears, bid ev'ry sigh depart,
And cast the load of anguish from thine heart:
From the cold shell of his great soul arise,
And look beyond, thou native of the skies;
There fix thy view, where fleeter than the wind
Thy *Leonard* mounts, and leaves the earth behind.
Thyself prepare to pass the vale of night
To join for ever on the hills of light:
To thine embrace his joyful spirit moves
To thee, the partner of his earthly loves;
He welcomes thee to pleasures more refin'd,
And better suited to th' immortal mind.

1772

TO THE BRIDE

from Freedom's Journal

Now, the nuptial knot is tied,
Su'da attends the lovely bride;
Crown her, ye celestial powers,
Flora, strew her path with flowers.

Ye nine, your golden harps employ;
To melting strains of nuptial joy;
Oh! Cupid prove the gentle guide!
To this new, this beauteous bride!

Lead her to the Elys'an bower,
Deck'd with every open flower;
The grove, where coos the Turtledove,
Emblem, fair of virtuous love.

Pom'na, th' cornucopia bear;
With fruit ambrosial for her fare;
Oh! may she ne'er taste of sorrow!
But, joys gild each op'ning morrow.
   HYMEN.

1828

CONNUBIAL FELICITY

George Moses Horton

The fairest soonest fade,
Young brides in flowers array'd,
   Will soon grow old,
   And prove a scold,
Tho' their forms decay'd.

But would you live with her at ease,
   Fly from the elf and leave her;
The only means a dame to please
   Is by your flight to grieve her.

The sweetest soonest pall,
The tallest soonest fall;
   The tender bloom,
   Of sweet perfume,
Will pine the first of all.

Little regard the ills of life,
   Her frowns are but to flatter;
So when your flight has grieved your wife,
   Come back and discord scatter.

The gaudy charms of May,
Are quickly past away;
   The honey moon
   Will change as soon,
And love to ills betray.

The fairest fruit upon the tree
   Is ever soonest rotten;
Know in as much the nuptial glee
   Must pass and be forgotten.

1845

THE FUGITIVE'S WIFE

Frances Ellen Watkins [Harper]

It was my sad and weary lot
    To toil in slavery;
But one thing cheered my lowly cot—
    My husband was with me.

One evening, as our children played
    Around our cabin door,
I noticed on his brow a shade
    I'd never seen before;

And in his eyes a gloomy night
    Of anguish and despair;-
I gazed upon their troubled light,
    To read the meaning there.

He strained me to his heaving heart—
    My own beat wild with fear;
I knew not, but I sadly felt
    There must be evil near.

He vainly strove to cast aside
    The tears that fell like rain:—
Too frail, indeed, is manly pride,
    To strive with grief and pain.

Again he clasped me to his breast,
    And said that we must part:
I tried to speak—but, oh! It seemed
    An arrow reached my heart.

"Bear not," I cried, "unto your grave,
    The yoke you've borne from birth;
No longer live a helpless slave,
    The meanest thing on earth!"

1857

THE OLD COUPLE

from the Christian Recorder

It stands in a sunny meadow,
The house so mossy and brown,
With its cumbrous, old stone chimneys,
And the gray roof sloping down.

The trees fold their green arms around it,
The trees, a century old;
And the winds go chanting through them,
And the sunbeams drop their gold.

The cowslips spring in the marshes,
And the roses bloom on the hill;
And beside the brook in the pastures,
The herds go feeding at will.

The children have gone and left them,
They sit in the sun alone!
And the old wife's ears are failing,
As she harks to the well-known tone

That won her heart in the girlhood,
That has soothed her in many a care,
And praises her now for the brightness
Her old face used to wear.

She thinks again of her bridal—
How, dressed in her robe of white,
She stood by her gay young lover
In the morning's rosy light

Oh, the morning is rosy as ever,
But the rose from her cheek is fled;
And the sunshine still is golden,
But it falls on a silvered head.

And the girlhood dreams, once vanished,
Come back in her winter time,
Till her feeble pulses tremble
With the thrill of spring-time's prime.

And looking forth from the window,
She thinks how the trees have grown,
Since, clad in her bridal whiteness,
She crossed the old door-stone.

Though dimmed her eye's bright azure,
And dimmer her hair's young gold;
The love in her girlhood plighted,
Has never grown dim nor old.

They sat in peace in the sunshine,
Till the day was almost done;
And then, at its close, an angel
Stole over the threshold stone.

He folded their hands together—
He touched their eyelids with balm;
And their last breath floated upward,
Like the close of a solemn psalm.

Like a bridal pair they traversed
The unseen, mystical road,
That leads to the beautiful city,
"Whose builder and maker is God."

Perhaps in that miracle country
They will give her lost youth back;
And the flowers of a vanished spring-time,
Will bloom in the spirit's track.

One draught from the living waters,
Shall call back his manhood's prime;
And eternal years shall measure
The love that outlived time.

But the shapes that they left behind them,
The wrinkles and silver hair,
Made holy to us by the kisses
The angel had printed there,—

We will hide away 'neath the willows,
When the day is low in the west;
Where the sunbeams cannot find them,
Nor the winds disturb their rest.

And we'll suffer no tell-tale tombstone,
With age and date to rise;
O'er the two who are old no longer,
In the Father's House in the skies.

1861

THE WIFE'S INVOCATION

John Menard Willis

"Love me, leave me not"—no never,
    Life is dark and full of woe;
We are one and cannot sever,
    Though the winds of sorrow blow!
True, I often sigh in sorrow—
    Sigh because your words are cold;
But the sunshine of the morrow,
Fills my heart with joy untold.

"Love me, leave me not," for dreary
    Are the days when you're away
And my heart grows sick and weary,
    As I vainly sigh and pray.
Once a warm love cheer'd my bosom,
    When our years were young and gay;
Now 'tis faded—but 'twill blossom,
    When this long night turns to day!

"Love me, leave me not," in anguish,
    Press your warm lips unto mine;
Then this heart no more will languish,
    If again you call me thine.
We have kiss'd and truly given
    Vows before the sacred shrine;
And we're one on earth—in Heaven—
    You are mine and I am thine!

Love me—claim this aching bosom,
    Press it once more to thine own!
And the flow'rs of Hope will blossom
    Where the pangs of sorrow burn!
Take me, I am thine forever—
    Soon from earth we'll pass away;
But we'll meet, when here we sever,
    In a brighter land of day.

1879

TO ELDER T. WELLINGTON HENDERSON

ON THE OCCASION OF THE TENTH ANNIVERSARY OF HIS
WEDDED LIFE THURSDAY, NOVEMBER 2, 1876

from the Christian Recorder

I.

Ten years have gone since first you won
A flower as fair as the sun shone on,
And plucked it from its parent stem,
A precious, rare, and priceless gem.

II.

Ten years have gone since vows were said,
And cake and wine,—a feast was spread,
And wedding bells rang far and wide
Told that the nuptial knot was tied.

III.

Ten years of wedded life, and yet
No word of sorrow or regret
For choice you made, or stern decree
Of fate that fixed your destiny.

IV.

Ten years! Yet love hath stronger grown,
You love now as you ne'er had known
Each day, each hour, your lives will be
More wedded for eternity.

V.

Your *crystal* nuptials five years hence
And five more, *China*—Heaven dispense!
Then Silver, Cotton, Silk, and *Gold*
When *fifty* wedded years have rolled.

VI.

May health attend, and joys as pure
As Heaven's nectar, ceaseless flow;
And when grim-visaged Death shall come,
Maybe he still find you *two* as *one*.

J. D. B.

1879

DEAREST

Robert C. O. Benjamin

I have loved thee fond and truly,
    In years that have passed away,
And I love thee now as dearly
    As upon our bridal day.

Yea, my heart is more thine own, dear,
    For I know thy priceless worth;
Of all, thou art the dearest,
    On this beautiful, bright earth.

In time of fiercest struggling,
    When cheerless was my life,
Thy, loving smile has armed me
    To conquer in the strife.

The voice of sweet encouragement
    Has nerved my fainting soul.
And brought me sweet contentment,
    And saved and made me whole.

So I love thee fond and truly, dear,
    And shall ever love thee so,
Until the messenger of death
    Has struck his fatal blow.

1883

TO MY ABSENT WIFE

A[lfred] G[ibbs] Campbell

My dear, true wife,
Life of my life,
And my heart's solace only,
Thou knowest not
How drear my lot
Without thee, and how lonely!

Yet well I know,
Come weal or woe,
Thy heart is mine forever:
Though far apart
From me thou art,
Our true souls naught can sever!

What though the pall
Of sorrow fall,
And shroud all things in sadness,
Love's holy light
Shall banish night,
And change the gloom to gladness!

Love cannot die!
'Tis Deity!
'Tis bliss, pure, bright, supernal;
Though worlds shall fall
To ruin,—all,
Yes, all of Love's eternal!

1883

TO MR. AND MRS. W. F. JOHNSON

ON THEIR TWENTY-FIFTH WEDDING ANNIVERSARY

Frances E[llen] W[atkins] Harper

God curtained from thy vision
    His great and glorious light,
But made for thee a pathway
    Which still was fair and bright.

Where death invades with sorrow
    And orphan children come,
Thou hast wrought within the shadow
    The Howard Orphan Home.

To-day I send my greeting
    To thee and thy dear wife,
Who has been in light and darkness
    True companion of thy life;

Always loving, true and truthful,
    To thy spirit more than sight;
May her heart be full of gladness—
    Her soul of love and light.

May the peace of God surround you,
    And his love with you abide
Till life's shadows all are faded
    And there's light at eventide.

When the storms of life are sweeping
    And the wolves of hunger bark,
May you leave upon the sands of time
    An ever shining mark.

May the children you have sheltered
    Within your earthly home.
Meet you mid the many mansions
    Where darkness cannot come.

1886

TIRED

Fenton Johnson

I am tired of work; I am tired of building up somebody else's civilization.

Let us take a rest, M'Lissy Jane.

I will go down to the Last Chance Saloon, drink a gallon or two of gin, shoot
a game or two of dice and sleep the rest of the night on one of Mike's
barrels.

You will let the old shanty go to rot, the white people's clothes turn to dust,
and the Calvary Baptist Church sink to the bottomless pit.

You will spend your days forgetting you married me and your nights hunting
the warm gin Mike serves the ladies in the rear of the Last Chance Saloon.

Throw the children into the river; civilization has given us too many. It is
better to die than to grow up and find that you are colored.

Pluck the stars out of the heavens. The stars mark our destiny. The stars
marked my destiny.

I am tired of civilization.

1919

Fiction

DIALOGUE BETWEEN A NEWLY MARRIED COUPLE

OR

MATRIMONIAL QUARRELS

from Provincial Freeman

"Behold how great a matter a little fire kindleth!"

"A pebble in the streamlet scant
Has turn'd the course of many a river,
A dew drop on the baby plant
Has warp'd the giant oak forever."

A young couple had passed the first few weeks of their marriage at the house of a friend. Having at length occupied their new home, they were taking their first breakfast, when the following scene took place.

The young husband was innocently opening a boiled egg in an egg-cup. The bride observed that he was breaking the shell at what she thought the wrong end. "How strange it looks," said she, "to see you break your egg at the small end, my dear! No one else does so; and it looks so odd."

"O, I think it is quite as good, in fact better than breaking it at the large end, my love; the egg runs over the top," replied the husband.

"But it looks very odd, when no one else does so," rejoined the wife.

"Well, now, I really do think it is not a nice way you have got of eating an egg. That dipping of strips of bread and butter into an egg, certainly is not tidy. But I do not object to your doing as you please, if you will let me break my egg at the small end," retorted the husband.

"I am sure my way is not so bad as eating fruit-pie with a knife, as you do, instead of using a fork; and you always eat the syrup, as if you were not accustomed to have such things. You really do not see how very bad it looks, or I am sure you would not do so," added the wife.

"The syrup is made to be eaten with the pie; and why should I send it away in the plate?" asked the husband.

"No well-bred persons clear up their plates, as if they were starved," said the bride, with a contemptuous cast of her head.

"Well, then, I am not a well-bred person," replied the husband, angrily.

"But you must be, if we are to live comfortably together," was the sharp answer of the fastidious lady.

"Well, I must break my egg at the small end, so it does not signify; and I must also eat the syrup."

"Then I will not have either fruit-pie or eggs at the table."

"But I will have them," petulantly exclaimed the husband.

"Then I wish I had not been married to you," cried the young wife, bursting into tears.

"And so do I," added the now incensed husband, as he rose, and walked out of the room.

This domestic quarrel was followed by others, equally trifling in their origin, and disgraceful in their character, until the silly couple made themselves so disagreeable to each other that their home became unendurable, and they separated.

"If ye bite and devour one another, take heed be not consumed one of another."
—Gal. v 15.

Guard well thy lips; none, none can know
What evils from the tongue may flow,

What guilt, what grief may be incurred
By one incautious hasty word.

1855

MR. PEPPER'S WIFE

from Provincial Freeman

"Mrs. Pepper, I labor under the impression that it is high time that you were getting breakfast. As my former housekeeper understood all my wishes with regard to these things, I found it unnecessary to give any orders respecting them; but with you it is different. As you have never got a meal in this house, of course you know nothing of the regulations of the household.

"In the first place you will make a fire in the kitchen, put on the kettle, &c.; then you will make a fire in here. That done, you will cook the breakfast and bring it in here, as I have always been accustomed to taking mine in bed, and do not consider it necessary to depart from the custom on your account; but should you prefer it, you can eat yours in the kitchen, as it is perfectly immaterial to me."

This occurred the morning after Mrs. Pepper went to housekeeping. Mrs. Pepper was a sensible woman—she made no reply to Mr. Pepper's commands; but as soon as her toilet was finished, she left the room, and sitting down in the kitchen, she thus ruminated:

"Make the kitchen fire! Yes, I'll do that. Then make a fire in the bedroom! I'll see to that too. Then take the breakfast to his bedside! Just see if I do!" And then Mrs. Pepper sat and thought deeply for a few minutes, when, apparently having arrived at a satisfactory conclusion, she proceeded to business.

Having got a nice fire kindled in the kitchen, she carried some coal into Mr. P.'s apartment, and filled up his stove, having first ascertained that there was not a spark of fire in it. That duty performed, she next prepared the breakfast, of which she partook with a great relish; and after matters and things were all set to rights in the kitchen, she went downtown on a shopping excursion.

Meanwhile Mr. Pepper began to grow impatient. He "labored under the impression" that the atmosphere of his room did not grow warm very fast, and he began to feel unpleasantly hungry. Peeping out from behind the bedcurtains he saw how affairs were with regard to the stove. Something like a suspicion of the real state of affairs began to dawn upon his mind. He listened for a few minutes, but all was still about the house.

Hastily dressing himself, he proceeded to investigate the affair. He soon comprehended the whole of it, and was very wrathful at first; but he comforted himself with the reflection that he had the power to punish Mrs. P., and he felt bound to do it, too. After some search he found the remains of the breakfast of which he partook with a gusto, and then sat down to wait for Mrs. P. She was a long time in coming, and he had ample time to nurse his wrath. While sitting there he thus soliloquized:

"That ever I, Philander Pepper, should be so treated, and, by a woman, too, is not to be believed. I can't believe it, no, nor I won't either. But she shan't escape that's certain; if she should my reputation for dignity would be forever gone! For havn't I told Solomon Simpleton all along how I was going to make *my* wife stand round, and how I was going to make her get up and make the fire every morning, and let me lie abed, and how I was going to shut her up, and feed her on bread and water, if she dared to say she wouldn't do it?"

"A cosy little arrangement, Mr. Pepper," said a soft voice behind him.

Mr. P. started up, and there stood Mrs. P. right behind his chair, laughing just as hard as she could. Mr. Pepper put on a severe look.

"Sit down in that chair madam," he said, pointing to the one he had just vacated, "while I have a little conversation with you."

"Now I shall be pleased to know why you did not obey my orders this morning, and where you have been, all the forenoon?"

"Where have I been this forenoon, Mr. Pepper, I have not the least objection to tell you; I have been down town doing a little shopping. I have purchased some lovely napkins; just look at them," said she, holding them up demurely for his inspection; "I only paid a dollar apiece for them—extremely cheap, don't you think so!" she added.

Mr. Pepper was astonished; how she dared to turn the conversation in this way was a mystery to him. Suddenly his bottled wrath broke loose. Turning fiercely upon her he said—

"Betsy Jane, you disgust me; you seem to make very light of this matter, but it is more serious than you imagine, as you will find to your cost presently. If you do not immediately beg my pardon in a submissive manner, I shall exert my authority to bring you to a proper sense of your misconduct, by imprisoning you in one of my chambers until you are willing to compromise strict obedience to my wishes."

At the close of this very eloquent and dignified speech, Mr. Pepper drew himself up to his full height, and stationed himself before Mrs. P., ready to receive expressions of sorrow and penitence; he had no doubt that she would fall down at his feet, and say—

"Dear Philander, won't you please forgive me this time, and I'll never do so no more!"

And he was going to say, "Betsy Jane, you'd better not," but instead of doing all this what do you think she did? Laughed him right in the face!

Mr. Pepper was awful wrathy. He spoke up in a voice of thunder, and said:

"Mrs. Pepper, walk right up stairs this very minute, and don't you let the grass grow under your feet while you are going neither. You have begun your antics in good season, Mrs. Pepper, but I'll have you know that it won't pay to continue them any length of time with me, Mrs. Pepper. Again I command you to walk up stairs."

"Well, really, Mr. P., it is not at all necessary for you to speak so loud—I am not so deaf as all that comes to; but as for walking up stairs I have not the least objection to doing so, if you will wait until I have recovered from my fatigue; but I can't think of doing so before."

"But you *must,* Mrs. P."

"Then all I've got to say is this, you'll have to carry me, for I *won't* walk!"

Mr. P. looked at his wife for a moment with the greatest astonishment; but as she began to laugh at him again, he thought to himself—

"She thinks I won't do it, and hopes to get off in that way; but it won't do; up stairs she's got to go, if I do have to carry her; so here goes," and taking the form of his lady in his arms, he soon had the satisfaction of seeing her safely lodged in her prison, and carefully locking her in, he stationed a little red-headed youth on the front door-steps to attend to callers and also to see that Mrs. P. did not escape; and then he betook himself to a restaurant for his dinner, and after despatching that, he hurried off to his office, and was soon engrossed in business.

About the middle of the afternoon, our young sentinel rushed into the office, never stopping to take breath:

"Mr. Pepper had better run home just as fast as he can, for that woman what's shut up be making an awful racket, and she be tearing around there, and rattling things the distressingest kind, and if she beant splitting up something or other, then I don't know what splitting be!"

Without waiting to hear more, Mr. P. seized his hat, and hurried off home at a most undignified pace.

Opening the hall door, he stole up stairs as carefully as possible, and applying his eyes to the keyhole, he beheld a sight which made him fairly boil with rage.

Mrs. P. was sitting in front of the fireplace reading his love-letters. The one she was engaged in perusing at that particular moment, was from a Miss Polly Primrose, who it appeared had once looked favorably on the suit of Mr. Pepper; but a more dashing lover appearing on the scene, Miss Polly sent him a letter of dismissal, promising her undying friendship, and accompanying the same with a lock of her hair, and some walnut meats.

But it was not the love letters alone that made Mr. P. so outrageous. He had been something of a traveller in his day, and had collected a great many curiosities in his rambles, which he had deposited in a cupboard in the very room where he had confined Mrs. P., and she had got at them.

She had split up an elegant writing-desk with his Indian battle axe, in order to have a fire, as the day was rather chilly. In one corner of the fire-place was Mr. P.'s best beaver filled up with love-letters.

On a small table, close to Mrs. P., was a beautiful flat China dish, filled with bear's oil, in which she had sunk Mr. P.'s best satin cravat, and having fired one end of it, it afforded her sufficient light for her labors—for Mr. P. had closed the blinds, for the better security of the culprit.

On some coals in front of the fire, was Mr. P.'s silver christening bowl, in which Mrs. P. was popping corn, which she ever and anon stirred, with the fiddle-bow, meanwhile, occasionally punching up the fire with the fiddle, for Mr. P. had with commendable foresight, removed the shovel and tongs.

Mr. P. condescended to peep through the key-hole, until he had obtained a pretty correct idea of what was going on within. Never was a Pepper so fired as he. He shook the door, it was securely fastened within, and resisted all his efforts to open it. He ordered Mrs. Pepper to open or take the consequences ; but as she did not open it, it is to be presumed that she preferred the consequences. Mr. Pepper darted down stairs like a madman.

"I must put a stop to this" he thought, "or I shall not have a rag of clothes to my back."

Procuring a ladder, he began to mount to the bedroom; but Mrs. P. was not to be taken so easily. She knew that he had left the door unlocked, for she examined it as soon as he had left; but she had left; but she had no idea of letting him have the benefit of her fire: so hastily seizing several bottles of cologne, she threw the contents upon the fire, and in a few minutes had the satisfaction of seeing it entirely extinguished. That duty performed, she left the apartment, and locking the door, she stationed herself in a convenient position to hear everything that transpired within.

In a few moments Mr. P. was safe in the apartment and as soon as he had closed the window, he stood bolt upright in the middle of the room, and said in a deep voice—

"Jezebel, come forth!"

No answer.

"Jade, do you think to escape?"

Still no response, Mr. P. begins to feel uneasy, and hastily begins to search the room, but had not proceeded far when he hears a slight titter in the vicinity of the door. He listens a moment, and it is repeated. Darting to the door, he attempts to open it, but finds himself a prisoner. There is one more chance, he thinks, and hurries to the window; but alas for Mr. Pepper, his wife has re-moved the ladder, and he cannot escape.

He sits down on a chair, and looks ruefully around him, and presently he arises and picks up a few fragments of a letter which is lying on the carpet, and finds it is from Polly Primrose. He wonders what she has done with the lock of hair.

At this moment his eye falls upon his daguerrotype, which is lying on the table before him—mechanically taking it up he opens it, and sees—what? nothing but his own face, all the rest of him being rubbed off, and around his lovely phiz the missing curl, and the walnut meats are carefully stowed away in the corner of the case. Mr. P. blubbered aloud.

Good! thought Mrs. P., when you find your level, I'll let you out, and not till then. A little wholesome advice will do you good, and I'm prepared to ad-minister it.

How long Mrs. Pepper kept her liege lord in durance vile, deponent saith not, and as to what passed between them when he was released from captivity, we are not any better informed, but of this we are sure, Mr. Pepper might have been seen, a morning or two afterwards, to put his head into the bedroom, and heard say in a meek manner—

"Betsy Jane, I've made the kitchen fire; and put on the tea kettle; won't you please to get up and get breakfast?"

1855

PATRICK BROWN'S FIRST LOVE

from the Anglo-African Magazine

> "Hail, love, young love, cream of all earthly bliss —
> The silken down of happiness complete."

> "The fire that's blawn on Beltane e'en,
>   May weel be black gin Yule:
> But blacker fa' befa' the heart
>   Where first fond love grows cule."

So sing the bards of love in freedom; but what is love in slavery? Can chattels love? Has the black code of slavery blotted out the kingly passion—the passion of passions—from the heart of the bondman? Pity but it had: for the written woes of slavery, none will compare with the unwritten, the unspeakable, the indescribable agonies with which slavery has torn the being of the negro lover—of a deeper, wilder, more passionate nature than the white man.

"These children of the sun"

love as the white man cannot; and, in blasted love, anguish as the white man cannot. Most of the deeds of violence perpetrated by the slaves, which reach the newspapers, have this passion as their source; and thousands of fierce, brave revenges, which never reach the public ear, are prompted in like manner. Many a white man, owner, or overseer, relying on the apparently soft and subdued character of their slaves, have invaded the slaves' married bed (which Judge Culver, to his infinite and everlasting infamy has pronounced *illegal*) and met the bloody end they deserved. In looking back at a recent tragedy enacted at Washington—the act, the trial, the acquittal—we could not help regarding it as a stone thrown upon the dark waters of slavery, whose circling ripple would some day be lashed up into a frightful tempest. Nature and passion are stern logicians; and what slave who heard and saw that tragedy and its end, could help reasoning thus: "If it be right and lawful to shoot the adulterer when the woman is willing, why is it not right, and lawful, and religious, for me also to slay the man who forces his beastly lust upon the shrieking resistance of the wife of my bosom? This is the LESSONS OF THE SICKLES TRAGEDY. It has touched as with living coals the fiery hearts of many a black Marylander and Virginian; and in some hour that we dream not of it, when smiling peace and content, and even joy, shall apparently beam out of the countenances of well-fed, and sleek, and *happy* slaves, there will be a blaze in the sky, and blood on the soil. Some one, half a century ago, looking to that successful insurrection, which has now almost dwindled into a myth, wrote that some negro preacher, wild with religious fanaticism, would stir up his fellows to resist the yoke of slavery. This idea was true as to insurrection, but wrong as to its source: the Bible, and its religion, teaches peace, not war, to the negro; submission, not resistance; to bear his cross, not to wield the sword: in a word, it inspires deep, trusting, earnest, loving nature, his wild imagination, with such glowing pictures of the New Jerusalem, and of the saints, and of the once suffering but now triumphant Jesus, that he is lifted out of this world by the prospective rewards and promised glories of the world to come. Had the Haytian slaves of 1793 been as pious, as christian as the half million of slaves of Virginia in 1859, there would have been no insurrection—no liberation. The Haytian insurrection was the product and the triumph of fetishism: it was the old African Vadoux—not the free principles of the Bible.

No! religious fanaticism will never goad the slaves to rebel. But some black-bosomed Virginius, crazed at the sight of his deflowered daughter, or some flame-colored hero, maddened at the sight of the wife of his bosom outraged in his very presence, will raise his bloody arm, and kindle the wild revenge of the ten thousands, in like manner, maddened; and there will be a short and bloody end to slavery.

What human power could resist them? What Northern bayonet could charge against them? What father, son, or brother could shoot them down—these men thrice armed in the eternal justice of their quarrel?

Patrick Brown was born to the doom of slavery. I saw him the other evening leap lightly from a moving avenue car, although the years of his life are three-score and ten. There may be a white hair here and there in his well-covered head; his face scarce betrays a wrinkle—it is smooth, pleasant, full and black. He has a square, iron chin, and a short, strongly-built nose, with full, not large, nostrils. His eyes I cannot describe; they are marked by the arcus senilis, and have a look out of them that makes you think they have looked at strange sights. He is short and stout, but has that quick, silent movement of limb, which you see in skilled boxers; and he impresses you with the idea, that even now, if need be, he "could strike a blow."

Patrick Brown was never emancipated; he never ran away; was not brought into a free State by his owner; yet he grew free in the far South. Slavery got tired of him—would have nothing to do with him—while he was yet young and in his prime of health and strength. He had been sold many times—was quick, willing, active and reliable—his word was his bond—yet slavery grew tired of him. He was, moreover, frank and plain-spoken—not so desirable a thing in a slave. He was mostly sold at auction, and *would* have his say after the auctioneer had enlarged upon his very apparent merits as a chattel serviceable. He would add: "Gentlemen, I will serve any one faithfully who treats me well, but I will not serve any man who strikes me without cause." This was a chuckling delight to a hard-featured, iron-framed negro-breaker, in Alabama, who bought him out of the gang brought down from Old Virginia, where Patrick Brown was born. He took his purchase out to his plantation, and took the earliest opportunity to knock his new slave almost senseless, with a whip-handle. Brown very humbly begged his pardon — was so submissive and intelligent, that he was promoted, within the year, to be the favored attendant on his owner, especially in hunting, to which the former was passionately addicted. Within the year, the twain went out to hunt together, when his horse threw the master, and killed him. In settling up the estate, Patrick Brown was sold at auction, and again made his little speech. The second owner, who was a kind-hearted man, but given to gusts of passion, after two or three years, one day struck Patrick. Within that year he and Patrick went out into the woods together on some errand, and Patrick returned alone. His master never afterwards was heard from. In like manner, owner after owner departed, and, while no one thought of suspecting the smooth, mild-looking Patrick Brown, and no one *saw him struck,* no one coupled his *speech* with the fate of his many owners. It began to be regarded as an *unlucky* thing to own him; and, finally, no one would buy him; and thus he became free.

And this man, in his early youth, had loved, with a mild, passionate, and boundless love. On the next plantation, in Virginia, there had grown up with him, from childhood, the girl who became his fate. Why waste words in describing her who was more than world, and stars, and life to him? She was the life of his life — the only entity he ever worshipped, and, perhaps, worships still. He does not remember ever to have spoken to her of love, yet the twain were one in all time and forever, and they were purified in the very depth and truthfulness of their love.

By some strange coincidence, they were both sold to the same trader, and manacled in the same gang, to make the overland journey to the far South. Keziah's mild beauty, which had been unnoticed on the plantation, attracted the eye of the trader. He soon showed favors to her on the march, and sought favors in return. She spurned him in her innocence. He tried threats, and ill-treatment, to no purpose. At length, one dark night, when they were camped in the depth of a forest, the trader ordered his wagon a little way off from the camp, and had Keziah conveyed into it, bound, and gagged.

No sound was heard of struggle nor shriek. Late the next morning, when one of the assistant drivers ventured near the wagon, and called, no answer came. On tearing aside the curtains, there lay the slave-driver, disemboweled; and there, unstained by his guilty touch, with death—beautiful; oh! how beautiful!—on her virgin brow, lay Patrick Brown's first love.

"It was a strange feeling," said Patrick Brown to me, as he finished this story of his love, "it was a strange feeling of horrid pity that reached back through my fingers, as I drove my sheath-knife through and through that man's bowels."

1859

AN OLD AND TRUE FRIEND

from the Christian Recorder

A gentleman played off a rich joke on his better half the other day. Being somewhat of an epicure, he took it into his head that morning that he would like to have a first rate dinner. So he addressed his wife a note politely informing her that a gentleman of her acquaintance—an old and true friend—would dine with her that day. As soon as she received it, all hands went to work to get everything in order. Precisely at twelve o'clock she was prepared to receive her guest. The house was clean as a new pin, a sumptuous dinner was on the table, and she was arrayed in her best attire. A gentle knock was heard, and she started with a palpitating heart to the door. She thought it must be an old friend, perhaps a brother from the place whence they once moved. On opening the door, she saw her husband, with a smiling countenance.

"Why, my dear," said she, in an anxious tone, "where is the gentleman of whom you spoke in your note."

"Why," replied the husband, complacently, "here he is."

"You said a gentlemen of my acquaintance, an old and true friend, would dine with us today."

"Well," said he, good humoredly, "am I not a gentleman of your acquaintance, an old and true friend?"

"Oh!" she cried, distressingly, "is there nobody but you?"

"No"

"Well, I declare this is too bad," said his wife, in an angry tone.

The husband laughed immoderately, but finally they sat down cozily together, and for once he had a good dinner without having company.

1869

OCTAROON SLAVE OF CUBA

Thomas Detter

Jane Gray was the daughter of a wealthy physician of New Orleans. She possessed all the requirements of a finished education. She was handsome and
charming. She swayed a magical influence over her associates. She moved in
the first circles of society; she made many friends—none had less enemies.
She was left an orphan at the tender age of one year and three months. Her
father's brother adopted her. They spared neither money nor pains to educate
her. Her father left her a handsome fortune at his death. Jane knew but little
concerning her mother. She often heard Mrs. James Gray remark what a beautiful girl his [*sic*] sister Louisa was. How unfortunate it was she had been kid-
napped. Jane never would have known that she had a sister, if it was not for
the information derived from Mrs. Gray. She had many admirers. Gentlemen
of refinement and wealth sought to capture her noble heart. These offers she
declined. Through the course of social events she made the acquaintance of a
Mr. Zevoe, a Cuban planter. He was by no means prepossessing or attractive,
but he was reported to be worth two millions of dollars.

He was not long in securing her consent to unite with him in the sacred
bonds of matrimony. Her adopted father and mother were not well pleased
with her choice, but offered no serious objections. They regretted it much, because their blood had been kept pure so many generations with but a slight
mixture of African blood coursing through Jane's veins (of which fact she was
ignorant), should now be corrupted with Spanish mixture. However, they
were married on the twenty-sixth day of September. Shortly after, they obtained passage on the old ship "Sea Monster," which was advertised to sail on
the first day of October for Cuba. They made every preparation that was necessary for the voyage. On the morning of the first of October, at half-past
eight o'clock, according to arrangement, a carriage was at the door of the residence. The morning was indeed lovely, and seemed to be the omen of happiness and joy to bride and groom. The two parlors were crowded with her
friends and acquaintances, who came to bid her farewell. Many who could not
gain access, rushed to the steamer to await their coming.

It was, indeed, a day long to be remembered. Women wept. Strong men
with warm hearts could not conceal their tears. The bride and groom entered
the coach, accompanied by her adopted parents. The driver was not long in
whirling them to the landing, where were congregated a host of her friends,
who crowded aboard of the steamer to bid her an affectionate farewell. The

captain, in the course of thirty minutes, gave orders to notify the guests to go ashore, which they did many with tears coursing down their cheeks. The signal was then given to cast off the moorings. Jane rushed on deck to gaze upon her friends ashore. By this time the steamer was drifting out in the deep and heading for the ocean. Jane Zevoe was so much affected, she could scarcely wave her handkerchief as a token of farewell. Jane lost sight of her friends in the distance. She then cast her weary eyes upon the stately domes and edifices of her native city. She looked eagerly upon them, until they faded from her view in the glorious sunlight of an Autumn day. Strange emotions filled her soul as the ocean widened the space between her and the home of her childhood. She retired to her state-room to reflect upon the scenes and pleasures of the past.

She wept long and bitterly. Her husband tried to soothe her grief by telling her to cast her all on him. To her he would be a father and a husband.

Nothing worthy of note transpired during the voyage. On the fifth day of October, the gallant ship cast anchor in the harbor of Havana. At half-past eight o'clock in the morning, Mr. and Mrs. Zevoe went ashore and ordered breakfast and a suite of rooms at the Planters' Hotel. Here they remained, recruiting themselves from the effects of their late voyage. Here she was the centre of attraction, and received many calls from the nobility of Cuba. She received the blessings of many who hoped that the radiant sunbeams of happiness and joy would shine brightly around her pathway.

On the twelfth day of October, her husband procured a carriage. They left early on that morning for his plantation, which was sixteen miles from the city of Havana. They arrived safe at four o'clock at their country mansion, which was not at all prepossessing to the bride for its architecture. Rachel, the negro servant, after shaking hands with her master, received a slight introduction to her new mistress, whom she escorted to the parlor, which looked cheerless and ancient to Mrs. Zevoe. The only furniture that it contained was a half dozen cane-bottom chairs, an old dingy desk, a settee, a rocking chair, and a plain old fashioned bureau. The floor was not robed with purple carpet, but was dressed with plain, common matting. Jane made herself as cheerful as circumstances would permit. She felt as though her brightest and happiest days had passed. Mr. Zevoe, after settling with the driver and arranging outside matters, entered the parlor.

He saw at a glance that she was neither cheerful nor happy. He engaged in conversation with her in regard to his future plans and prospects. While they were conversing, Rachel was busying herself preparing for supper. When the repast was ready she notified Mr. and Mrs. Zevoe. They entered the dining-room, which exhibited neither taste nor style. She partook of the supper, which did not suit her palate or appetite. After supper she concluded to take an observation of the rooms in the dwelling. Rachel, being delighted with her appearance, offered to escort her, which offer was accepted. They were not long in exploring the premises. She was more disappointed than she had been previously. They contained nothing worthy of note. She told Rachel she felt greatly disappointed in the appearance of things, but requested Rachel not to speak of it to her Master. She returned to the parlor unable to disguise her feelings.

He again renewed the conversation and asked her how she liked the appearance of things. She smiled, but not cheerfully, and said: "I suppose it will do."

He then told her that he intended to furnish the house complete, and had left his order in New York, which he expected would arrive in thirty days. She thought it very strange that he did not have the house furnished previous to their arrival. He offered some slight excuse. The clock chimed ten, and they retired to bed. They arose next morning at eight and breakfasted, after which they took a morning walk. The air was pure, invigorating and fragrant with the odor of flowers. The sun was just climbing the eastern horizon, spreading its golden rays over Nature's favored landscape. The birds were pouring forth their melodies. All Nature seemed to lend its beauties and loveliness to welcome Jane Zevoe. Ye she was not happy. She told her husband of a strange dream she had during the night about her long lost sister. She saw her and conversed with her. He asked her under what circumstances she left.

"I only know what I learned from my adopted parents concerning Louisa," said Jane; "she was playing with some children in the neighborhood. She was not more than six or seven years of age at the time and was induced to follow a man under the promise of presenting her with candy and toys. She has never been seen from that day to this. They say they advertised for her in every paper in the State and offered large rewards for her recovery. That is all I know about it. I would give the world, with all its wealth, to see her. They tell me she is the striking likeness of my father."

"My dear, I sympathize with you. A sister's love is incomprehensible to one like myself. I have not a relative living on earth; but I will use my endeavors to assist you to recover her. I have a slave on this plantation that anybody would take to be you, not knowing that she had African blood in her veins."

"Ah, indeed," said Mrs. Zevoe; "I am sure she is not a relative of mine, for my family are of pure Saxon blood; nevertheless I would like to see her."

By this time they had returned to the house. He excused himself and left to attend some business on the plantation. Mrs. Zevoe entered into conversation with Rachel and asked:

"Have you ever seen a colored woman on the plantation that your master says resembles me so much?"

"I have; she resembles you slightly."

"Where did you come from, Rachel?" asked Mrs. Zevoe.

"I came from New Orleans."

"Is it possible," says Mrs. Zevoe, "that you come from my native state? Tell me who you belonged to there."

"I was owned when quite small, by a man named William Jackson. His property was attached for debt; myself and mother, including other slaves, were sold at public auction in New Orleans. A Doctor Gray purchased me to take care of a little girl called Jane, whose mother and an older sister the doctor sold, because she displeased him. He took a fancy to little Jane, and concluded to raise and educate her."

"Did you ever see the woman and child he sold?"

"No, madam; they were sold before I went to live with the doctor."

"How old do you think the girl was when she was sold?"

"I have heard others say she was between six and seven."

"How old was this child Jane, when you went to nurse her?"

"She was just able to toddle around a chair; indeed, I often felt sorry for the dear little creature, although I took great care of it. It ate and slept with me."

"How long did you live with the doctor?"

"Nine months."

"Why did you leave him?"

"He died during the nine months. His brother was left executor of the doctor's estate; they concluded to adopt little Jane as their own child. The doctor's brother was opposed to holding slaves; he sold me to a minister, who promised to take good care of me. I went to live with him; his wife's health was very poor. They concluded to take a trip to Cuba to improve her health. We arrived here safe. I waited upon her day and night; by constant care and attention a change took place for the better, and in six months she finally recovered. For my faithful attention to her, they promised never to part with me. After remaining here eight months, they concluded again to return to Louisiana. The day before they left I was notified, by a gentleman, that I was his individual property. This I could not believe; I rushed into the sitting-room, where my mistress was, and asked her if such were the facts. She replied:

" 'Rachel, our means are about exhausted. Mr. Cook was compelled to dispose of you to raise funds, as he did not wish to send home for more means. I think, Rachel, you have a good master in Mr. Zevoe, and a comfortable home, so you must endeavor to make yourself contented.' Tears coursed down my cheeks as those words fell from her lips. I long entertained the hope of return-ing home with them."

"Indeed, they treated you very mean. But you must put your trust in God. His blessings and His mercies He bestows upon the just and the good. His vengeance and His wrath shall visit the unjust. I shall do all in my power to make matters pleasant for you during my stay."

Rachel thanked her kindly.

The following morning Mrs. Zevoe and Rachel prepared themselves to call and see Louisa. Rachel remarked before leaving the house:

"Mr. Zevoe would not like it, as he notified me to have no communication with her whatever, and I have not seen her but once I have been here."

"What does she do, Rachel?"

"I don't think she does anything more than take care of her house and chil-dren when they are at home."

"Is not her children with her?"

"No, madam; Mr. Zevoe wrote from New Orleans before he started, to have the children moved to the Lower Plantation, which orders were com-plied with."

"Who is the father of her children?"

Rachel smiled, and said:

"Indeed, I could not say."

"Whether it pleases or displeases Mr. Zevoe, we shall call to see her. What is the distance from here to her house?"

"Three miles."

"It will be a pleasant walk for us."

They started and by half-past nine o'clock stood in front of a neat cabin, covered with honey-suckles. They knocked. The door was opened by a woman who was fairer than her master, prepossessing in her appearance and affable. Rachel remarked to Louise:

"I wish to introduce you to our new mistress, Mrs. Zevoe."

Here stood the handmaid of slavery and the queen of refinement. Louisa acknowledged her superiority with a polite bow. Mrs. Zevoe saw at a glance a striking resemblance between Louisa and her father's portrait, which hung in the parlors of her adopted parents. They entered into conversation, during which Mrs. Zevoe asked Louisa where she was from. She answered:

"I was born in the city of New Orleans."

"When did you leave there?"

"I suppose it is now about eighteen years."

"Under what circumstances did you leave?"

"My mother and I were sold to a planter in Texas, by the name of Cravan. He promised not to separate us. After living with him one year, he sold me to a man by the name of Hood, whom I must say had neither principle nor honor. I declared I would not live with him. He sold me to Mr. Zevoe, the father of your husband."

"How long have you been here?"

"Nearly ten years."

"Are you married?"

"I am not, although the mother of three children."

"Pray tell me who is the father of your children?"

Louisa hesitated a few moments and said:

"It is not for me to say; you will know, perhaps, if you remain on the plantation."

Mrs. Zevoe could scarcely suppress her love and affection for Louisa. She believed her to be her long-lost sister. She asked:

"I suppose you have some knowledge of your mother?"

"I have; I often see her tall form and her cheerful countenance in my mind."

"Was she handsome?"

"She was not; but she had one of the sweetest dispositions that a woman was ever blessed with."

"What was her complexion?"

"She was a brown-copper color, with long wavy hair and good features."

"Had she any other children besides yourself?"

"She had a baby called Jane, of which I have a faint recollection."

Louisa and Rachel both noticed that Mrs. Zevoe labored under great mental embarrassment which she was endeavoring to overcome. Louis and Rachel were intelligent and might be regarded as judges of human nature. They knew not what wrought upon her feelings, unless she believed that Mr. Zevoe was the father of Louisa's children.

"Louisa," said Mrs. Zevoe, "I pity your condition."

Here again, her feelings showed signs of distress.

"I may be of service to you. If I can possibly better your condition, I shall use my best endeavors to do so."

She bade her good-bye, and promised to see her at an early day. She was convinced Louisa was her sister, and that Rachel had watched over her when [she was] a little infant; but she revealed the secret to neither of them. She remarked to Rachel on their return:

"I want you to tell me, confidentially, what you think of Mr. Zevoe. I have, in a degree, lost confidence in the man. I believe he gambles. My reasons for thinking so is—he sat up two nights on our voyage and came in to the state-room several times to get sums of money. Besides I have detected him in several stories."

"If I can speak with you confidentially, I will post you a little," replied Rachel.

"You can place implicit confidence in me. I will never divulge a word of it."

"I am sorry for you; I know him well. He is not the man to make you happy. I am expecting every day to see every thing on this plantation attached for debt, myself included."

"Can it be possible?"

"Yes; it is mortgaged for every dollar it is worth."

"Oh heavens! What silly creatures women are to be duped by such men. But say nothing. I will endeavor by stratagem to secure your freedom. Do you believe he left his orders in New York for furniture to be shipped?"

Rachel shook her head, and said:

"You don't know the man."

"I have made up my mind firmly to make my stay here but short. Has he anything?"

"He has a small plantation south of here, which I believe is not mortgaged. The overseer claims it in order to keep off his creditors. It is said to be worth thirty or forty thousand dollars."

"If such is the fact, I shall try to revenge myself upon him."

When they returned home, Mr. Zevoe was there. He had been absent nearly the entire day. Mrs. Zevoe approached him affectionately and kissed him.

He said:

"Dear Jane, I could not live without your presence."

"I am happy to know that you love me, and love me dearly," replied Mrs. Zevoe.

"Have you been taking a walk?"

"I called to see your white slave."

"I am surprised at your thinking that she is white."

He continued the conversation by asking her what she thought of Louisa. Mrs. Zevoe carelessly remarked:

"I think she would make me a good waiting-maid. With her and Rachel, I think I could run this establishment, and make myself contented. I have one request to make of you."

"What is it, my dear?"

"I want you to make me out a bill of sale in my own name for Louisa and Rachel, making them my own individual property."

Mr. Zevoe laughed and said:

"That is just what I intended doing."

"Louisa has three children, has she not?"

He seemed for a moment silent. After recovering himself, he replied:

"She has."

"Who is the father of her children?"

"That is a matter I have not troubled myself to ascertain. We are glad to have our property increase. It pays good interest on the money invested."

Mrs. Zevoe smiled, and said:

"You will not think I am at all inquisitive. It is a matter that interests me but little."

"To-morrow I will get Lawyer Wilson to draw up the papers. He will be in the neighborhood, and he promised to make me a call before returning."

Accordingly, the lawyer arrived the following morning. Mr. Zevoe was not in at the time. The madam and [he] entered into conversation. She informed him what she desired him to do. Lawyer Wilson asked her if she had the consent of her husband, and if he would sign the papers. Mrs. Zevoe said he would. He then said:

"It will be a capital thing for you. I have been his attorney for years."

"How does his business matters stand?"

"They are not in a healthy condition. I shall advise him also to make over the Lower Plantation to you."

"I hope you will. I think you have influence enough with him to affect it."

During the conversation, Mr. Zevoe made his appearance and expressed himself highly gratified to see Lawyer Wilson. After conversing a few moments, he told the counsellor what he desired him to do in reference to Rachel and Louisa.

"It is a wise act upon your part."

The lawyer asked him to step outside; he wished to have a private conversation with him. They walked out and had quite a consultation. His attorney said:

"Your affairs are in critical condition. The mortgage on your property will be due in a few days. I am satisfied you are not in a condition to meet it. If so, you had better give your wife a deed also of the Lower Plantation."

"You are aware that my overseer, Mr. Lamar, has a deed of that property."

"I am satisfied he will cancel it if agreeable to you."

"Perfectly."

"Where is he?"

"He left here a short time since for Havana on business; he will not return for several days."

"I will see him in the city and have a talk with him about it."

They then returned to the house and took the names of Louisa and Rachel, and their ages.

"The documents will be prepared day after to-morrow. You must sign them, and I will have them recorded," said Lawyer Wilson.

"I shall be in town in a day or two, and will call at your office."

After dining, the lawyer bade them good day. The following day he met Mr. Lamar in the streets of Havana and spoke to him on the subject. He said he was perfectly willing to resign his claims to the plantation, notwithstanding Mr. Zevoe owed him some twelve hundred dollars; yet he had confidence that Mr. Zevoe would pay every dollar. Lawyer Wilson took him to the Recorder's office to cancel his claim, with the understanding that Mr. Zevoe would give him his note, with an endorser for the amount. The lawyer gave him his word that it would be done, and made out the papers, turning the estate, together with Louisa and her children and Rachel, over to Mrs. Zevoe. The second day following, Mr. Zevoe arrived in the city. The documents were signed and recorded.

Mr. Zevoe told Lawyer Wilson that his wife wished him to call out and see her in the course of a few days. He said he would go and bring the documents with him. Owing to a pressure of business he was detained. He wrote her a letter congratulating her on her success—telling her he would call and see her as soon as an opportunity would afford. She wrote a reply asking him to make out free papers for Rachel and Louisa and her children, and to bring them when he came, but not to divulge it to any living soul.

Mr. Zevoe was absent some days before returning. During this time, Mrs. Zevoe again called upon Louisa and said:

"Louisa, the lost is found."

"What have you lost and found?"

"I lost a beloved sister years ago."

She threw her arms around her neck, embraced and kissed her, and said: "You are my beloved sister."

"Oh heavens!" exclaimed Louisa, "can it be that this is my dear sister Jane?"

Mrs. Zevoe was overcome and could not utter a sentence. When she recovered, she said:

"This is Jane. Oh! how I have longed to see you. But much to my surprise and shame, I find you the victim of slavery and the concubine of your own master, who regards you and your children as *chattels*. What a cursed institution slavery is! How damning its effects! It fetters the intellect and robs virtue of its purest jewel. It brings shame and disgrace to the door of many a woman who would be an ornament to society, were it not for the cursed sin. Though a woman's skin be black, her soul can be as pure as the purest Saxon. I have been reared in the lap of luxury. I am the favored child of fortune."

"Can you not redeem me from this life of shame and degradation?" asked Louisa.

"I will free you and your children at all hazards."

They again embraced each other and wept. Jane said:

"You shall be as free as the air that blows. I desire you to keep this a secret to the grave. Do not reveal that I am the daughter of a Negro woman or the sister of a slave. It would blast my hopes forever in this life. It would leave a stain upon me that never could be wiped out. You know the prejudices that are entertained against persons in whose veins course the slightest mixture of African blood. I have moved in the first circles of society and have been the guest of the wealthiest families of my State. I was educated to believe I was of the purest Saxon blood. How humiliating it would be to me to be rejected and scorned because of my origin. I myself entertain no prejudices against caste, and acknowledge God to be the common father of the human family. But, Louisa, be cheerful. I will be your benefactor."

She bade Louisa good-bye and requested her to call and bring the children to the house on the following Thursday. She then left for home. When she arrived Rachel told her that Lawyer Wilson had called and left a package for her, and that he regretted her absence.

"I should have liked so much to have seen him," said Mrs. Zevoe.

She took a seat and opened the package. It contained the documents making Rachel, Louisa and her children, and the Lower Plantation, her individual property. She felt much delighted, but did not mention it to Rachel. Mr. Zevoe returned from Havana the following morning. He did not find Mrs. Zevoe as cheerful as he expected. He told her what he had done in making her the sole owner of certain property. She thanked him and asked if the plantation on which they lived was free from debt. He said it was.

"I heard in Havana that your home plantation was mortgaged for every dollar it was worth," said Mrs. Zevoe.

"Nonsense; you know there are persons in this world who attend to everybody's business but their own. Such characters, my dear, envy you your wealth."

Little did he think that she knew the depth of his purse and the amount of his liabilities. He supposed he had a young woman that would give herself more concern about social pleasures than business matters. But such was not the case. Mr. Zevoe, after they had quite a chat, asked her if she would not loan him fifteen hundred dollars as he had a speculation in view which would pay him well for the amount invested.

"You are aware that you have already used some twenty-five hundred dollars of my money."

"I am; I will have a check from New York in a few days for ten thousand dollars. Then I will return you the amount."

"As you are expecting it in a few days, you had better not make any investment until you receive it."

Mrs. Zevoe winked at Rachel and smiled. Mr. Zevoe left the house. Mrs. Zevoe laughed, and remarked to Rachel:

"I judge he takes me to be an unsophisticated wife."

"I think so too."

"Rachel, you will see a change here on Thursday next."

"Do you intend leaving us so soon?"

"You will know when the time comes."

Rachel was totally ignorant of what Mrs. Zevoe had in contemplation, or of the relationship existing between Louisa and Mrs. Zevoe.

"I trust you will never leave me here," said Rachel.

"Keep a good heart. Be hopeful. God works in mysterious ways, His wonders to perform."

"That is true. I have been a believer in His goodness and His mercy for a number of years."

"Still trust in Him," said Mrs. Zevoe.

Mr. Zevoe returned to the house, but did not seem to be in very good humor.

Nothing special transpired until Thursday morning, when Louisa arrived with her children. Mr. Zevoe was the first person Louisa met when she approached the house. He remarked:

"How do you do, Louisa? I suppose you have called to make your mistress a visit."

She smiled. He then spoke to her in a tone not audible. Rachel was busying herself about the kitchen, yet she had an eye on her master and Louisa. Mr. Z. requested her to go in the kitchen and take a seat and he would notify her mistress of her arrival. He walked into the parlor and told Mrs. Zevoe that her maid had come.

"Who?" she asked.

"Louisa and her brats."

"Ask her to walk in the parlor."

On her entering the parlor, neither Jane nor Louisa betrayed any signs of friendship. Mrs. Zevoe remarked to Louisa:

"Are those your children?"

"Yes," replied Louisa.

"They are fine and healthy looking."

Mr. Zevoe sat without taking any part in the conversation. It was the first time that Mrs. Zevoe had seen Louisa's children. After learning the names of the children, she took little Eddy by the hand and said in an excited tone:

"Mr. Zevoe, I have the painful duty of introducing you to your own children. They are bone of your bone, flesh of your flesh."

He started from his seat, saying:

"Madam, I deny the charge."

Mrs. Zevoe, pointing to little Eddy, said:

"That child alone is sufficient evidence to convict you of the charge in any Court; he is, indeed, a photograph of the man who disowns his own children, that a king would be proud of."

"Your brain, madam, must be diseased."

"Louisa, upon this issue is hinged your freedom and future happiness. I ask you a question to-day that I never asked you before. Are not these children Charles Zevoe's?"

Louisa hung her head and blushed.

"I wish you to tell me the whole truth," said Mrs. Zevoe.

Louisa, in a tremulous voice, said:

"They are."

Mr. Zevoe rushed towards Louisa like a madman. Jane stepped between them, as fearless as a Roman soldier, and defied him to lay his hands upon her at the peril of his life, and exclaimed:

"I have sworn this day, in the presence of high heaven, never to live with you again. I have decreed my own divorce. She, sir, was as pure as the fleeting snow until you robbed her of chastity and liberty. If you possessed a spark of manhood, you would love her and honor her children. You regard her as your inferior, because a tinge of African blood courses through her veins. She is too noble a creature to be your slave or your wife."

Under that roof, slavery and freedom met hope and despair. Joy and sorrow each struggled to defend freedom's claims. Jane, armed with the weapons of Justice and Truth, struck slavery a terrible blow. Her soul was inflamed, her feelings aroused and her pride wounded, to find her sister the subject of slavery.

Jane continued:

"It is to her, sir, you owe your love and affection. She has borne you three lovely children."

Louisa was much affected; Rachel stood by with tears in her eyes. Mr. Zevoe remained silent. His very soul wrung with bitterness. She took Louisa by the hand and led her affectionately to where he was seated.

"Charles Zevoe, I ask you to-day—will you not accept of Louisa to be your wedded wife. My name is no longer Jane Zevoe, but Jane Gray."

He spoke not a sentence. Mrs. Zevoe said:

"Louisa, by power in me invested, I install you mistress of this castle. Here are papers securing to you and your children freedom. I will also make you a deed to the Lower Plantation. I will secure Lawyer Wilson to see that you are protected in your liberty and property. God forbid! I should reap the benefits of that which justly belongs to you and your children. Be careful and do not allow yourself to be swindled out of the property I shall deed to you. I stand here to-day as a minister of justice and the advocate of human rights. I ask you, Charles Zevoe, in the presence of high heaven, will you not take Louisa to be your wife? Treat her as a companion, not a slave. Your silence, I suppose, gives consent."

She then placed her hand in his. Lifting her eyes heavenward, [she] offered a fervent and devout prayer, and pronounced them man and wife. She kissed each of them and blessed the children. She then said to Louisa:

"I wish to speak to you privately."

They entered the adjoining room. She said:

"To-morrow morning I shall bid you farewell!"

Neither could subdue their feelings.

"Dear sister," said Louisa, "do you intend to leave me? What will become of me?"

"I am ever your sister in the bonds of affection; you must write me often— under an assumed name. I expect a carriage to arrive here every moment. If it arrives we shall be off to-morrow morning, bright and early."

"Do you intend to take Rachel with you?"

"Yes, poor thing. I could not think of leaving her behind. She will be the only recompense I will have for the twenty-five hundred dollars that Mr. Zevoe used of my money. I have her free papers in my possession and will give them to her when we arrive in New Orleans."

On her return to the room she said:

"Charles Zevoe, I freely forgive you for the injuries I received at your hands. I will not expose you. My parting request is to treat Louisa as becomes a husband. Educate your children and respect her. I will wear the weeds of mourning for you when I return to that home where the sunshine of gladness, joy and peace ever shed its effulgent rays. No night of gloom or sadness entered its chambers. If you are asked for I will tell my friends I have buried you in the sea of forgetfulness. However unpleasant it may be, circumstances compel me to pursue this course. However sacred the bonds of matrimony may be regarded, I look upon it as being a civil contract between the parties, and when either willfully and knowingly violate its duties, I hold it to be the duty of the injured party to seek redress. There is no law, temporal or Divine, that can compel a woman or a man to live with those who are repugnant to them. It behooves every individual to seek happiness, regardless of the smiles and frowns of the world. Personal pride induce many to eke out a miserable existence, who have married persons not adapted to them in feeling or disposition. I, this day, decree my own divorce. Whether censured or sustained by public sentiment—I care not. Honesty, virtue, truth and diligence cling together and hang around the neck of memory."

"Can it be that you had discarded my affections, deceived and betrayed my confidence?" asked Mr. Zevoe.

"I look not to the fleeting shadows of time, but to eternity. Where the secrets of all hearts shall be revealed. If I have done good, I shall be the recipient of the mercies of a just God. If wrong, even in this case, I shall receive His condemnation. Conscience, sir, like a thorn, is ever pricking the soul of the wicked, warning them to repent. It is the faithful sentinel of God. I wish you not to entertain the slightest hopes of me. I am dead to you—dead forever! I intend again to launch this frail bark upon the ocean of chance, never, I hope, to be captured by a pirate in disguise!"

"Do you consider me to be a pirate?" asked he.

"I do; one of the deepest dye."

"What have I robbed you of?"

"Of my good name and my happiness."

Mr. Zevoe stood like a prisoner, condemned without hope.

"Shall crime, guilt and sin outlive Justice, Truth, and Righteousness. No! never! My soul was sick within me when I entered this castle. It bore the signs of misery, distress and unhappiness. I have, sir, one request to ask of you. Will you treat Louisa as your bosom companion?"

About seven o'clock P.M., the coach arrived; they intended starting early the following morning. Miss Jane and Rachel prepared themselves for the trip. Rachel was greatly overjoyed when Miss Jane informed her that she intended taking her to New Orleans. She charged Rachel, on her arrival home, never to speak of the circumstances. If she did, to say Charles Zevoe was dead. Rachel promised to do as requested.

Mr. Zevoe and Rachel are still ignorant of the relationship of Jane to Louisa.

Nothing occurred during the evening. After supper, the new bride and her children occupied the room of the late Mrs. Zevoe. Miss Gray and Rachel slept together. Strange to say, she arose with a complexion as fair as ever after sleeping with a Negro woman. They bade Louisa an affectionate farewell, and kissed the children. Mr. Zevoe was so much enraged that he left the house before breakfast and did not return.

The parting scene was truly affecting. Jane promised Louisa, faithfully, she would write on her arrival at New Orleans. They stepped into the carriage and bade Mr. Zevoe and his plantation a final adieu.

1871

THE WIFE OF HIS YOUTH

Charles W. Chesnutt

I

Mr. Ryder was going to give a ball. There were several reasons why this was an opportune time for such an event.

Mr. Ryder might aptly be called the dean of the Blue Veins. The original Blue Veins were a little society of colored persons organized in a certain Northern city shortly after the war. Its purpose was to establish and maintain correct social standards among a people whose social condition presented almost unlimited room for improvement. By accident, combined perhaps with some natural affinity, the society consisted of individuals who were, generally speaking, more white than black. Some envious outsider made the suggestion that no one was eligible for membership who was not white enough to show blue veins. The suggestion was readily adopted by those who were not of the favored few, and since that time the society, though possessing a longer and more pretentious name, had been known far and wide as the "Blue Vein Society," and its members as the "Blue Veins."

The Blue Veins did not allow that any such requirement existed for admission to their circle, but, on the contrary, declared that character and culture were the only things considered; and that if most of their members were light-colored, it was because such persons, as a rule, had had better opportunities to qualify themselves for membership. Opinions differed, too, as to the usefulness of the society. There were those who had been known to assail it violently as a glaring example of the very prejudice from which the colored race had suffered most; and later, when such critics had succeeded in getting on the inside, they had been heard to maintain with zeal and earnestness that the society was a lifeboat, an anchor, a bulwark and a shield,—a pillar of cloud by day and of fire by night, to guide their people through the social wilderness. Another alleged prerequisite for Blue Vein membership was that of free birth; and while there was really no such requirement, it is doubtless true that very few of the members would have been unable to meet it if there had been. If there were one or two of the older members who had come up from the South and from slavery, their history presented enough romantic circumstances to rob their servile origin of its grosser aspects.

While there were no such tests of eligibility, it is true that the Blue Veins had their notions on these subjects, and that not all of them were equally liberal in regard to the things they collectively disclaimed. Mr. Ryder was one of the most conservative. Though he had not been among the founders of the society, but had come in some years later, his genius for social leadership was such that he had speedily become its recognized adviser and head, the custodian of its standards, and the preserver of its traditions. He shaped its social policy, was active in providing for its entertainment, and when the interest fell off, as it sometimes did, he fanned the embers until they burst again into a cheerful flame.

There were still other reasons for his popularity. While he was not as white as some of the Blue Veins, his appearance was such as to confer distinction upon them. His features were of a refined type, his hair was almost straight; he was always neatly dressed; his manners were irreproachable, and his morals above suspicion. He had come to Groveland a young man, and obtaining employment in the office of a railroad company as messenger had in time worked himself up to the position of stationery clerk, having charge of the distribution of the office supplies for the whole company. Although the lack of early training had hindered the orderly development of a naturally fine mind, it had not prevented him from doing a great deal of reading or from forming decidedly literary tastes. Poetry was his passion. He could repeat whole pages of the great English poets; and if his pronunciation was sometimes faulty, his eye, his voice, his gestures, would respond to the changing sentiment with a precision that revealed a poetic soul and disarmed criticism. He was economical, and had saved money; he owned and occupied a very comfortable house on a respectable street. His residence was handsomely furnished, containing among other things a good library, especially rich in poetry, a piano, and some choice engravings. He generally shared his house with some young couple, who looked after his wants and were company for him; for Mr. Ryder was a single man. In the early days of his connection with the Blue Veins he had been regarded as quite a catch, and young ladies and their mothers had manoeuvred [*sic*] with much ingenuity to capture him. Not, however, until Mrs. Molly Dixon visited Groveland had any woman ever made him wish to change his condition to that of a married man.

Mrs. Dixon had come to Groveland from Washington in the spring, and before the summer was over she had won Mr. Ryder's heart. She possessed many attractive qualities. She was much younger than he; in fact, he was old enough to have been her father, though no one knew exactly how old he was. She was whiter than he, and better educated. She had moved in the best colored society of the country, at Washington, and had taught in the schools of that city. Such a superior person had been eagerly welcomed to the Blue Vein

Society, and had taken a leading part in its activities. Mr. Ryder had at first been attracted by her charms of person, for she was very good looking and not over twenty-five; then by her refined manners and vivacity of her wit. Her husband had been a government clerk, and at his death had left a considerable life insurance. She was visiting friends in Groveland, and, finding the town and the people to her liking, had prolonged her stay indefinitely. She had not seemed displeased at Mr. Ryder's attentions, but on the contrary had given him every proper encouragement; indeed, a younger and less cautious man would long since have spoken. But he had made up his mind, and had only to determine the time when he would ask her to be his wife. He decided to give a ball in her honor, and at some time during the evening of the ball to offer her his heart and hand. He had no special fears about the outcome, but, with a little touch of romance, he wanted the surroundings to be in harmony with his own feelings when he should have received the answer he expected.

Mr. Ryder resolved that this ball should mark an epoch in the social history of Groveland. He knew, of course,—no one could know better,—the entertainments that had taken place in past years, and what must be done to surpass them. His ball must be worthy of the lady in whose honor it was to be given, and must, by the quality of its guests, set an example for the future. He had observed of late a growing liberality, almost a laxity, in social matters, even among members of his own set, and had several times been forced to meet in a social way persons whose complexions and callings in life were hardly up to the standard which he considered proper for the society to maintain. He had a theory of his own.

"I have no race prejudice," he would say, "but we people of mixed blood are ground between the upper and the nether millstone. Our fate lies between absorption by the white race and extinction in the black. The one doesn't want us yet, but may take us in time. The other would welcome us, but it would be for us a backward step. 'With malice towards none, with charity for all,' we must do the best we can for ourselves and those who are to follow us. Self-preservation is the first law of nature."

His ball would serve by its exclusiveness to counteract leveling tendencies, and his marriage with Mrs. Dixon would help to further the upward process of absorption he had been wishing and waiting for.

II

The ball was to take place on Friday night. The house had been put in order, the carpets covered with canvas, the halls and stairs decorated with palms and potted plants; and in the afternoon Mr. Ryder sat on his front porch, which the shade of a vine running up over a wire netting made a cool and pleasant lounging place. He expected to respond to the toast "The Ladies" at the supper, and from a volume of Tennyson—his favorite poet—was fortifying himself with apt quotations. The volume was open at "A Dream of Fair Women." His eyes fell on these lines, and he read them aloud to judge better of their effect:—

"At length I saw a lady within call,
    Stiller than chisell'd marble, standing there;
A daughter of the gods, divinely tall,
    And most divinely fair."

He marked the verse, and turning the page read the stanza beginning,—

"O sweet pale Margaret,
    O rare pale Margaret."

He weighed the passage a moment, and decided that it would not do. Mrs. Dixon was the palest lady he expected at the ball, and she was of a rather ruddy complexion, and of lively disposition and buxom build. So he ran over the leaves until his eye rested on the description of Queen Guinevere:—

"She seem'd a part of joyous Spring:
A gown of grass-green silk she wore,
Buckled with golden clasps before;
A light-green tuft of plumes she bore
Closed in a golden ring.
        .   .   .
"She look'd so lovely, as she sway'd
The rein with dainty finger-tips,
A man had given all other bliss,
And all his worldly worth for this,
To waste his whole heart in one kiss
Upon her perfect lips."

As Mr. Ryder murmured these words audibly, with an appreciative thrill, he heard the latch of his gate click, and a light footfall sounding on the steps. He turned his head, and saw a woman standing before his door.

She was a little woman, not five feet tall, and proportioned to her height. Although she stood erect, and looked around her with very bright and restless eyes, she seemed quite old; for her face was crossed and re-crossed with a hundred wrinkles, and around the edges of her bonnet could be seen protruding here and there a tuft of short gray wool. She wore a blue calico gown of ancient cut, a little red shawl fastened around her shoulders with an old-fashioned brass brooch, and a large bonnet profusely ornamented with faded red and yellow artificial flowers. And she was very black,—so black that her toothless gums, revealed when she opened her mouth to speak, were not red, but blue. She looked like a bit of the old plantation life, summoned up from the past by the wave of a magician's wand, as the poet's fancy had called into being the gracious shapes of which Mr. Ryder had just been reading.

He rose from his chair and came over to where she stood.

"Good-afternoon, madam," he said.

"Good-evenin', suh," she answered, ducking suddenly with a quaint curtsy. Her voice was shrill and piping, but softened somewhat by age. "Is dis yere hwat Mistuh Ryduh lib, suh?" she asked, looking around her doubtfully, and glancing into the open windows, through which some of the preparations for the evening were visible.

"Yes," he replied, with an air of kindly patronage, unconsciously flattered by her manner, "I am Mr. Ryder. Did you want to see me?"

"Yes, suh, ef I ain't 'sturbin' of you too much."

"Not at all. Have a seat over here behind the vine, where it is cool. What can I do for you?"

"'Scuse me, suh," she continued, when she had sat down on the edge of a chair, "'scuse me, suh, I's lookin for my husban'. I heerd you wuz a big man an' had libbed heah a long time, an' I 'lowed you would n't min' ef I'd come roun' an' ax you ef you'd ever heerd of a merlatter man by the name er Sam Taylor 'quirin' roun' in de chu'ches ermongs' de people for his wife 'Liza Jane?"

Mr. Ryder seemed to think for a moment.

"There used to be many such cases right after the war," he said, "but it has been so long that I have forgotten them. There are very few now. But tell me your story, and it may refresh my memory."

She sat back farther in her chair so as to be more comfortable, and folded her withered hands in her lap.

"My name's 'Liza," she began, "'Liza Jane. W'en I wuz young I us'ter b'long ter Marse Bob Smif, down in ole Missoura. I wuz bawn down dere. W'en I wuz a gal I wuz married ter a man named Jim. But Jim died, an' after dat I married a merlatter man named Sam Taylor. Sam wuz free-bawn, but his mammy and daddy dies, an' w'ite folks 'prenticed him ter my marster fer ter work fer 'im 'tel he wuz growed up. Sam worked in de fiel', and I wuz de cook. One day Ma'y Ann, old miss's maid, came rushin' out ter de kitchen, an' says she, 'Liza Jane, ole marse gwine sell yo' Sam down de ribber.'

"'Go way f'm yere,' says I; 'my husban's free!'

"'Don' make no diff'ence. I heerd ole marse tell ole miss he wuz gwine take yo' Sam 'way wid 'im ter-morrow, fer he needed money, an' he knowed whar he could git a t'ousan' dollars for Sam an' no questions axed.'

"W'en Sam come home f'm de fiel' dat night, I tole him 'bout ole marse gwine steal 'im, an' Sam run erway. His time wuz mos' up, an' he swo' dat w'en he wuz twenty-one he would come back an' he'p me run erway, er else save up de money ter buy my freedom. An' I know he'd 'a' done it, fer he thought a heap er me, Sam did. But w'en he come back he did n' fin' me, fer I wuz n' dere. Ole marse had heerd dat I warned Sam, so he had me whip' an' sol' down de ribber.

"Den de wah broke out, an' w'en it wuz ober de cullud folks wuz scattered. I went back ter de ole home; but Sam wuz n' dere, an' I couldn' l'arn nuffin' 'bout 'im. But I knowed he'd be'n dere to look fer me an' hadn' foun' me, an' had gone erway ter hunt fer me.

"I's be'n lookin' fer 'im eber sence," she added simply, as though twenty-five years were but a couple of weeks, "an' I knows he's be'n lookin' fer me. Fer he sot a heap er sto' by me, Sam did, an' I know he's be'n huntin' fer me all dese years,—'less'n he's be'n sick er sump'n so he could n' work, er out'n his head, so he could n' 'member his promise. I went back down de ribber, fer I 'lowed he'd gone down dere lookin' fer me. I's be'n ter Noo Orleens, an' Atlanty, an' Charleston, an' Richmon'; an' w'en I'd be'n all ober de Souf I come ter de Norf. Fer I knows I'll fin' 'im some er dese days," she added softly, "er he 'll fin' me, an' den we 'll bofe be as happy in freedom as we wuz in de ole days befo' de wah." A smile stole over her withered countenance as she paused a moment, and her bright eyes softened into a faraway look.

This was the substance of the old woman's story. She had wandered a little here and there. Mr. Ryder was looking at her curiously when she finished.

"How have you lived all these years?" he asked.

"Cookin', suh. I's a good cook. Does you know anybody w'at needs a good cook, suh? I's stoppin' wid a cullud fam'ly roun' de corner younder 'tel I kin git a place."

"Do you really expect to find your husband? He may be dead long ago."

She shook her head emphatically. "Oh no, he ain't dead. De signs an' de tokens tells me. I dremp three nights runnin' on'y dis las' week dat I foun' him."

"He may have married another woman. Your slave marriage would not have prevented him, for you never lived with him after the war, and without that your marriage does n't count."

"Wouldn' make no diff'ence wid Sam. He wouldn' marry no yuther 'ooman 'tel he foun' out 'bout me. I knows it," she added. "Sump'n 's be'n tellin' me all dese years dat I's gwine fin' Sam 'fo' I dies."

"Perhaps he's outgrown you, and climbed up in the world where he wouldn't care to have you find him."

"No, indeed, suh," she replied, "Sam ain't dat kin' er man. He wuz good ter me, Sam wuz, but he wuz n' much good ter nobody e'se, fer he wuz one er de triflin'es' han's on de plantation. I 'spec's ter haf suppo't 'im w'en I fin' 'im, fer he nebber would work 'less'n he had ter. But den he wuz free, an he did n' git no pay fer his work, an' I don't blame 'im much. Mebbe he's done better sence he run erway, but I ain' 'spectin' much."

"You may have passed him on the street a hundred times during the twenty-five years, and not have known him; time works great changes."

She smiled incredulously. "I'd know 'm 'mongs' a hund'ed men. Fer dey wuz n' no yuther merlatter man like my man Sam, an' I coul n' be mistook. I's toted his picture roun' wid me twenty-five years."

"May I see it?" asked Mr. Ryder. "It might help me to remember whether I have seen the original."

As she drew a small parcel from her bosom he saw that it was fastened to a string that went around her neck. Removing several wrappers, she brought to light an old-fashioned daguerreotype in a black case. He looked long and intently at the portrait. It was faded with time, but the features were still distinct, and it was easy to see what manner of man it had represented.

He closed the case, and with a slow movement handed it back to her.

"I don't know of any man in town who goes by that name," he said, "nor have I heard of any one making such inquiries. But if you will leave me your address, I will give the matter some attention, and if I find out anything I will let you know."

She gave him the number of a house in the neighborhood, and went away, after thanking him warmly.

He wrote the address on the fly-leaf of the volume of Tennyson, and, when she had gone, rose to his feet and stood looking after her curiously. As she walked down the street with mincing step, he saw several persons whom she passed turn and look back at her with a smile of kindly amusement. When she had turned the corner, he went upstairs to his bedroom, and stood for a long time before the mirror of his dressing-case, gazing thoughtfully at the reflection of his own face.

III

At eight o'clock the ballroom was a blaze of light and the guests had begun to assemble; for there was a literary programme and some routine business of the society to be gone through with before the dancing. A black servant in evening dress waited at the door and directed the guests to the dressing-rooms.

The occasion was long memorable among the colored people of the city; not alone for the dress and display, but for the high average of intelligence and culture that distinguished the gathering as a whole. There were a number of school-teachers, several young doctors, three or four lawyers, some professional singers, an editor, a lieutenant in the United States army spending his furlough in the city, and others in various polite callings; these were colored, though most of them would not have attracted even a casual glance because of any marked difference from white people. Most of the ladies were in evening costume, and dress coats and dancing pumps were the rule among the men. A band of string music, stationed in an alcove behind a row of palms, played popular airs while the guests were gathering.

The dancing began at half past nine. At eleven o'clock supper was served. Mr. Ryder had left the ballroom some little time before the intermission, but reappeared at the supper-table. The spread was worthy of the occasion, and the guests did full justice to it. When the coffee had been served, the toastmaster, Mr. Solomon Sadler, rapped for order. He made a brief introductory speech, complimenting host and guests, and then presented in their order the toasts of the evening. They were responded to with a very fair display of after-dinner wit.

"The last toast," said the toast-master, when he reached the end of the list, "is one which must appeal to us all. There is no one of us of the sterner sex who is not at some time dependent upon woman,—in infancy for protection, in manhood for companionship, in old age for care and comforting. Our good host has been trying to live alone, but the fair faces I see around me to-night prove that he too is largely dependent upon the gentler sex for most that makes life worth living,—the society and love of friends,—and rumor is at fault if he does not soon yield entire subjection to one of them. Mr. Ryder will now respond to the toast,—The Ladies."

There was a pensive look in Mr. Ryder's eyes as he took the floor and adjusted his eyeglasses. He began by speaking of woman as the gift of Heaven to man, and after some general observations on the relations of the sexes he said: "But perhaps the quality which most distinguishes woman is her fidelity and devotion to those she loves. History is full of examples, but has recorded none more striking than one which only to-day came under my notice."

He then related, simply but effectively, the story told by his visitor of the afternoon. He gave it in the same soft dialect, which came readily to his lips, while the company listened attentively and sympathetically. For the story had awakened a responsive thrill in many hearts. There were some present who had seen, and others who had heard their fathers and grandfathers tell, the wrongs and sufferings of this past generation, and all of them still felt, in their darker moments, the shadow hanging over them. Mr. Ryder went on:—

"Such devotion and confidence are rare even among women. There are many who would have searched a year, some who would have waited five years, a few who might have hoped ten years; but for twenty-five years this woman has retained her affection for and her faith in a man she has not seen or heard of in all that time.

"She came to me to-day in the hope that I might be able to help her find this long-lost husband. And when she was gone I gave my fancy rein, and imagined a case I will put to you.

"Suppose that this husband, soon after his escape, had learned that his wife had been sold away, and that such inquiries as he could make brought no information of her whereabouts. Suppose that he was young, and she much older than he; that he was light, and she was black; that their marriage was a slave marriage, and legally binding only if they chose to make it so after the war. Suppose, too, that he made his way to the North, as some of us have done, and there, where he had larger opportunities, had improved them, and had in the course of all these years grown to be as different from the ignorant boy who ran away from fear of slavery as the day is from the night. Suppose, even, that he had qualified himself, by industry, by thrift, and by study, to win the friendship and be considered worthy the society of such people as these I see around me to-night, gracing my board and filling my heart with gladness; for I am old enough to remember the day when such a gathering would not have been possible in this land. Suppose, too, that, as the years went by, this man's memory of the past grew more and more indistinct, until at last it was rarely, except in his dreams, that any image of this bygone period rose before his mind. And then suppose that accident should bring to his knowledge the fact that the wife of his youth, the wife he had left behind him,—not one who had walked by his side and kept pace with him in his upward struggle, but one upon whom advancing years and a laborious life had set their mark,—was alive and seeking him, but that he was absolutely safe from recognition or discovery, unless he chose to reveal himself. My friends, what would the man do? I will presume that he was one who loved honor, and tried to deal justly with all men. I will even carry the case further, and suppose that perhaps he had set his heart upon another, whom he had hoped to call his own. What would he do, or rather what ought he to do, in such a crisis of a lifetime?

"It seemed to me that he might hesitate, and I imagined that I was an old friend, a near friend, and that he had come to me for advice; and I argued the case with him. I tried to discuss it impartially. After we had looked upon the matter from every point of view, I said to him, in words that we all know:—

"This above all: to thine own self be true,
And it must follow, as the night the day,
Thou canst not then be false to any man."

Then, finally, I put the question to him, 'Shall you acknowledge her?'

"And now, ladies and gentlemen, friends and companions, I ask you, what should he have done?"

There was something in Mr. Ryder's voice that stirred the hearts of those who sat around him. It suggested more than mere sympathy with an imaginary situation; it seemed rather in the nature of a personal appeal. It was observed, too, that his look rested more especially upon Mrs. Dixon, with a mingled expression of renunciation and inquiry.

She had listened, with parted lips and streaming eyes. She was the first to speak: "He should have acknowledged her."

"Yes," they all echoed; "he should have acknowledged her."

"My friends and companions," responded Mr. Ryder, "I thank you, one and all. It is the answer I expected, for I knew your hearts."

He turned and walked toward the closed door of an adjoining room, while every eye followed him in wondering curiosity. He came back in a moment, leading by the hand his visitor of the afternoon, who stood started and trembling at the sudden plunge into this scene of brilliant gayety. She was neatly dressed in gray, and wore the white cap of an elderly woman.

"Ladies and gentlemen," he said, "this is the woman, and I am the man, whose story I have told you. Permit me to introduce to you the wife of my youth."

1899

BRO'R ABR'M JIMSON'S WEDDING

A CHRISTMAS STORY

Pauline E. Hopkins

It was a Sunday in early spring the first time that Caramel Johnson dawned on the congregation of —— Church in a populous New England city.

The Afro-Americans of that city are well-to-do, being of a frugal nature, and considering it a lasting disgrace for any man among them, desirous of social standing in the community, not to make himself comfortable in this world's goods against the coming time, when old age creeps on apace and renders him unfit for active business.

Therefore the members of the said church had not waited to be exhorted by reformers to own their unpretentious homes and small farms outside the city limits, but they vied with each other in efforts to accumulate a small competency urged thereto by a realization of what pressing needs the future might bring, or it might have been because of the constant example of white neighbors, and a due respect for the dignity which *their* foresight had brought to the superior race.

Of course, these small Vanderbilts and Astors of a darker hue must have a place of worship in accord with their worldly prosperity, and so it fell out that —— Church was the richest plum in the ecclesiastical pudding, and greatly sought by scholarly divines as a resting place for four years,—the extent of the time-limit allowed by conference to the men who must be provided with suitable charges according to the demands of their energy and scholarship.

The attendance was unusually large for morning service, and a restless movement was noticeable all through the sermon. How strange a thing is nature; the change of the seasons announces itself in all humanity as well as in the trees and flowers, the grass, and in the atmosphere. Something within us responds instantly to the touch of kinship that dwells in all life.

The air, soft and balmy, laden with rich promise for the future, came through the massive, half-open windows, stealing in refreshing waves upon the congregation. The sunlight fell through the colored glass of the windows in prismatic hues, and dancing all over the lofty star-gemmed ceiling, painted the hue of the broad vault of heaven, creeping down in crinkling shadows to touch the deep garnet cushions of the sacred desk, and the rich wood of the altar with a hint of gold.

The offertory was ended. The silvery cadences of a rich soprano voice still lingered on the air, "O, Worship the Lord in the beauty of holiness." There was a suppressed feeling of expectation, but not the faintest rustle as the minister rose in the pulpit, and after a solemn pause, gave the usual invitation:

"If there is anyone in this congregation desiring to unite with this church, either by letter or on probation, please come forward to the altar."

The words had not died upon his lips when a woman started from her seat near the door and passed up the main aisle. There was a sudden commotion on all sides. Many heads were turned—it takes so little to interest a church audience. The girls in the choir-box leaned over the rail, nudged each other and giggled, while the men said to one another, "She's a stunner, and no mistake."

The candidate for membership, meanwhile, had reached the altar railing and stood before the man of God, to whom she had handed her letter from a former Sabbath home, with head decorously bowed as became the time and the holy place. There was no denying the fact that she was a pretty girl; brown of skin, small of feature, with an ever-lurking gleam of laughter in eyes coal black. Her figure was slender and beautifully moulded, with a seductive grace in the undulating walk and erect carriage. But the chief charm of the sparkling dark face lay in its intelligence, and the responsive play of facial expression which was enhanced by two mischievous dimples pressed into the rounded cheeks by the caressing fingers of the god of Love.

The minister whispered to the candidate, coughed, blew his nose on his snowy clerical handkerchief, and, finally, turned to the expectant congregation:

"Sister Chocolate Caramel Johnson—"

He was interrupted by a snicker and a suppressed laugh, again from the choir-box, and an audible whisper which sounded distinctly throughout the quiet church,—

"I'd get the Legislature to change that if it was mine, 'deed I would!" then silence profound caused by the reverend's stern glance of reproval bent on the offenders in the choir-box.

"Such levity will not be allowed among the members of the choir. If it occurs again, I shall ask the choir master for the names of the offenders and have their places taken by those more worthy to be gospel singers."

Thereupon Mrs. Tilly Anderson whispered to Mrs. Nancy Tobias that, "them choir gals is the mos' deceivines' hussies in the church, an' for my part, I'm glad the pastor called 'em down. That sister's too good lookin' fer 'em, an' they'll be after her like er pack o' houn's, min' me, Sis' Tobias."

Sister Tobias ducked her head in her lap and shook her fat sides in laughing appreciation of the sister's foresight.

Order being restored the minister proceeded:

"Sister Chocolate Caramel Johnson brings a letter to us from our sister church in Nashville, Tennessee. She has been a member in good standing for ten years, having been received into fellowship at ten years of age. She leaves them now, much to their regret, to pursue the study of music at one of the large conservatories in this city, and they recommend her to our love and care. You know the contents of the letter. All in favor of giving Sister Johnson the right hand of fellowship, please manifest the same by a rising vote." The whole congregation rose.

"Contrary minded? None. The ayes have it. Be seated, friends. Sister Johnson it gives me great pleasure to receive you into this church. I welcome you to its joys and sorrows. May God bless you, Brother Jimson?" (Brother Jimson stepped from his seat to the pastor's side.) "I assign this sister to your class. Sister Johnson, this is Brother Jimson, your future spiritual teacher."

Brother Jimson shook the hand of the new member, warmly, and she returned to her seat. The minister pronounced the benediction over the waiting congregation; the organ burst into richest melody. Slowly the crowd of worshippers dispersed.

Abraham Jimson had made his money as a janitor for the wealthy people of the city. He was a bachelor, and when reproved by some good Christian brother for still dwelling in single blessedness always offered as an excuse that he had been too busy to think of a wife, but that now he was "well fixed," pecuniarily, he would begin to "look over" his lady friends for a suitable companion.

He owned a house in the suburbs and a fine brick dwelling-house in the city proper. He was a trustee of prominence in the church; in fact, its "solid man," and his opinion was sought and his advice acted upon by his associates on the Board. It was felt that any lady in the congregation would be proud to know herself his choice.

When Caramel Johnson received the right hand of fellowship, her aunt, the widow Maria Nash, was ahead in the race for the wealthy class-leader. It had been neck-and-neck for a while between her and Sister Viney Peters, but, finally it had settled down to Sister Maria with a hundred to one, among the sporting members of the Board, that she carried off the prize, for Sister Maria owned a house adjoining Brother Jimson's in the suburbs, and property counts these days.

Sister Nash had "no idea" when she sent for her niece to come to B. that the latter would prove a rival; her son Andy was as good as engaged to Caramel. But it is always the unexpected that happens. Caramel came, and Brother Jimson had no eyes for the charms of other women after he had gazed into her coal black orbs, and watched her dimples come and go.

Caramel decided to accept a position as housemaid in order to help defray the expenses of her tuition at the conservatory, and Brother Jimson interested himself so warmly in her behalf that she soon had a situation in the home of his richest patron where it was handy for him to chat with her about the business of the church, and the welfare of her soul, in general. Things progressed very smoothly until the fall, when one day Sister Maria had occasion to call, unexpectedly, on her niece and found Brother Jimson basking in her smiles while he enjoyed a sumptuous dinner of roast chicken and fixings.

To say that Sister Maria was "set way back" would not accurately describe her feelings; but from that time Abraham Jimson knew that he had a secret foe in the Widow Nash.

Before many weeks had passed it was publicly known that Brother Jimson would lead Caramel Johnson to the altar "come Christmas." There was much sly speculation as to the "widder's gittin' left," and how she took it from those who had cast hopeless glances toward the chief man of the church. Great preparations were set on foot for the wedding festivities. The bride's trousseau was a present from the groom and included a white satin wedding gown and a costly gold watch. The town house was refurnished, and a trip to New York was in contemplation.

"Hump!" grunted Sister Nash when told the rumors, "there's no fool like an ol' fool. Car'mel's a han'ful he'll fin', ef he gits her."

"I reckon he'll git her all right, Sis' Nash," laughed the neighbor, who had run in to talk over the news.

"I've said my word an' I ain't goin' change it, Sis'r. Min' me. I says, *ef he gits her*, an, I mean it."

Andy Nash was also a member of Brother Jimson's class; he possessed, too, a strong sweet baritone voice which made him of great value to the choir. He was an immense success in the social life of the city, and had created sad havoc with the hearts of the colored girls; he could have his pick of the best of them because of his graceful figure and fine easy manners. Until Caramel had been dazzled by the wealth of her elderly lover, she had considered herself fortunate as the lady of his choice.

It was Sunday, three weeks before the wedding that Andy resolved to have it out with Caramel.

"She's been hot an' she's been col', an' now she's luke warm, an' today ends it before this gent-man sleeps," he told himself as he stood before the glass and tied his pale blue silk tie in a stunning knot, and settled his glossy tile at a becoming angle.

Brother Jimson's class was a popular one and had a large membership; the hour spent there was much enjoyed, even by visitors. Andy went into the vestry early resolved to meet Caramel if possible. She was there, at the back of the room sitting alone on a settee. Andy immediately seated himself in the vacant place by her side. There were whispers and much head-shaking among the few early worshippers, all of whom knew the story of the young fellow's romance and his disappointment.

As he dropped into the seat beside her, Caramel turned her large eyes on him intently, speculatively, with a doubtful sort of curiosity suggested in her expression, as to how he took her flagrant desertion.

"Howdy, Car'mel?" was his greeting without a shade of resentment.

"I'm well; no need to ask how you are," was the quick response. There was a mixture of cordiality and coquetry in her manner. Her eyes narrowed and glittered under lowered lids, as she gave him a long side-glance. How could she help showing her admiration for the supple young giant beside her? "Surely," she told herself, "I'll have long time enough to git sick of old rheumatics," her pet name for her elderly lover.

"I ain't sick much," was Andy's surly reply.

He leaned his elbow on the back of the settee and gave his recent sweetheart a flaming glance of mingled love and hate, oblivious to the presence of the assembled class-members.

"You ain't over friendly these days, Car'mel, but I gits news of your capers 'roun' 'bout some of the members."

"My—Yes?" she answered as she flashed her great eyes at him in pretended surprised. He laughed a laugh not good to hear.

"Yes," he drawled. Then he added with sudden energy, "Are you goin' to tie up to old Rheumatism sure 'nuff, come Chris'mas?"

"Come Chris'mas, Andy, I be. I hate to tell you but I have to do it."

He recoiled as from a blow. As for the girl, she found a keen relish in the situation; it flattered her vanity.

"How comes it you've changed your mind, Car'mel, 'bout you an' me? You've tol' me often that I was your first choice."

"We—ll," she drawled, glancing uneasily about her and avoiding her aunt's gaze, which she knew was bent upon her every movement, "I did reckon once I would. But a man with money suits me best, an' you ain't got a cent."

"No more have you. You ain't no better than other women to work an' help a man along, is you?"

The color flamed an instant in her face turning the dusky skin to a deep, dull red.

"Andy Nash, you always was a fool, an' as ignerunt as a wil' Injun. I mean to have a sure nuff brick house an' plenty of money. That makes people respec' you. Why don' you quit bein' so shifless and save your money. You ain't worth your salt."

"Your head's turned with pianorer-playin' an' livin' up North. Ef you'll turn *him* off an' come back home, I'll turn over a new leaf, Car'mel," his voice was soft and persuasive enough now.

She had risen to her feet; her eyes flashed, her face was full of pride.

"I won't. I've quit likin' you, Andy Nash."

"Are you in earnest?" he asked, also rising from his seat.

"Dead earnes'."

"Then there's no more to be said."

He spoke calmly, not raising his voice above a whisper. She stared at him in surprise. Then he added as he swung on his heel preparatory to leaving her:

"You ain't got him yet, my gal. But remember, I'm waitin' for you when you need me."

While this whispered conference was taking place in the back part of the vestry, Brother Jimson had entered, and many an anxious glance he cast in the direction of the couple. Andy made his way slowly to his mother's side as Brother Jimson rose in hos place to open the meeting. There was a commotion on all sides as the members rustled down on their knees for prayer. Widow Nash whispered to her son as they knelt side by side:

"How did you make out, Andy?"

"Didn't make out at all, mammy; she's as obstinate as a mule."

"Well, then, there's only one thing mo' to do."

Andy was unpleasant company for the remainder of the day. He sought, but found nothing to palliate Carmel's treachery. He had only surly, bitter words for his companions who ventured to address him, as the outward expression of inward tumult. The more he brooded over his wrongs the worse he felt. When he went to work on Monday morning he was feeling vicious. He had made up his mind to do something desperate. The wedding should not come off. He would be avenged.

Andy went about his work at the hotel in gloomy silence unlike his usual gay hilarity. It happened that all the female help at the great hostelry was white, and on that particular Monday morning it was the duty of Bridget McCarthy's watch to clean the floors. Bridget was also not in the best of humors, for Pat McCloskey, her special company, had gone to the priest's with her rival, Kate Connerton, on Sunday afternoon, and Bridget had not got over the effects of a strong rum punch taken to quiet her nerves after hearing the news.

Bridget had scrubbed a wide swath of the marble floor when Andy came through with a rush order carried in scientific style high above his head, balanced on one hand. Intent upon satisfying the guest who was princely in his "tips," Andy's unwary feet became entangled in the maelstrom of brooms, scrubbing-brushes and pails. In an instant the "order" was sliding over the floor in a general mix-up.

To say Bridget was mad wouldn't do her state justice. She forgot herself and her surroundings and relieved her feelings in elegant Irish, ending a tirade of abuse by calling Andy a "wall-eyed, bandy-legged nagur."

Andy couldn't stand that from "common, po' white trash," so calling all his science into play he struck out straight from the shoulder with his right, and brought her a swinging blow on the mouth, which seated her neatly in the five-gallon bowl of freshly made lobster salad which happened to be standing on the floor behind her.

There was a wail from the kitchen force that reached to every department. It being the busiest hour of the day when they served dinner, the dish-washers and scrubbers went on a strike against the "nagur who struck Bridget McCarthy, the baste," mingled with cries of "lynch him!" Instantly the great basement floor was a battle ground. Every colored man seized whatever was handiest and ranged himself by Andy's side, and stood ready to receive the onslaught of the Irish brigade. For the sake of peace, and sorely against his inclinations, the proprietor surrendered Andy to the police on a charge of assault and battery.

On Wednesday morning of that eventful week, Brother Jimson wended his way to his house in the suburbs to collect the rent. Unseen by the eye of man, he was wrestling with a problem that had shadowed his life for many years. No one on earth suspected him unless it might be the widow. Brother Jimson boasted of his consistent Christian life—rolled his piety like a sweet morsel beneath his tongue, and had deluded himself into thinking that *he* could do no sin. There were scoffers in the church who doubted the genuineness of his pretensions, and he believed that there was a movement on foot against his power led by Widow Nash.

Brother Jimson groaned in bitterness of spirit. His only fear was that he might be parted from Caramel. If he lost her he felt that all happiness in life was over for him, and anxiety gave him a sickening feeling of unrest. He was tormented, too, by jealousy; and when he was called upon by Andy's anxious mother to rescue her son from the clutches of the law, he had promised her fair enough, but in reality resolved to do nothing but—tell the judge that Andy was a dangerous character whom it was best to quell by severity. The pastor and all the other influential members of the church were at court on Tuesday, but Brother Jimson was conspicuous by his absence.

Today Brother Jimson resolved to call on Sister Nash, and, as he had heard nothing of the outcome of the trial, make cautious inquiries concerning that, and also sound her on the subject nearest his heart.

He opened the gate and walked down the side path to the back door. From within came the rhythmic sound of a rubbing board. The brother knocked, and then cleared his throat with a preliminary cough.

"Come," called a voice within. As the door swung open it revealed the spare form of the widow, who with sleeves rolled above her elbows stood at the tub cutting her way through piles of foaming suds.

"Mornin', Sis' Nash! How's all?"

"That you, Bro'r Jimson? How's yourself? Take a cheer an' make yourself to home."

"Cert'nly, Sis' Nash; don' care ef I do," and the good brother scanned the sister with an eagle eye. "Yas'm, I'm purty tol'rable these days, thank God. Bleeg'd to you, Sister, I jes' will stop an' res' myself befo' I repair myself back to the city." He seated himself in the most comfortable chair in the room, tilted it on the two back legs against the wall, lit his pipe and with a grunt of satisfaction settled back to watch the white rings of smoke curl about his head.

"These are mighty ticklish times, Sister. How's you continue on the journey? Is you strong in the faith?"

"I've got the faith, my brother, but I ain't on no mountain top this week. I'm way down in the valley; I'm jes' coaxin' the Lord to keep me sweet," and Sister Nash wiped the suds from her hands and prodded the clothes in the boiler with the clothes-stick, added fresh pieces and went on with her work.

"This is a worl' strewed with wrecks an' floatin' with tears. It's the valley of tribulation. May your faith continue. I hear Jim Jinkins has bought a farm up Taunton way."

"Wan' ter know!"

"Doctor tells me Bro'r Waters is comin' after Chris-mus. They do say as how he's stirrin' up things turrible; he's easin his min' on this lynchin' business, an' it's high time—high time."

"Sho! Don' say so! What you reck'n he's goin' tell us now, Brother Jimson?"

"Suthin' 'stonishin', Sister; it'll stir the country from end to end. Yes'm, the Council is powerful strong as an organ'zation."

"Sho! sho!" and the "thrub, thrub" of the board could be heard a mile away.

The conversation flagged. Evidently Widow Nash was not in a talkative mood that morning. The brother was disappointed.

"Well, it's mighty comfort'ble here, but I mus' be goin'."

"What's your hurry, Brother Jimson?"

"Business, Sister, business," and the brother brought his chair forward preparatory to rising. "Where's Andy? How'd he come out of that little difficulty?"

"Locked up."

"You don't mean to say he's in jail?"

"Yes; he's in jail 'tell I git's his bail."

"What might the sentence be, Sister?"

"Twenty dollars fine or six months at the Islan'." There was silence for a moment, broken only by the "thrub, thrub" of the washboard, while the smoke curled upward from Brother Jimson's pipe as he enjoyed a few last puffs.

"These are mighty ticklish times, Sister. Po' Andy, the way of the transgressor is hard."

Sister Nash took her hands out of the tub and stood with arms akimbo, a statue of Justice carved in ebony. Her voice was like the trump of doom.

"Yes; an' men like you is the cause of it. You leadin' men with money an' chances don' do your duty. I arst you, I arst you fair, to go down to the jedge an' bail that po' chile out. Did you go? No; you hard-faced old devil, you lef him be there, an' I had to git the money from my white folks. Yes, an' I'm breakin' my back now, over that pile of clo's to pay that twenty dollars. Um! all the trouble comes to us women."

"That's so, Sister; that's the livin' truth," murmured Brother Jimson furtively watching the rising storm and wondering where the lightning of her speech would strike next.

"I tell you what it is our receiptfulnes to each other is the reason we don' prosper an' God's a-punishin' us with fire an' with sward 'cause we's so jealous an' snaky to each other."

"That's so, Sister; that's the livin' truth."

"Yes, sir' a nigger's boun' to be a nigger 'tell the trump of doom. You kin skin him, but he's a nigger still. Broadcloth, biled shirts an' money won't make him more or less, no, sir."

"That's so, Sister; that's jes' so."

"A nigger can't holp himself. White folks can run agin the law all the time an' they never gits caught, but a nigger! Every time he opens his mouth he puts his foot in it—got to hit that po' white trash gal in the mouth an' git jailed, an' leave his po'r ol' mother to work her fingers to the secon' jint to get him out. Um!"

"These are mighty ticklish times, Sister. Man's boun' to sin; it's his nat'ral state. I hope this will teach Andy humility of the sperit."

"A little humility'd be good for yourself, Abra'm Jimson." Sister Nash ceased her sobs and set her teeth hard.

"Lord, Sister Nash, what compar'son is there 'twixt me an' a worthless nigger like Andy? My business is with the salt of the earth, an' so I have dwelt ever since I was consecrated."

"Salt, of the earth! But ef the salt have los' its saver how you goin' salt it ergin'? No, sir, you cain't do it; it mus' be cas' out an' trodded under foot of men. That's who's goin' happen you Abe Jimson, hyar me? An' I'd like to trod on you with my foot, an' every ol' good fer nuthin' bag o' salt like you," shouted Sister Nash. "You're a snake in the grass; you done stole the boy's gal an' then try to git him sent to the Islan'. You cain't deny it, fer the jedge done tol' me all you said, you ol' rhinoceros-hided hypercrite. Salt of the earth! You!"

Brother Jimson regretted that Widow Nash had found him out. Slowly, he turned, settling his hat on the back of his head.

"Good mornin', Sister Nash. I ain't no hard feelin's agains' you. I'm too near to the kindom to let trifles jar me. My bowels of compassion yearns over you, Sister, a pilgrim an' a stranger in this unfriendly worl'."

No answer from Sister Nash. Brother Jimson lingered.

"Good mornin', Sister," still no answer.

"I hope to see you at the weddin', Sister."

"Keep on hopin'; I'll be there. That gal's my own sister's chile. What in time she wants of a rheumatic ol' sap-head like you for, beats me. I wouldn't marry you for no money, myself; no, sir; it's my belief that you've done goophered her."

"Yes, Sister; I've hearn tell of people refusin' befo' they was ask'd," he retorted, giving her a sly look.

For answer the widow grabbed the clothes-stick and flung it at him in speechless rage.

"My, what a temper it's got," remarked Brother Jimson soothingly as he dodged the shovel, the broom, the coalhod and the stove-covers. But he sighed with relief as he turned into the street and caught the faint sound of the washboard now resumed.

· · · · ·

To a New Englander the season of snow and ice with its clear biting atmosphere, is the ideal time for the great festival. Christmas morning dawned in royal splendor; the sun kissed the snowy streets and turned the icicles into brilliant stalactites. The bells rang a joyous call from every steeple, and soon the churches were crowded with eager worshippers—eager to hear again the oft-repeated, the wonderful story on which the heart of the whole Christian world feeds its faith and hope. Words of tender faith, marvelous in their simplicity fell from the lips of a world-renowned preacher, and touched the hearts of the listening multitude:

"The winter sunshine is not more bright and clear than the atmosphere of living joy, which stretching back between our eyes and that picture of Bethlehem, shows us its beauty in unstained freshness. And as we open once again those chapters of the gospel in which the ever fresh and living picture stands, there seems from year to year always to come some newer, brighter meaning into the words that tell the tale.

"St. Matthew says that when Jesus was born in Bethlehem the wise men came from the East to Jerusalem. The East means man's search after God; Jerusalem means God's search after man. The East means the religion of the devout soul; Jerusalem means the religion of the merciful God. The East means Job's cry, 'Oh, that I knew where I might find him!' Jerusalem means Immanuel—God with us.'"

Then the deep-toned organ joined the grand chorus of human voices in a fervent hymn of praise and thanksgiving:

"Lo! the Morning star appeareth,
    O'er the world His beams are cast;
He the Alpha and Omega,
    He, the Great, the First the Last!
Hallelujah! hallelujah!
    Let the heavenly portal ring!
Christ is born, the Prince of glory!
    Christ the Lord, Messiah, King!"

Everyone of prominence in church circles had been bidden to the Jimson wedding. The presents were many and costly. Early after service on Christmas morning the vestry room was taken in hand by leading sisters to prepare the tables for the supper, for on account of the host of friends bidden to the feast, the reception was to be held in the vestry.

The tables groaned beneath their loads of turkey, salads, pies, puddings, cakes and fancy ices.

Yards and yards of evergreen wreaths encircled the granite pillars; the altar was banked with potted plants and cut flowers. It was a beautiful sight. The main aisle was roped off for the invited guests, with white satin ribbons.

Brother Jimson's patrons were to be present in a body, and they had sent the bride a solid silver service so magnificent that the sisters could only sigh with envy.

The ceremony was to take place at seven sharp. Long before that hour the ushers in full evening dress were ready to receive the guests. Sister Maria Nash was among the first to arrive, and even the Queen of Sheba was not arrayed like unto her. At fifteen minutes before the hour, the organist began an elaborate instrumental performance. There was an expectant hush and much head-turning when the music changed to the familiar strains of the "Wedding March." The minister took his place inside the railing ready to receive the party. The groom waited at the altar.

First came the ushers, then the maids of honor, then the flower girl—daughter of a prominent member—carrying a basket of flowers which she scattered before the bride, who was on the arm of the best man. In the bustle and confusion incident to the entrance of the wedding party no one noticed a group of strangers accompanied by Andy Nash, enter and occupy seats near the door.

The service began. All was quiet. The pastor's words fell clearly upon the listening ears. He had reached the words:

"If any man can show just cause, etc.," when like a thunder-clap came a voice from the back part of the house—an angry excited voice, and a woman of ponderous avoirdupois advanced up the aisle.

"Hol' on thar, pastor, hol'on! A man cain't have but one wife 'cause it's agin' the law. I'm Abe Jimson's lawful wife, an' hyars his six children—all boys—to pint out their daddy." In an instant the assembly was in confusion.

"My soul," exclaimed Viney Peters, "the ol' sarpen'! An' to think how near I come to takin' up with him. I'm glad I ain't Car'mel."

Sis'r Maria said nothing, but a smile of triumph lit up her countenance.

"Brother Jimson, is this true?" demanded the minister, sternly. But Abraham Jimson was past answering. His face was ashen, his teeth chattering, his hair standing on end. His shaking limbs refused to uphold his weight; he sank upon his knees on the steps of the altar.

But now a hand was laid upon his shoulder and Mrs. Jimson hauled him up on his feet with a jerk.

"Abe Jimson, you know me. You run'd 'way from me up North fifteen years ago, an' you hid yourself like a groun' hog in a hole, but I've got you. There'll be no new wife in the Jimson family this week. I'm yer fus' wife an' I'll be yer las' one. Git up hyar now, you mis'able sinner an' tell the pastor who I be." Brother Jimson meekly obeyed the clarion voice. His sanctified air had vanished; his pride humbled into the dust.

"Pastor," came in trembling tones from his quivering lips. "These are mighty ticklish times." He paused. A deep silence followed his words. "I'm a weak-kneed, mis'able sinner. I have fallen under temptation. This is Ma' Jane, my wife, an' these hyar boys is my sons, God forgive me."

The bride, who had been forgotten now, broke in:

"Abraham Jimson, you ought to be hung. I'm goin' to sue you for breach of promise." It was a fatal remark. Mrs. Jimson turned upon her.

"You will, will you? Sue him, will you? I'll make a choc'late Car'mel of you befo' I'm done with you, you 'ceitful hussy, hoodooin' hones' men from thar wives."

She sprang upon the girl, tearing, biting, rendering. The satin gown and gossamer veil were reduced to rags. Caramel emitted a series of ear-splitting shrieks, but the biting and tearing went on. How it might have ended no one can tell if Andy had not sprang over the backs of the pews and grappled with the infuriated woman.

The excitement was intense. Men and women struggled to get out of the church. Some jumped from the windows and others crawled under the pews, where they were secure from violence. In the midst of the melee, Brother Jimson disappeared and was never seen again, and Mrs. Jimson came into possession of his property by due process of law.

In the church Abraham Jimson's wedding and his fall from grace is still spoken of in eloquent whispers.

. . . . .

In the home of Mrs. Andy Nash a motto adorns the parlor walls worked in scarlet wool and handsomely framed in gilt. The text reads: "Ye are the salt of the earth; there is nothing hidden that shall not be revealed."

1901

Nonfiction

WHISPER TO A WIFE

from Colored American

In the matrimonial character, gentle lady, no longer let your fancy wander to scenes of pleasure or disappointment. Let home be now your empire, your world! Let home be now the sole scene of your wishes, your thoughts, your plans, your exertions. Let home be now the stage on which, in the varied character of wife, or mother, and of mistress, you strive to act and shine with splendor. In its sober, quiet scenes, let your heart cast its anchor—let your feelings and pursuits all be centered. And beyond the spreading oaks that shadow and shelter your dwelling, gentle lady, let not your fancy wander. Leave to your husband to distinguish himself by his valor or his talents. Do you seek for fame at home! and let the applause of your God, of your children, and your servants, weave for your brow a never-fading chaplet.

An ingenious writer says—"If a painter wished to draw the very finest object in the world, it would be the picture of a wife, with eyes expressing the serenity of her mind, and countenance beaming with benevolence; one hand lulling to rest on her bosom a lovely infant, the other employed in presenting a moral page to a second sweet baby, who stands at her knee—listening to the words of truth and wisdom from its incomparable mother.

1837

THE INTEMPERATE HUSBAND

Charles Sprague, from Colored American

The common calamities of life may be endured. Poverty, sickness, and even death may be met—but there is that which, while it brings all these with it, is worse than all these together. When the husband and father forgets the duties he once delighted to fulfill, and by slow degrees becomes the creature of intemperance, there enters into his house the sorrow that rends the spirit—that cannot be alleviated, that will not be comforted.

It is here, above all, where she, who has ventured every thing, feels that every thing is lost. Woman, silent-suffering, devoted woman, here bends to her direst affliction. The measure of her woe is, in truth, full, whose husband is a drunkard. Who shall protect her when he is her insult, her oppressor? What shall delight her, when she shrinks from the sight of his face, and trembles at the sound of his voice? The heart is indeed dark, that he has made desolate. There, through the dull midnight hour, her griefs are whispered to herself, her bruised heart bleeds in secret. There, while the cruel author of her distress is drowned in distant revelry, she holds her solitary vigil, waiting, yet dreading his return, that will only wring from her, by his unkindness, tears even more scalding than those she shed over his transgression. To fling a deeper gloom across the present, memory turns back, and broods upon the past. Like the recollection of the sun-stricken pilgrim, of the cool spring that he drank at in the morning, the joys of other days come over her, as if only to mock her parched and weary spirit. She recalls the ardent lover, whose graces won her from the home of her infancy—the enraptured father, who bent with such delight over his new-born child—and she asks if this can really be him— this sunken being, who has now nothing for her but the sot's disgusting brutality—nothing for those abashed and trembling children, but the sot's disgusting example! Can we wonder, that amid these agonizing moments, the tender cords of violated affection should snap asunder? That the scorned and deserted wife should confess, "there is no killing like that which kills the heart?" That though it would have been hard for her to kiss, for the last time, the cold lips of her dead husband, and lay his body for ever in the dust, it is harder to behold him so debasing life, that even his death would be greeted in mercy? Had he died in the light of his goodness, bequeathing to his family the inheritance of an untarnished name, the example of virtues that should blossom for his sons and daughters from the tomb—though she would have wept bitterly indeed, the tears of grief would not have been the tears of shame. But to behold him, fallen away from the station he adorned, degraded from the station he adorned, degraded from eminence to ignominy—at home, turning his dwelling to darkness, and his holy endearments to mockery—abroad thrust from the companionship of the worthy, a self-branded outlaw. This is the woe that the wife feels is more dreadful than death, that she mourns over, as worse than widowhood.

1837

TELL YOUR WIFE

from Pacific Appeal

Yes, the only way is to tell your wife just how you stand. Show her your balance sheet. Let her look over the items. You think it will hurt her feelings. No, it will not do any such thing. She has been taught to believe that money was with you, just as little boys think it is with their fathers—terribly hard to reach, inexhaustible. She has had her suspicions already; she has guessed you were not so prosperous as you talked; but you have so befogged your money affairs that she, poor thing, knows nothing about them. Tell it right out to her, that you are living outside your income. Take her into partnership, and I will warrant you will never regret it; there may be a slight shower at first, but that is natural. Let her see your estimates, and when you come home again she will show you that you have put her bills too high—true she has had an eight dollar bonnet last winter, but it is just as good as ever; a few bits will provide it with new strings and refit it a little; the shape, she says, is almost as they wear them now. She will surprise you with a new vest, not exactly unfamiliar somehow, looking as if in another shop you had seen it before. You will find a wonderful change in her tastes and appetites, whereas she always fancied what was a little out of season, or just coming into market. Now, if beef is dear, she thinks boiled mutton is delightful—as tender as chicken—if lamb rises, and fish are plenty, she thinks salmon or rock cod is so good occasionally, and always insists on having it on Friday. Before you have thought much about it, you will find yourself spending evenings at home, and such evenings too; so full of domestic enjoyment and fireside pleasure, that you will look with wonder on the record of last year's expenses. My friend, if your outgoes threaten to exceed your incomes, be sure and tell your wife of it—not in a tone and manner that will lead her to think you do not want her to buy furs this winter—but just as if you wanted a counselor in the day of your trouble; and if she does not come up, heart and soul, and most successfully to your relief, put me down for no judge.

    M. E. R.

1862

A CHAPTER FOR YOUNG HUSBANDS

from the Christian Recorder

Walking the other day with a valued friend who had been confined a week or two by sickness to his room, he remarked that a husband might learn a good lesson by being confined occasionally to his house, by having in this way an opportunity of witnessing the cares and never-ending toils of his wife, whose burden and duties and patient endurance he might never otherwise have understood. There is a great deal in this thought, perhaps enough for an "editorial." Men, especially young men, are called by their business during the day mostly away from home, returning only at the hours for meals; and as they then see nearly the same routine of duty, they begin to think it is their own lot to perform all the drudgery, and to be exercised with all the weight of care and responsibility. But such a man has got a very wrong view of the case; he needs an opportunity for more extended observation, and it is perhaps for this very reason that a kind Providence arrests him by sickness, that he may learn in pain what he would fail to observe in health. We have seen recently a good many things said in the papers to wives, especially to young wives, exposing their faults, perhaps magnifying them, in none of the kindest terms, their duty and the offices pertaining to a woman's sphere. No, we believe that wives, as a whole, are really better than they are generally admitted to be. We doubt if there can be found a large number of wives who are disagreeable and negligent, without some palpable coldness or shortcoming on the part of their husbands. So far as we have had an opportunity for observation, they are far more devoted and faithful than those who style themselves their lords, and who, by the customs of society, have other and generally more pleasant and varied duties to perform. We protest, then, against those lectures so often and so obtrusively addressed to the ladies, and insist upon it that they must—most of them—have been written by some fusty bachelors who knew no better, or by some inconsiderate husbands who deserve to have been old bachelors to the end of their lives. But is there nothing to be said on the other side? Are husbands so generally the perfect, amiable, injured beings they are so often represented? Men sometimes declare that their wives' extravagances have picked their pockets—that their never-ceasing tongues have robbed them of their peace, and their general disagreeableness has driven them to the tavern and gambling-table; but this is generally the wicked excuse for a most wicked life on their own part. The fact is, men often lose their interest in their homes by their own neglect to make their homes interesting and pleasant. It should never be forgotten that the wife has her rights—as sacred after marriage as before—and a good husband's devotion to the wife after marriage will concede to her quite as much attention as his gallantry did while a lover. If it is otherwise, he most generally is at fault. Take a few examples. Before marriage a young man would feel some delicacy about accepting an invitation to spend an evening in company where his lady love had not been invited. After marriage is he always as particular? During the days of courtship his gallantry would demand that he should make himself agreeable to her; after marriage it often happens that he thinks more of being agreeable to himself. How often it happens that married men, after having been away from home the live-long day, during which the wife has toiled at her duties, go at evening again to some place of amusement, and leave her to toil on alone, uncheered and unhappy. How often it happens that her kindest offices pass unobserved, and unrewarded even by a smile, and her best efforts are condemned by the fault-finding husband. How often it happens, even when the evening is spent at home, that it is employed in silent reading, or some other way that does not recognise the wife's right to share in the enjoyments even of the fireside.

Look, ye husbands, a moment, and remember what your wife was when you took her, not from compulsion, but from your own choice; a choice based, probably, on what you then considered her superiority to all others. She was young—perhaps the idol of a happy home; she was gay and blithe as the lark, and the brothers and sisters at her father's fireside cherished her as an object of endearment. Yet she left all to join her destiny with yours; to make your home happy, and to do all that woman's love could prompt and woman's ingenuity devise to meet your wishes and lighten the burdens which might press upon you in your pilgrimage. She, of course, had her expectations too. She could not entertain feelings which promised so much, without forming some idea of reciprocation on your part, and she did expect you would after marriage perform those kind offices of which you were so lavish in the days of betrothment. She became your wife! left her own home for yours—burst asunder, as it were, the bands of love which had bound her to her father's fireside, and sought no other boon than your affections; left, it may be, the case [sic] and delicacy of a home of indulgence—and now, what must be her feelings if she gradually awakes to the consciousness that you love her less than before; that your evenings are spent abroad, that you only came home at all to satisfy the demands of your hunger, and to find a resting-place for your head when weary, or a nurse for your sick-chamber when diseased.

Why did she leave the bright hearth of her youthful days? Why did you ask her to give up the enjoyment of a happy home? Was it simply to darn your stocking, mend your clothes, take care of your children, and watch over your sick bed? Was it simply to conduce to your own comfort? Or was there some understanding that she was to be made happy in her connection with the man she cared to love?

Nor is it sufficient answer that you reply that you give her a home; that you feed and clothe her. You do this for your help; you would do it for an indifferent housekeeper. She is your wife, and unless you attend to her wants, and in some way answer the reasonable expectations you raised by your attentions before marriage, you need not wonder if she be dejected, and her heart sink into insensibility; but if this be so, think well who is the cause of it. We repeat, very few women make indifferent wives, whose feelings have not met with some outward shock by the indifference or thoughtlessness of their husbands. It is our candid opinion that in a large majority of the instances of domestic misery the man is the aggressor.

1864

A TIN WEDDING

from the Christian Recorder

On the evening of Thursday, the 2nd inst., Bethel Chapel—A.M.E. Church—Leavenworth, was crowded with the friends of Rev. T. W. Henderson and wife, it being the tenth anniversary of their married life. The following from the Leavenworth *Times* will serve to inform the readers of the good time:

TIN WEDDING

"On Thursday evening, the many friends of Rev. T. W. Henderson and his amiable wife, assembled from Lawrence, assembled from Topeka and Kansas City, together with those of Leavenworth, at the A.M.E. Church, of which Mr. Henderson is the pastor, to celebrate the tenth anniversary of their marriage. The Ceremony was performed by Rev. R. Ricketts, of Kansas City, assisted by Rev. J. H. Hubbard, of Topeka, and Rev. Mr. Lucas, of Tonganozie.

After the happy couple were re-united, they were congratulated by their friends, among whom were Miss M. Young, Nathaniel Harris, J. D. Bowser and wife, and others from Kansas City. Mr. W. B. Townsend then proceeded to call off the names of those who gave presents, which were many; he also read a letter from the friends of the newly married couple accompanied with handsome presents, regretting their inability to be present, but sent their tokens of friendship and respect. Mr. Henderson then made a little speech, returning to them his heart felt thanks for the donations he had received. After which the assembly enjoyed themselves until half past ten, when they were dismissed to re-assemble at the silver wedding of the happy pair."

1876

A BEREAVED WIFE

from the Christian Recorder

A bereaved wife, Lucy Booker, writes us from San Antonio a long and sad letter concerning her husband, who has deserted her and fled with a young girl but fifteen years old, all the dear woman says we cannot print; but the following sentence is too touching to be kept from the eyes of the public. Telling of the years she has been married—eight—and of the four children begotten, together with the sad plight in which he left her, she pathetically says:

"I think if he could have seen in his house and heard the weeping of his children, he surely would have felt very sad. One of the little ones that is sick now said to me when I was weeping, 'Mamma, God will be a papa to us.'"

Alas! Alas! What is it that the spirit of sin will not do.

1880

Letters

NOTICE

Having understood from unquestionable authority, that my husband, James Stephens, formerly of this city, is now representing himself as a man without family, in the city of New York: and in endeavouring to justify his conduct to those who have demanded an explanation of his unnatural conduct, he has attempted to asperse and caluminate my character; conceiving it my duty to preserve the only thing he left behind after deserting me and his three small children, I have thought it my duty to make him known to the public as a base, mean, false and unprincipled man.

I will also inform the public, that three years after I was united to him, I understand for the first time, that he had been previously married to another, amiable woman, who, when she understood that he was again married, died of a broken heart. In informing the public of his deserting his family, without just cause of provocation on my part, I do it in self-defence, and can support my assertions by many of the most respectable families in this city.

JANE STEPHENS

City of Washington, (D.C.) Oct. 5, 1827.

NOTICE.—A communication having appeared in the "Freedom's Journal," of October 12th, in which a certain woman who signs herself, "Jane Stephens," takes the liberty of appearing before the public as my wife, and denouncing me on account of substantial abandonment, as "a base, mean, false and unprincipled man"; regard to my own character, and respect to my many friends through the community, call upon me to lay a true statement before the public.

For a correct understanding of the subject, it is necessary to premise certain events, which the said Jane Stephens alias Jane Mushit has seen proper to introduce in her insolent notice. In the year 1813, I was married by the Rev. Mr. Conner of Maryland, to Miss Anne Johnson, with whom I lived in peace and harmony until particular business called me to a distant part of the country. Not succeeding in my expectations, and unable from want of funds to return at the time appointed, I was much astonished in 1817, at the receipt of a letter from my wife, which informed me that she had married a man by the name of Stephen Broadwater, belonging to Accomack county, Virginia.

In the year 1820, my wife who had now become Mrs. Broadwater died; since which time I have remained a single man, notwithstanding Jane Stephens, alias Mushit, has the audacity to style herself my wife.

I have deceived no woman, nor defrauded any man, as the many friends who know me in this and other cities can testify. Jane Stephen's alias Mushit, always knew from the first of our acquaintance, that I was a married man, and it appears somewhat foolish and silly to come before the public at this late period, pleading ignorance of certain facts which she must certainly have known. Jane Mushit has never been my wife, and of course can have no right to assume the name of Jane Stephen's. As for the friends who have advised Miss Jane Mushit to pursue the course which she has, I think it would become them to look at home, paying no attention to my affairs, and by so doing, I am sure they would gain more credit to themselves.

JAMES STEPHENS,
Formerly of Baltimore.
New York, Nov. 27, 1827.

FROM GEORGE PLEASANT TO AGNES HOBBS

Shelbyville, 6 September 1833.

Mrs. Agnes Hobbs.

DEAR WIFE: My dear biloved wife I am more than glad to meet with opportunity writee thes few lines to you by my Mistress who ar now about starterng to virginia, and sevl others of my old friends are with her; in compeney Mrs. Ann Rus the wife of master Thos Rus and Dan Woodiard and his family and I am very sorry that I havn the chance to go with them as I feele Determid to see you If life last again. I am now here and out at this pleace so I am not abble to get of at this time. I am write well and hearty and all the rest of masters family. I heard this eveng by Mistress that ar just from theree all sends love to you and all my old friends. I am a living in a town called Shelbyville and I have wrote a greate many letters since Ive beene here and almost been reeady to my selfe that its out of the question to write any more at tall: my dear wife I don't feeld no whys like giving out writing to you as yet and I hope when you get this letter that you be Inncougege to write me a letter. I am well satisfied at my living at this place I am a making money for my own benifit and I hope that its to yours also If I live to Nexct year I shall have my own time from master by giving him 100 and twenty Dollars a year and I thinke I shall be doing good business at that and heve something more thean all that. I hope with gods helpe that I may be abble to rejoys with you on the earth and In heaven lets meet when will I am detemnid to nuver stope praying, not in this earth and I hope to praise god In glory there weel meet to part no more forever. So my dear wife I hope to meet you In paradase to prase god forever * * * I want Elizabeth to be a good girl and not to thinke that because I am bound so fare that gods not abble to open the way * * *

GEORGE PLEASANT,
Hobbs a servant of Grum.

Charlottesville Oct. 5, 1852

Dear Husband   I write you a letter to let you know of my distress   my master has sold Albert to a trader on Monday court day and myself and other child is for sale also and I want you to let [me] hear from you very soon   Before next cort if you can   I don't know when   I don't want you to wait till Christmas   I want you to tell Dr. Hamilton your master if either will buy me they can attend to it know and then I can go afterwards

I don't want a trader to get me   they asked me if I had got any person to buy me and I thold them no   they told me to the court house too

They never put me up   A man buy the name of brady bought albert and is gone I don't know whare   they say he lives in scottsville   my things is in several places   some is in stanton and if I would be sold I don't know what will become of them   I don't expect to meet with the luck to get that way till I am quite heart sick   nothing more   I am and ever will be your kind wife

Marie Perkins

FROM ABREAM SCRIVEN TO WIFE

September 19, 1858

My Dear Wife,

I take the pleasure of writing you these few with much regret to inform you that I am sold to a man by the name of Peterson atreader and Stays in new orleans. I am here yet But I expect to go before long but when I get there I will write and let you know where I am. My Dear I want to Send you some things but I donot know who to Send them by but I will thry to get them to you and my children. Give my love to my father and mother and tell them good Bye for me. and if we Shall not meet in this world I hope to meet in heaven. My Dear wife for you and my children my pen cannot Express the griffe I feel to be parted from you all

I remain your truly husband until death

Abream Scriven

FROM HARRIET NEWBY TO DANGERFIELD NEWBY

Brentville, April 11th, 1859.

DEAR HUSBAND:

I mus now write you apology for not writing you before this, but I know you will excuse me when I tell you Mrs. Gennings has been very sick. She has a baby—a little girl; ben a grate sufferer; her breast raised, and she has had it lanced, and I have had to stay with her day and night; so you know I had no time to write, but she is now better, and one of her own servent is now sick. I am well; that is of the grates importance to you. I have no news to write you, only the children are all well. I want to see you very much, but am looking forward to the promest time of your coming. Oh, Dear Dangerfield, com this fall without fail, monny or no monney. I want to see you so much. That is one bright hope I have before me. Nothing more at present, but remain

Your affectionate wife,

HARRIET NEWBY

P.S. Write soon, if you please.

FROM HARRIET NEWBY TO DANGERFIELD NEWBY

Brentville, April 22d, 1859.

DEAR HUSBAND:

I received your letter to-day, and it gives much pleasure to here from you, but was sorry to [hear] of your sikeness; hope you may be well when you receive this. I wrote to you several weeks ago, and directed my letter to Bridge Port, but I fear you did not receive it, as you said nothing about it in yours. You must give my love to Brother Gabial, and tell him I would like to see him very much. I wrote in my last letter that Miss Virginia had a baby—a little girl. I had to narse her day and night. Dear Dangerfield, you cannot imagine how much I want to see you. Com as soon as you can, for nothing would give more pleasure than to see you. It is the grates Comfort I have in thinking of the promist time when you will be here. Oh, that *bless* hour when I shall see you once more. My baby commenced to crall to-day; it is very delicate. Nothing more at present, but remain

Your affectionate wife,

HARRIET NEWBY

P.S. Write soon.

FROM HARRIET NEWBY TO DANGERFIELD NEWBY

Brentville, August 16, 1859

DEAR HUSBAND;

Your kind letter came only to hand, and it gave me much pleasure to here from you, and especely to here you are better off [with] your rhumatism, and hope when I here from you again, you may be entirely well. I want you to buy me as soon as possible, for if you do not get me some body else will. The servents are very disagreeable; they do all they can to set my mistress against me. Dear Husband you [know], not the trouble I see; the last two years has ben like a trouble dream to me. It is said Master is in want of monney. If so, I know not what time he may sell me, an then all my bright hops of the futer are blasted, for their has ben one bright hope to cheer me in all my troubles, that is to be with you, for if I thought I shoul never see you this earth would have no charms for me. Do all you can for me, witch I have no doubt you will. I want to see you so much. The children are all well. The baby can not walk yet [at] all. It can step around everything by holding on. It is very much like Agnes. I must bring my letter to a Close, as I have no newes to write. You mus write soon and say when you think you can come.

Your affectionate wife,

HARRIET NEWBY

January 19, 1864 from Paris, Missouri

My Dear Husband,

I r'ecd your letter dated Jan. 9th also one dated Jan'y 1st but have got no one till now to write for me. You do not know how bad I am treated. They are treating me worse and worse every day. Our child cries for you. Send me some money as soon as you can for me and my child are almost naked. My cloth is yet in the loom and there is no telling when it will be out. Do not send any of your letters to Hogsett especially those having money in them as Hogsett will keep the money. George Combs went to Hannibal soon after you did so I did not get that money from him. Do the best you can and do not fret too much for me for it wont be long before I will be free and then all we make will be ours.

Your affectionate wife,

Ann

p.s. Send our little girl a string of beads in your next letter to remember you by. Ann

Autobiographical Accounts

JARENA LEE

from Life and Religious Experience of Jarena Lee

MY MARRIAGE

In the year 1811, I changed my situation in life, having married Mr. Joseph Lee, pastor of a Society at Snow Hill, about six miles from the city of Philadelphia. It became necessary therefore for me to remove. This was a great trial at first, as I knew no person at Snow Hill, except my husband, and to leave my associates in the society, and especially those who composed the *band* of which I was one. None but those who have been in sweet fellowship with such as really love God, and have together drank bliss and happiness from the same fountain, can tell how dear such company is, and how hard it is to part from them.

At Snow Hill, as was feared, I never found that agreement and closeness in communion and fellowship, that I had in Philadelphia, among my young companions, nor ought I to have expected it. The manners and customs at this place were somewhat different, on which account I became discontented in the course of a year, and began to importune my husband to remove to the city. But this plan did not suit him, as he was the Pastor of the Society, he could not bring his mind to leave them. This afflicted me a little. But the Lord showed me in a dream what his will was concerning this matter.

I dreamed that as I was walking on the summit of a beautiful hill, that I saw near me a flock of sheep, fair and white, as if but newly washed; when there came walking toward me a man of a grave and dignified countenance, dressed entirely in white, as it were in a robe, and looking at me, said emphatically, "Joseph Lee must take care of these sheep, or the wolf will come and devour them." When I awoke I was convinced of my error, and immediately, with a glad heart, yielded to the right spirit in the Lord. This also greatly strengthened my faith in his care over them, for fear the wolf should by some means take any of them away. The following verse was beautifully suited to our condition, as well as to all the little flocks of God scattered up and down this land:

"Us into Thy protection take,
    And gather with Thine arm;

Unless the fold we first forsake,
   The wolf can never harm."

After this, I fell into a state of general debility, and in an ill state of health, so much so, that I could not sit up; but a desire to warn sinners to flee the wrath to come, burned vehemently in my heart, when the Lord would send sinners into the house to see me. Such opportunities I embraced to press home on their consciences the things of eternity, and so effectual was the word of exhortation made through the Spirit, that I have seen them fall to the floor crying aloud for mercy.

From this sickness I did not expect to recover, and there was but one thing which bound me to earth, and this was, that I had not as yet preached the gospel to the fallen sons and daughters of Adam's race, to the satisfaction of my mind. I wished to go from one end of the earth to the other, crying, Behold, behold the lamb! To this end I earnestly prayed the Lord to raise me up, if consistent with his will. He condescended to hear my prayer, and to give me a token in a dream, that in due time I should recover my health. The dream was as follows: I thought I saw the sun rise in the morning, and ascend to an altitude of about half an hour high, and then become obscured by a dense black cloud, which continued to hide its rays for about one-third part of the day, and then it burst forth again with renewed splendor.

This dream I interpreted to signify my early life, my conversion to God, and this sickness, which was a great affliction, as it hindered me, and I feared would forever hinder me from preaching the gospel, was signified by the cloud; and the bursting forth of the sun, again, was the recovery of my health, and being permitted to preach.

I went to the throne of grace on this subject, where the Lord made this impressive reply in my heart, while on my knees: "Ye shall be restored to thy health again, and worship God in full purpose of heart."

This manifestation was so impressive, that I could but hide my face as if some one was gazing upon me, to think of the great goodness of the Almighty God to my poor soul and body. From that very time I began to gain strength of body and mind, glory to God in the highest, until my health was fully recovered.

For six years from this time I continued to receive from above, such baptisms of the Spirit as mortality could scarcely bear. About that time I was called to suffer in my family, by death—five, in the course of about six years, fell by his hand; my husband being one of the number, which was the greatest affliction of all.

I was now left alone in the world, with two infant children, one of the age of about two years, the other six months, with no other dependence than the promise of Him who hath said—I will be the widow's God, and a father to the fatherless. Accordingly, he raised me up friends, whose liberality comforted and solaced me in my state of widowhood and sorrows, I could sing with the greatest propriety the words of the poet.

"He helps the stranger in distress,
The widow and the fatherless,
And grants the prisoner sweet release."

I can say even now, with the Psalmist, "Once I was young, but now I am old, yet I have never seen the righteous forsaken, nor his seed begging bread." I have ever been fed by his bounty, clothed by his mercy, comforted and healed when sick, succored when tempted, and every where upheld by his hand.

1836

LUNSFORD LANE

from Narrative of Lunsford Lane

I began, slave as I was, to think about taking a wife. So I fixed my mind upon Miss Lucy Williams, a slave of Thomas Devereax, Esq., an eminent lawyer in the place; but failed in my undertaking. Then I thought I never would marry; but at the end of two or three years my resolution began to slide away, till finding I could not keep it longer, I set out once more in pursuit of a wife. So I fell in with her to whom I am now united, MISS MARTHA CURTIS, and the bargain between *us* was completed. I next went to her master, Mr. Boylan, and asked him, according to the custom, if I might "marry his woman." His reply was, "Yes, if you will behave yourself." I told him I would. "And make her behave herself?" To this I also assented: and then proceeded to ask the approbation of my master, which was granted. So in May, 1828, I was bound as fast in wedlock as a slave can be. God may at any time sunder that band in a freeman; either master may do the same at pleasure in a slave. The bond is not recognized in law. But in my case it has never been broken; and now it cannot be, except by a higher power.

When we had been married nine months and one day, we were blessed with a son, and two years afterwards with a daughter. My wife also passed from the hands of Mr. Boylan into those of MR. BENJAMIN B. SMITH, a merchant, a member and class-leader in the methodist church, and in much repute for his deep piety and devotion to religion. But grace (of course,) had not wrought in the same *manner* upon the heart of Mr. Smith as nature had done upon that of Mr. Boylan, who made no religious profession. This latter gentleman used to give my wife, who was a favorite slave (her mother nursed every one of his own children,) sufficient food and clothing to render her comfortable, so that I had to spend for her but little, except to procure such small articles of extra comfort as I was prompted to from time to time. Indeed, Mr. Boylan was regarded as a very kind master to all the slaves about him,—that is, to his house-servants; nor did he personally inflict much cruelty, if any, upon his field hands. The overseer on his nearest plantation (I knew but little about the rest,) was a very cruel man; in one instance, as it was said among the slaves, he whipped a man *to death;* but of course he denied that the man died in consequence of the whipping. Still it was the choice of my wife to pass into the hands of Mr. Smith, as she had become attached to him in consequence of belonging to the same church, and receiving his religious instruction and counsel as her class-leader, and in consequence of the peculiar devotedness to the cause of religion for which he was noted, and which he always seemed to manifest. But when she became his slave, he withheld both from her and her children the needful food and clothing, while he exacted from them to the uttermost all the labor they were able to perform. Almost every article of clothing worn either by my wife or children, especially every article of much value, I had to purchase; while the food he furnished the family amounted to less than a meal a day, and that of the coarser kind. I have no remembrance that he ever gave us a blanket, or any other article of bedding, although it is considered a rule at the south that the master shall furnish each of his slaves with one blanket a year. So that, both as to food and clothing, I had in fact to support both my wife and the children, while he claimed them as his property, and received all their labor.

1848

HENRY BIBB

From The Life and Adventures of Henry Bibb

The circumstances of my courtship and marriage, I consider to be among the most remarkable events of my life while a slave. To think that after I had determined to carry out the great idea which is so universally and practically acknowledged among all the civilized nations of the earth, but I would be free or die, I suffered myself to be turned aside by the fascinating charms of a female, who gradually won my attention from an object so high as that of liberty; and an object which I held paramount to all others.

But when I had arrived at the age of eighteen, which was in the year of 1833, it was my lot to be introduced to the favor of a mulatto slave girl named Malinda, who lived in Oldham County, Kentucky, about four miles from the residence of my owner. Malinda was a medium sized girl, graceful in her walk, of an extraordinary make, and active in business. Her skin was of a smooth texture, red cheeks, with dark and penetrating eyes. She moved in the highest circle of slaves, and free people of color. She was also one of the best singers I ever heard, and was much esteemed by all who knew her, for her benevolence, talent and industry. In fact, I considered Malinda to be equalled by few, and surpassed by none, for the above qualities, all things considered.

It is truly marvellous to see how sudden a man's mind can be changed by the charms and influence of a female. The first two or three visits that I paid this dear girl, I had no intention of courting or marrying her, for I was aware that such a step would greatly obstruct my way to the land of liberty. I only visited Malinda because I liked her company, as a highly interesting girl. But in spite of myself, before I was aware of it, I was deeply in love; and what made this passion so effectual and almost irresistable, I became satisfied that it was reciprocal. There was a union of feeling, and every visit made the impression stronger and stronger. One or two other young men were paying attention to Malinda, at the same time; one of whom her mother was anxious to have her marry. This of course gave me a fair opportunity of testing Malinda's sincerity. I had just about opposition enough to make the subject interesting. That Malinda loved me above all others on earth, no one could deny. I could read it by the warm reception with which the dear girl always met me, and treated me in her mother's house. I could read it by the warm and affectionate shake of the hand, and gentle smile upon her lovely cheek. I could read it by her always giving me the preference of her company; by her pressing invitations to visit even in opposition to her mother's will. I could read it in the language of her bright and sparkling eye, penciled by the unchangable finger of nature, that spake but could not lie. These strong temptations gradually diverted my attention from my actual condition and from liberty, though not entirely.

But oh! that I had only then been enabled to have seen as I do now, or to have read the following slave code, which is but a stereotyped law of American slavery. It would have saved me I think from having to lament that I was a husband and am the father of slaves who are still left to linger out their days in hopeless bondage. The laws of Kentucky, my native State, with Maryland and Virginia, which are said to be the mildest slaves States in the Union, noted for their humanity, Christianity and democracy, declare that "Any slave, for rambling in the night, or riding horseback without leave, or running away, may be punished by whipping, cropping and branding in the cheek, or otherwise, not rendering him unfit for labor." "Any slave convicted of petty larceny, murder, or wilfully burning of dwelling houses, may be sentenced to have his right hand cut off; to be hanged in the usual manner, or the head severed from the body, the body divided into four quarters, and head and quarters stuck up in the most public place in the county, where such act was committed."

At the time I joined my wife in holy wedlock, I was ignorant of these ungodly laws; I knew not that I was propogating victims for this kind of torture and cruelty. Malinda's mother was free, and lived in Bedford, about a quarter of a mile from her daughter; and we often met and passed off the time pleasantly. Agreeable to promise, on one Saturday evening, I called to see Malinda, at her mother's residence, with an intention of letting her know my mind upon the subject of marriage. It was a very bright moonlight night; the dear girl was standing in the door, anxiously waiting my arrival. As I approached the door she caught my hand with an affectionate smile, and bid me welcome to her mother's fireside. After having broached the subject of marriage, I informed her of the difficulties which I conceived to be in the way of our marriage; and that I could never engage myself to marry any girl only on certain conditions; near as I can recollect the substance of our conversation upon the subject, it was, that I was religiously inclined; that I intended to try to comply with the requisitions of the gospel, both theoretically and practically through life. Also that I was decided on becoming a free man before I died; and that I expected to get free by running away, and going to Canada, under the British Government. Agreement on those two cardinal questions I made my test for marriage.

I said, "I never will give my heart nor hand to any girl in marriage, until I first know her sentiments upon the all-important subjects of Religion and

Liberty. No matter how well I might love her, nor how great the sacrifice in carrying out these God-given principles. And I here pledge myself from this course never to be shaken while a single pulsation of my heart shall continue to throb for Liberty." With this idea Malinda appeared to be well pleased, and with a smile she looked me in the face and said, "I have long entertained the same views, and this has been one of the greatest reasons why I have not felt inclined to enter the married state while a slave; I have always felt a desire to be free; I have long cherished a hope that I should yet be free, either by purchase or running away. In regard to the subject of Religion, I have always felt that it was a good thing, and something that I would seek for at some future period." After I found that Malinda was right upon these all important questions, and that she truly loved me well enough to make me an affectionate wife, I made proposals for marriage. She very modestly declined answering the question then, considering it to be one of a grave character, and upon which our future destiny greatly depended. And notwithstanding she confessed that I had her entire affections, she must have some time to consider the matter. To this I of course consented, and was to meet her on the next Saturday night to decide the question. But for some cause I failed to come, and the next week she sent for me, and on the Sunday evening following I called on her again; she welcomed me with all the kindness of an affectionate lover, and seated me by her side. We soon broached the old subject of marriage, and entered upon a conditional contract of matrimony, viz: that we would marry if our minds should not change within one year; that after marriage we would change our former course and live a pious life; and that we would embrace the earliest opportunity of running away to Canada for our liberty. Clasping each other by the hand, pledging our sacred honor that we would be true, we called on high heaven to witness the rectitude of our purpose. There was nothing that could be more binding upon us as slaves than this; for marriage among American slaves, is disregarded by the laws of this country. It is counted a mere temporary matter; it is a union which may be continued or broken off, with or without the consent of a slaveholder, whether he is a priest or a libertine.

There is no legal marriage among the slaves of the South; I never saw nor heard of such a thing in my life, and I have been through seven of the slave states. A slave marrying according to law, is a thing unknown in the history of American Slavery. And be it known to the disgrace of our country that every slaveholder, who is the keeper of a number of slaves of both sexes, is also the keeper of a house or houses of ill-fame. Licentious white men, can and do, enter at night or day the lodging places of slaves; break up the bonds of affection in families; destroy all their domestic and social union for life; and the laws of the country afford them no protection. Will any man count, if they can be counted, the churches of Maryland, Kentucky, and Virginia, which have slaves connected with them, living in an open state of adultery, never having been married according to the laws of the State, and yet regular members of these various denominations, but more especially the Baptist and Methodist churches? And I hazard nothing in saying, that this state of things exists to a very wide extent in the above states.

I am happy to state that many fugitive slaves, who have been enabled by the aid of an over-ruling providence to escape to the free North with those whom they claim as their wives, notwithstanding all their ignorance and superstition, are not at all disposed to live together like brutes, as they have been compelled to do in slaveholding Churches. But as soon as they get free from slavery they go before some anti-slavery clergyman, and have the solemn ceremony of marriage performed according to the laws of the country. And if they profess religion, and have been baptized by a slaveholding minister, they repudiate it after becoming free, and are re-baptized by a man who is worthy of doing it according to the gospel rule.

The time and place of my marriage, I consider one of the most trying of my life. I was opposed by friends and foes; my mother opposed me because she thought I was too young, and marrying she thought would involve me in trouble and difficulty. My mother-in-law opposed me, because she wanted her daughter to marry a slave who belonged to a very rich man living near by, and who was well known to be the son of his master. She thought no doubt that his master or father might chance to set him free before he died, which would enable him to do a better part by her daughter than I could! And there was no prospect then of my ever being free. But his master has neither died nor yet set his son free, who is now about forty years of age, toiling under the lash, waiting and hoping that his master may die and will him to be free.

The young men were opposed to our marriage for the same reason that Paddy opposed a match when the clergyman was about to pronounce the marriage ceremony of a young couple. He said, "if there be any present who have any objections to this couple being joined together in holy wedlock, let them speak now, or hold their peace henceforth." At this time Paddy sprang to his feet and said, "Sir, I object to this." Every eye was fixed upon him. "What is your objection?" said the clergyman. "Faith," replied Paddy, "Sir I want her myself."

The man to whom I belonged was opposed, because he feared my taking off from his farm some of the fruits of my own labor for Malinda to eat, in the shape of pigs, chickens, or turkeys, and would count it not robbery. So we formed a resolution, that if we were prevented from joining in wedlock, that we would run away, and strike for Canada, let the consequences be what they might. But we had one consolation; Malinda's master was very much in favor of the match, but entirely upon selfish principles. When I went to ask his permission to marry Malinda, his answer was in the affirmative with but one condition, which I consider to be too vulgar to be written in this book. Our marriage took place one night during the Christmas holydays; at which time we had quite a festival given us. All appeared to be wide awake, and we had quite a jolly time at my wedding party. And notwithstanding our marriage was without license or sanction of law, we believed it to be honorable before God, and the bed undefiled. Our christmas holydays were spent in matrimonial visiting among our friends, while it should have been spent in running away to Canada, for our liberty. But freedom was little thought of by us, for several months after marriage. I often look back to that period even now as one of the most happy seasons of my life; notwithstanding all the contaminating and heart-rending features with which the horrid system of slavery is marked, and must carry with it to its final grave, yet I still look back to that season with sweet remembrance and pleasure, that yet hath power to charm and drive back dull cares which have been accumulated by a thousand painful recollections of slavery. Malinda was to me an affectionate wife. She was with me in the darkest hours of adversity. She was with me in sorrow, and joy, in fasting and feasting, in trial and persecution, in sickness and health, in sunshine and in shade.

Some months after our marriage, the unfeeling master to whom I belonged, sold his farm with the view of moving his slaves to the State of Missouri, regardless of the separation of husbands and wives forever; but for fear of my resuming my old practice of running away, if he should have forced me to leave my wife, by my repeated requests, he was constrained to sell me to his brother, who lived within seven miles of Wm. Gatewood, who then held Malinda as his property. I was permitted to visit her only on Saturday nights, after my work was done, and I had to be at home before sunrise on Monday mornings or take a flogging. He proved to be so oppressive, and so unreasonable in punishing his victims, that I soon found that I should have to run away in self-defence. But he soon began to take the hint, and sold me to Wm. Gatewood the owner of Malinda. With my new residence I confess that I was much dissatisfied. Not that Gatewood was a more cruel master than my former owner—not that I was opposed to living with Malinda, who was then the centre and object of my affections—but to live where I must be eye witness to her insults, scourgings and abuses, such as are common to be inflicted upon slaves, was more than I could bear. If my wife must be exposed to the insults and licentious passions of wicked slave-drivers and overseers; if she must bear the stripes of the lash laid on by an unmerciful tyrant; if this is to be done with impunity, which is frequently done by slaveholders and their abettors, Heaven forbid that I should be compelled to witness the sight.

Not many months after I took up my residence on Wm. Gatewood's plantation, Malinda made me a father. The dear little daughter was called Mary Frances. She was nurtured and caressed by her mother and father, until she was large enough to creep over the floor after her parents, and climb up by a chair before I felt it to be my duty to leave my family and go into a foreign country for a season. Malinda's business was to labor out in the field the greater part of her time, and there was no one to take care of poor little Frances, while her mother was toiling in the field. She was left at the house to creep under the feet of an unmerciful old mistress, whom I have known to slap with her hand the face of little Frances, for crying after her mother, until her little face was left black and blue. I recollect that Malinda and myself came from the field one summer's day at noon, and poor little Frances came creeping to her mother smiling, but with large tear drops standing in her dear little eyes, sobbing and trying to tell her mother that she had been abused, but was not able to utter a word. Her little face was bruised black with the whole print of Mrs. Gatewood's hand. This print was plainly to be seen for eight days after it was done. But oh! this darling child was a slave; born of a slave mother. Who can imagine what could be the feelings of a father and mother, when looking upon their infant child whipped and tortured with impunity, and they placed in a situation where they could afford it no protection. But we were all claimed and held as property; the father and mother were slaves!

On this same plantation I was compelled to stand and see my wife shamefully scourged and abused by her master; and the manner in which this was done, was so violently and inhumanly committed upon the person of a female, that I despair in finding decent language to describe the bloody act of cruelty. My happiness or pleasure was then all blasted; for it was sometimes a pleasure to be with my little family even in slavery. I loved them as my wife and child. Little Frances was a pretty child; she was quiet, playful, bright, and interesting. She had a keen black eye, and the very image of her mother was stamped upon her cheek; but I could never look upon the dear child without being filled with sorrow and fearful apprehensions, of being separated by slaveholders, because she was a slave, regarded as property. And unfortunately for me, I am the father of a slave, a word too obnoxious to be spoken by a fugitive slave. It calls fresh to my mind the separation of husband and wife; of stripping, tying up and flogging; of tearing children from their parents, and selling them on the auction block. It calls to mind female virtue trampled under foot with impunity. But oh! when I remember that my daughter, my only child, is still there, destined to share the fate of all these calamities, it is too much to bear. If ever there was any one act of my life while a slave, that I have to lament over it is that of being a father and a husband of slaves. I have the satisfaction of knowing that I am only the father of one slave. She is bone of my bone, and flesh of my flesh; poor unfortunate child. She was the first and shall be the last slave that ever I will father, for chains and slavery on this earth.

1849

JOSIAH HENSON

from Father Henson's Story of His Own Life

ESCAPE FROM BONDAGE

During the bright and hopeful days I spent in Ohio, while away on my preaching tour, I had heard much of the course pursued by fugitives from slavery, and
became acquainted with a number of benevolent men engaged in helping
them on their way. Canada was often spoken of as the only sure refuge from
pursuit, and that blessed land was now the desire of my longing heart. Infinite
toils and perils lay between me and that haven of promise; enough to daunt the
stoutest heart; but the fire behind me was too hot and fierce to let me pause to
consider them. I knew the North Star—blessed be God for setting it in the
heavens! Like the Star of Bethlehem, it announced where my salvation lay.
Could I follow it through forest, and stream, and field, it would guide my feet
in the way of hope. I thought of it as my God-given guide to the land of promise far away beneath its light. I knew that it had led thousands of my poor,
hunted brethren to freedom and blessedness. I felt energy enough in my own
breast to contend with privation and danger; and had I been a free, untram-
meled man, knowing no tie of father or husband, and concerned for my own
safety only, I would have felt all difficulties light in view of the hope that was
set before me. But, alas! I had a wife and four dear children; how should I provide for them? Abandon them I could not; no! Not even for the blessed boon of
freedom. They, too, must go. They, too, must share with me the life of liberty.

It was not without long thought upon the subject that I devised a plan of
escape. But at last I matured it. My mind fully made up, I communicated the
intention to my wife. She was overwhelmed with terror. With a woman's in-
stinct she clung to hearth and home. She knew nothing of the wide world
beyond, and her imagination peopled it with unseen horrors. We should die
in the wilderness,—we should be hunted down with blood-hounds,—we
should be brought back and whipped to death. With tears and supplications
she besought me to remain at home, contented. In vain I explained to her
our liability to be torn asunder at any moment; the horrors of the slavery I
had lately seen; the happiness we should enjoy together in a land of freedom,
safe from all pursuing harm. She had not suffered the bitterness of my lot,
nor felt the same longing for deliverance. She was a poor, ignorant, unrea-
soning slave woman.

I argued the matter with her at various times, till I was satisfied that argu-
ment alone would not prevail. I then told her deliberately, that though it

would be a cruel trial for me to part with her, I would nevertheless do it, and take all the children with me except the youngest, rather than remain at home, only to be forcibly torn from her, and sent down to linger out a wretched existence in the hell I had lately visited. Again she wept and entreated, but I was sternly resolute. The whole night long she fruitlessly urged me to relent; exhausted and maddened, I left her, in the morning, to go to my work for the day. Before I had gone far, I heard her voice calling me, and waiting till I came up, she said, at last, she would go with me. Blessed relief! My tears of joy flowed faster than had hers of grief.

Our cabin, at this time, was near the landing. The plantation itself extended the whole five miles from the house to the river. There were several distinct farms, all of which I was over-seeing, and therefore I was riding about from one to another every day. Our oldest boy was at the house with Master Amos; the rest of the children were with my wife.

The chief practical difficulty that had weighed upon my mind, was connected with the youngest two of the children. They were of three and two years, respectively, and of course would have to be carried. Both stout and healthy, they were a heavy burden, and my wife had declared that I should break down under it before I had got five miles from home. Sometime previously I had directed her to make me a large knapsack of tow cloth, large enough to hold them both, and arranged with strong straps to go round my shoulders. This done, I had practised carrying them night after night, both to test my own strength and accustom them to submit to it. To them it was fine fun, and to my great joy I found I could manage them successfully. My wife's consent was given on Thursday morning, and I resolved to start on the night of the following Saturday. Sunday was a holiday; on Monday and Tuesday I was to be away on farms distant from the house; thus several days would elapse before I should be missed, and by that time I should have got a good start.

At length the eventful night arrived. All things were ready, with the single exception that I had not yet obtained my master's permission for little Tom to visit his mother. About sundown I went up to the great house to report my work, and after talking for a time, started off, as usual, for home; when, suddenly appearing to recollect something I had forgotten, I turned carelessly back, and said, "O, Master Amos, I most forgot. Tom's mother wants to know if you won't let him come down a few days; she wants to mend his clothes and fix him up a little." "Yes, boy, yes; he can go." "Thankee, Master Amos; good night, good night. The Lord bless you!" In spite of myself I threw a good deal of emphasis into my farewell. I could not refrain from an inward chuckle at the thought—how long a good night that will be! The coast was all clear now, and, as I trudged along home, I took an affectionate look at the well-known objects on my way. Strange to say, sorrow mingled with my joy; but no man can live anywhere long without feeling some attachment to the soil on which he labors.

It was about the middle of September, and by nine o'clock all was ready. It was a dark, moonless night, when we got into the little skiff, in which I had induced a fellow slave to set us across the river. It was an anxious moment. We sat still as death. In the middle of the stream the good fellow said to me, "It will be the end of me if this is ever found out; but you won't be brought back alive, Sie, will you?" "Not if I can help it," I replied; and I thought of the pistols and knife I had bought some time before of a poor white. "And if they're too many for you, and you get seized, you'll never tell my part in this business?" "Not if I'm shot through like a sieve." "That's all," said he, "and God help you." Heaven reward him. He, too, has since followed in my steps; and many a time in a land of freedom have we talked over that dark night on the river.

In due time we landed on the Indiana shore. A hearty, grateful farewell, such as none but companions in danger can know, and I heard the oars of the skiff propelling him hom[e]. There I stood in the darkness, my dear ones with me, and the all unknown future before us. But there was little time for reflection. Before daylight should come on, we must put as many miles behind us as possible, and be safely hidden in the woods. We had no friends to look to for assistance, for the population in that section of the country was then bitterly hostile to the fugitive. If discovered, we should be seized and lodged in jail. In God was our only hope. Fervently did I pray to him as we trudged on cautiously and steadily, and as fast as the darkness and the feebleness of my wife and boys would allow. To her, indeed, I was compelled to talk sternly; she trembled like a leaf, and even then implored me to return.

For a fortnight we pressed steadily on, keeping to the road during the night, hiding whenever a chance vehicle or horseman was heard, and during the day burying ourselves in the woods. Our provisions were rapidly giving out. Two days before reaching Cincinnati they were utterly exhausted. All night long the children cried with hunger, and my poor wife loaded me with reproaches for bringing them into such misery. It was a bitter thing to hear them cry, and God knows I needed encouragement myself. My limbs were weary, and my back and shoulders raw with the burden I carried. A fearful dread of detection ever pursued me, and I would start out of my sleep in terror, my heart beating against my ribs, expecting to find the dogs and slave-hunters after me. Had I been alone I would have borne starvation, even to exhaustion, before I would have ventured in sight of a house in quest of food.

But now something must be done; it was necessary to run the risk of exposure by daylight upon the road.

The only way to proceed was to adopt a bold course. Accordingly, I left our hiding-place, took to the road, and turned towards the south, to lull any suspicion that might be aroused were I to be seen going the other way. Before long I came to a house. A furious dog rushed out at me, and his master following to quiet him, I asked if he would sell me a little bread and meat. He was a surly fellow. "No, he had nothing for niggers!" At the next I succeeded no better, at first. The man of the house met me in the same style; but his wife, hearing our conversation, said to her husband, "How can you treat any human being so? If a dog was hungry I would give him something to eat." She then added, "We have children, and who knows but they may some day need the help of a friend." The man laughed, and told her that she might take care of niggers, he wouldn't. She asked me to come in, loaded a plate with venison and bread, and, when I laid it into my handkerchief, and put a quarter of a dollar on the table, she quietly took it up and put it in my handkerchief, with an additional quantity of venison. I felt the hot tears roll down my cheeks as she said "God bless you"; and I hurried away to bless my starving wife and little ones.

A little while after eating the venison, which was quite salt, the children become very thirsty, and groaned and sighed so that I went off stealthily, breaking the bushes to keep my path, to find water. I found a little rill, and drank a large draught. Then I tried to carry some in my hat; but alas! it leaked. Finally, I took off both shoes, which luckily had no holes in them, rinsed them out, filled them with water, and carried it to my family. They drank it with great delight. I have since then sat at splendidly furnished tables in Canada, the United States, and England; but never did I see any human beings relish anything more than my poor famishing little ones did that refreshing draught out of their father's shoes. That night we made a long run, and two days afterward we reached Cincinnati.

1858

NOAH DAVIS

from A Narrative of the Life of Rev. Noah Davis

* * I had now been in Baltimore more than a year. My wife and seven children were still in Virginia. I went to see them as often as my circumstances permitted—three or four times a year. About this time, my wife's mistress agreed to sell to me my wife and our two youngest children. The price fixed, was eight hundred dollars cash, and she gave me twelve months to raise the money. The sun rose bright in my sky that day; but before the year was out, my prospects were again in darkness. Now I had two great burdens upon my mind: one to attend properly to my missionary duty, the other to raise eight hundred dollars. During this time we succeeded in getting a better place for the Sabbath school, and there was a larger attendance upon my preaching, which demanded reading and study, and also visiting, and increased my daily labors. On the other hand, the year was running away, in which I had to raise eight hundred dollars. So that I found myself at times in a great strait.

My plan to raise the money was, to secure the amount, first, by pledges, before I collected any. * * Finally, the year was more than passed away, and I had upon my subscription list about one half of the money needed. It was now considered that the children had increased in value one hundred dollars, and I was told that I could have them, by paying in cash six hundred dollars, and giving a bond, with good security, for three hundred more, payable in twelve months. I had six weeks, in which to consummate this matter. I felt deeply, that this was a time to pray the Lord to help me, and for this my wife's prayers were fervently offered with my own. I had left my wife in Virginia, and come to Baltimore, a distance of over a hundred miles; I had been separated thus for nearly three years; I had been trying to make arrangements to have her with me, for over twelve months, and as yet had failed. We were oppressed with the most gloomy forebodings, and could only kneel down together and pray for God's direction and help.

I was in Fredericksburg, and had but one day longer to stay, and spend with my wife. What could be done, must be done quickly. I went to my old friend, Mr. Wright, and stated my case to him. After hearing of all I had done, and the conditions I had to comply with, he told me that if I would raise the six hundred dollars cash, he would endorse my bond for the remaining three hundred.—This promise inspired me with new life. The next thing was, how could the six hundred dollars be obtained in six weeks. I had upon my subscription list and in pledges nearly four hundred dollars. But this had to be collected from friends living in Fredericksburg, Washington city, Baltimore, and Philadelphia.

I left Fredericksburg and spent a few days in Washington, to collect what I could of the money promised to me there; and met much encouragement, several friends doubling their subscriptions. When I arrived in Baltimore and made known the peculiar strait I was in, to my joyful surprise, some of the friends who had pledged five dollars, gave me ten; and one dear friend who had promised me ten dollars, for this object, and who had previously contributed largely in the purchase of myself, now gave me fifty. I began to count up, and in two weeks from the time I commenced collecting, I had in hand four hundred dollars. Presently, another very dear friend enquired of me how I was getting along; and when I told him, he said, "Bring your money to me." I did so. It lacked two hundred dollars to make the purchase. This, the best friend I ever had in the world, made up the six hundred dollars, and said, "Go, get your wife; and you can keep on collecting, and repay the two hundred dollars when you get able."

I was now overcome with gratitude and joy, and knew not what to say; and when I began to speak, he would not have any of my thanks. I went to my boarding house, and shut myself up in my room, where I might give vent to the gratitude of my heart: and, O, what a melting time I had! It was to me a day of thanksgiving.

Having now in hand the six hundred dollars, and the promise of Mr. Wright's security for three hundred more, I was, by twelve o'clock, next day in Fredericksburg.

At first sight, my wife was surprised that I had come back so soon; for it was only two weeks since I had left her; and when I informed her that I had come after her and the children, she could hardly believe me. In a few days, having duly arranged all things relative to the purchase and removal, we left for Baltimore, with feelings commingled with joy and sorrow—sorrow at parting with five of our older children, and our many friends; and rejoicing in the prospect of remaining together permanently in the missionary field, where God had called me to labor. I arrived in Baltimore, with my wife and two little ones, November 5th, 1851, and stopped with sister Hester Ann Hughes, a worthy member of the M. E. Church, with whom I had been boarding for four years.

1859

J. D. GREEN

from the Narrative of the Life of J. D. Green

When I arrived at the age of 20, my master told me I must marry Jane, one of the slaves. We had been about five months married when she gave birth to a child, I then asked who was the father of the child, and she said the master, and I had every reason to believe her, as the child was nearly white, had blue eyes and veins, yet notwithstanding this we lived happily together, and I felt happy and comfortable, and I should never have thought of running away if she had not been sold. We lived together six years and had two children. Shortly after my marriage my master's wife died, and when he fixed upon Tillotson's daughter as his future wife, she made a condition that all female slaves whom he had at any time been intimate with must be sold, and my wife being one was sold with the children as well as any other female slaves. My wife was sold while I was away on an errand at Centreville, and any one situated as I was may imagine my feelings when I say that I left them in the morning all well and happy, in entire ignorance of any evil, and returned to find them all sold and gone away, and from then until now I have never seen any of them. I went to my master and complained to him, when he told me he knew nothing about it, as it was all done by his wife. I then went to her and she said she knew nothing about, as it was all done by my master, and I could obtain no other satisfaction; I then went to my master to beg him to sell me to the same master as he had sold my wife, but he said he could not do that, as she was sold to a trader.

1864

ELIZABETH KECKLEY

from Behind the Scenes

Some time afterwards he told me that he had reconsidered the question; that I had served his family faithfully; that I deserved my freedom, and that he would take $1200 for myself and boy.

This was joyful intelligence for me, and the reflection of hope gave a silver lining to the dark cloud of my life—faint, it is true, but still a silver lining.

Taking a prospective glance at liberty, I consented to marry. The wedding was a great event in the family. The ceremony took place in the parlor, in the presence of the family and a number of guests. Mr. Garland gave me away, and the pastor, Bishop Hawks, performed the ceremony, who had solemnized the bridals of Mr. G.'s own children. The day was a happy one, but it faded all too soon. Mr. Keckley—let me speak kindly of his faults—proved dissipated, and a burden instead of a helpmate. More than all, I learned that he was a slave instead of a free man, as he represented himself to be. With the simple explanation that I lived with him eight years, let charity draw around him the mantle of silence.

1868

PART FIVE

Family Trees Rooted—in Love

Lyrics

DAUGHTER'S INQUIRY

Ann Plato

I asked if father's to return,
    He left some years ago,
And I have never seen him since,—
    That all sad parting blow.

I said, my father, if you please
    Do guide the ship no more,
Some other can your place fulfill,
    And others can explore.

If not, dear father, do resign
    This ever roaming life,
Oh, do not spend your life in this,
    An ever mournful strife.

Perchance that you may ne'er return,
    The billows thence your grave,
O'er which no storied wind shall rise,
    No music but the wave.

Thus you have roam'd the southern seas,
    And riches with you flow;
You have beheld the bread fruit tree,
    The yam and millet grow.

You've been around the world again,
    And view'd it o'er and o'er;
Then why do you thus wish to go,
    And speed the parting hour?

I never may behold you more,
    Or seek advice so dear;
Oh! how can I to strangers tell,
    Or trust a feeling near.

Some say there's danger on the sea,
    No more than on the land;
I think we're liable to this,
    On sea, or desert sand.

I begged him, father do not go,
    For when you left me last,
You said you would not go again:
    My childish joys are past.

Then speed the long farewell;
    You must depart in haste,
The seamen are on board her decks,
    To plough the billow's waste.

He knelt, and pray'd of God above,
    My dearest daughter spare;
If not on earth, in heaven to meet,
    Sure trusting in Thy care.

And oft I sit me down, and think
    My father's absence long;
I wonder if he will return,
    To bless my childish song.

Some say, "he must be dead, I think,
    Or we should from him hear;"
Sometimes I think it must be true,
    And shed a mournful tear.

If then he is on distant shores,
    May God his steps approve,
And find a rest in heaven at last,
    And then with Christ to move.

1841

OUR FAMILY TREE

Joseph Cephas Holly

> *On the death of my sister Cecilia—the last of five*
> *members of the family, who died successively.*

Our family tree is in the sear
   And yellow leaf of life;
Branch after branch, year after year,
   Yields to death's pruning knife.
First, youngest born, as if 'twere meet,
   The sacrifice should be,
"The last of earth," the first to meet
   Th' unknown eternity.
'Twas God who gave, 'twas He who took,
   His voice let us obey,
So that in his eternal book,
   Our names shine bright as day.

1853

MY CHILD

from Provincial Freeman

Where is she now, my little bright-eyed daughter—
She who in gladness sported by blue Potomac's water?
Joy of my life, of my lone home the blessing,
No more her soft arms twine round me, caressing.

Scarce had three summer suns her young life gladdened,
And ne'er had toil or care its brightness saddened;
Like a bright flower in desert wild upspringing,
Comfort and joy by its sweet fragrance giving!

Rosa, my darling! Life's sole, only treasure,
My love for thee no human words can measure;
My very life-blood in thy pulse seemed bounding,
And like sweet music was thy glad voice's sounding!

Thy father, far away, is in the nice-fields pining,
And Hope's bright sun for him no more is shining;
They sold him from my side, and left me broken-hearted,
How can I, darling, from thee too, be parted!

Dark, dark and lonely now the hours are seeming,
And my sad heart to grief's lone plaint is beating
A dirge-like strain, from crushed affections gushing;
The life of joy and hope forever hushing.

Far, far away, beyond the rushing Santee,
To the Slave-mart, my child, they now have borne thee;
No mother's heart of love may shield thee ever—
And her fond words again shall cheer thee never.

And thou, as pure and [] what will be thy future!
And who will seek in thy young heart to nurture
Virtue's fair flowers, and save thee from the tempter,
When thou a maiden, shalt life's threshhold enter?

Oh! Wert thou in the grave, but calmly sleeping—
The wild vine and the daisy o'er thee creeping,
No sin strain resting on thy spirit's brightness,
No sorrow shadowing its sunny lightness.

Oh, mother! That in anguish wild art weeping,
And o'er thy baby's grave sad vigil keeping—
Think of the slave's sad lot—of her deep sorrow;
For her there is no joy, no bright to-morrow.

Pity her woes! and oh! let her not languish,
Uncared for and forgot, in her deep anguish;
Give her thy prayer—the prayer of high endeavor—
Rest not till Truth each gailing chain can sever.

CARRIE

1855

OLD GRIMES' SON

from Life of William Grimes

Old Grimes' boy lives in our town,
    A clever lad is he,—
He's long enough, if cut in half,
    To make two men like me.

He has a sort of waggish look,
    And cracks a harmless jest;
His clothes are rather worse for wear,
    Except his Sunday's best.

He is a man of many parts,
    As all who know can tell;
He sometimes reads the list of goods,
    And rings the auction bell.

He's kind and lib'ral to the poor,
    That is, to number one;
He sometimes saws a load of wood,
    And piles it when he's done.

He's always ready for a job—
    (When paid)—whate'er you choose;
He's often at the Colleges,
    And brushes boots and shoes.

Like honest men, he pays his debts,
    No fears has he of duns;
At leisure he prefers to walk,
    And when in haste, he runs.

In all his intercourse with folks,
    His object is to please;
His pantaloons curve out before,
    Just where he bends his knees.

His life was written sometime since,
    And many read it through;
He makes a racket when he snores,
    As other people do.

When once oppressed he prov'd his blood
    Not covered with the yoke;
But now he sports a freeman's cap,
    And when it rains, a cloak!

He's drooped beneath the southern skies,
    And tread on northern snows;
He's taller by a foot or more,
    When standing on his toes.

In Church he credits all that's said,
    Whatever preacher rise;
They say he has been seen in tears,
    When dust got in his eyes.

A man remarkable as this,
    Must sure immortal be,
And more than all, because he is
    Old Grimes' posterity!

1855

THE HOME FOR ME

from the Christian Recorder

I.

The home of peace, is the home for me,
Where parents both are seen agree.
Where little sister's voice is heard
To give assent to brother's word.
The home of peace, is the home for me,
Where all abide in happiest gree. [*sic*]

II.

The home for me, is the home of song,
I'll guarantee few things go wrong
Where sisters, brothers, parents sing,
And make the very welkin ring.
The home for me, is the home of song;
For there you'll find few things go wrong.

III.

There's music sweet, in the home for me
—Music of heavenly symphony,
Where all the girls, and all the boys,
Thus give increase to common joys.
There's music sweet, in the home for me
—Music of heavenly symphony.

IV.

The home for me, is the home of prayer,
To Him, who condescends to hear
And graciously accept the praise,
That's rendered through the life long days.
The home for me is the home of prayer,
To Him who condescends to hear.

    B. T. T(ANNER)

1872

THE LONELY MOTHER

(A NEGRO SPIRITUAL)

Fenton Johnson

I

Oh, my mother's moaning by the river,
My poor mother's moaning by the river,
For her son who walks the earth in sorrow.
Long my mother's moaned beside the river,
And her tears have filled an angel's pitcher,
"Lord of Heaven, bring to me my honey,
Bring to me the darling of my bosom,
For a lonely mother by the river."

II

Cease O mother, moaning by the river,
Cease, good mother, moaning by the river;
I have seen the star of Michael shining
Michael shining at the Gates of Morning;
Row, O mighty angel, down the twilight,
Row until I find a lonely woman,
Swaying long beneath a tree of cypress,
Swaying for her son who walks in sorrow.

1916

Fiction

CHARLES AND CLARA HAYES

Mrs. Lucie S. Day

The mansion of Mr. Hayes was pleasantly situated on one of the bluffs which forms a part of the bank of the Mississippi. It was evening, at that mansion all the pride of that section was gathered; sounds of revelry and mirth echoed through the apartments, bright forms flitted by the open windows, and women's low musical laugh told of happy hearts within.

Come away from this crowded scene, and let us stroll toward the bank of the river. But another is here before us—Clara, the daughter of Mr. Hayes. But why is she not with the other daughter of his, the admired of all? Her features, you see, are as perfect, her eye as intelligent, her form as graceful, as that other sister's. We soon learn she is—a slave. That settles all the mystery.

Another form approaches her—a tall youth. He whispers, "Sister." She looked up with a smile, but soon an expression of anxiety passed over her face, as she saw a stain of blood upon his breast, and on his brow the traces of recent passion, while his eye yet flashed with fire.

"Charles, what is the matter?"

"Matter? Are we not slaves, mere cyphers, who dare not call our lives, our souls, our own? Nothing belongs to us, but thought and feeling. I *will* yet escape and tell my wrongs to those who will hear and sympathize. Hush! do not tell me God is just—*I* never felt his justice. What I am, they have made me, and if I sink down, down to deep despair, I will sink under the pressure of their tyranny. All that *I* have learned, all that raises me above the brute, I gained myself, being my own teacher. I knew they wished me not to read, yet to do what they wished not was pleasure. Do not think me wild; I have been tempted almost beyond what I could bear. A little while ago, as I sat on yonder rock, gazing upon the bright stars, I wondered if they were worlds, inhabited like ours, and if so, were slaves there. There came many bitter thoughts; I spake aloud, when suddenly I received a blow in the face, followed by these words—'Slave, let *that* teach you what to think!' I arose from the ground, almost blind with rage, and there stood master Henry, grinning with pleasure. It was too much. I glanced at him—then at the steep bank; something within me whispered and I obeyed. With all the strength of madness and revenge, I seized and held him over the water. Another instant, and he would have floated a mangled corpse on the dark waves of this river; but I looked down and saw the reflection of the stars on the water. They looked like your bright eyes. I thought of you and spared him. But [] . . . to our little cottage; we will collect a few things, and long ere the morning light we will be far [from] hence.

Clara threw her arms around her brother's neck, and bending her head low, that he might not see the tears, said—"I cannot go. Do not say I do not love you; who else have I to love? Our mother is dead—our father is worse than none—I have no one to love but you. I dare not render your escape doubtful by going with you."

The morn was near its dawning, and still Clara knelt in earnest prayer. Her uplifted face was covered with tears; her accents fell not unheard on the ear of Him who hath said by the mouth of his Apostle—"And if we know that he heard us, whatsoever we ask we know that we have the petition that we desired of Him."

Clara seized hold upon that promise, and she felt that her entreaty to her brother's safety would be [] from that long communion with God, and with comparative cheerfulness went about her daily task. When it was reported that Charles was to be found nowhere on the plantation, and the company of hunters went forth with blood-hounds, pistols and the other accompaniments which Slavery uses on such occasions, Clara's faith remained unshaken.

But let us look forward and watch the fate of that brother. All night has he been making his way through the thick forest—now parting, with already lacerated hands, the vines that clustered in his path; now crawling through the dense underwood—he made his way until the bright sun peeped through the overhanging leaves. Plunging farther still into the forest, he came to a brook, which he crossed and recrossed, then threw himself down to rest in the welcome shelter of a cane-brake. Here he lay still and unmolested until near noon, when he heard the bay of the leader of the hounds, who had separated from the others, and reached the stream. In he dashed—again he crossed, and came on through the rustling cane. Charles' heart beat wildly—he shuddered; it was only for a moment. Drawing his knife, he waited in silence the coming of his savage foe. The animal approached, and, for a moment, shrank beneath the acknowledged supremacy which flashes in the eye of man. Charles seized that moment and catching him by the neck, buried the knife in his throat. He gave a low bay and all was over.

Charles had saved himself for a short time, but at a great risk, for when his pursuers discovered the dog, they would be certain that their victim was near. Just then, as he heard the bay of the dead hound's companions, there was a rustling near him in another direction, and a large animal of the wolf kind appeared, falling upon the dead dog to devour him. Charles, recrossing the brook as noiselessly as possible, pressed on until he was compelled to rest from pure exhaustion.

He remained, until he was aware, from the quiet around, that his pursuers were gone. Thanking God in his heart for his preservation, he pursued his toilsome way until he found a place of rest on the free shores of Canada; British Monarchy being freer than American Republicanism.

Though among strangers, without money, and almost without clothing, he was comparatively happy. He knew that no one dared to lay hand upon him and say "you are mine." He found a friend good, and true, in Mr. Stanhope, who, like himself, was a refugee from Slavery, and who feeling for "those in bonds as bound with them," supplied him with the necessaries of life, and procured him employment. Charles felt that what he earned was his own, and he went about his work with a will to accomplish it.

The light of Christianity at length dawned upon his mind. Clara's prayers were answered. Often did he wish to see that sister, but he knew that under present circumstances, it would be impossible. By industry and perseverance he gained a home; had land and a home of his own. This was a new and joyful era in his life. He had suffered enough to realize all that there is in life of joy.

In the mean time, he had become attached to Mary, the daughter of Mr. Stanhope, his friend. It was true, Charles had more knowledge of books then herself, for before he came from the South he could read and write, and since he had been free, had improved every opportunity. Mary's parents, being untaught themselves, did not pay that attention to her education which they should have done; but hers was the inward teaching of a meek and quiet spirit. She had that wisdom which "cometh from above," and when she gave her hand to Charles Hayes, felt that there was duty involved in that as in everything else; consequently there was happiness in their relation to each other. One cloud alone darkened their horizon—a sister was in the far South. Charles had sent for her once; but the person sent was not able to obtain her, and it was reported she was sold.

Five years, with all their untold trials, have been added to the lives of the family, who are the subjects of this memoir. It was the Spring of 1830. The winter in that section of country had been unusually severe, and though it was now April, the snow still covered the ground, and the wind blew piercingly through the naked branches of the trees. In the evening, around the clean hearth of his neat cottage, Mr. Hayes and his little family assembled for devotions. The father read a portion of the Scriptures, by the Prophet Isaiah, and the little children even, seemed to realize that it was the word of God. The last verse of the chapter he repeated—"And I will feed them that oppress thee with their own flesh; and they shall be drunken with their own blood, as with sweet wine; and all flesh shall know that I the Lord am thy Savior and thy Redeemer, the Mighty One of Jacob." The good man knelt in prayer, [] and impressive, as, in the full confidence of faith, he asked for strength to accomplish every duty; but as he prayed for his brethren in the South, his voice faltered; and when he mentioned his sister, it failed him. His sympathies, tuned by the hand of Sorrow, overcame him. He began to doubt the promises of his God, as he had applied them to his sister, and to despair of ever again meeting her. This it was that overwhelmed him. The family all wept with him. A few moments and he resumed his supplication. He settled down upon the promises; he believed and repeated the words—"I the Lord am thy Savior and thy Redeemer, the Mighty One of Jacob."

It was at a different hour of the same evening that a low knock was heard at the door, and as Mr. Hayes opened it, a familiar voice—"Brother!"

Yes, that brother and sister were united.

1853

DIALOGUE BETWEEN A MOTHER AND HER CHILDREN ON THE PRECIOUS STONES

Mrs. Sarah Douglas

Caroline—Here comes dear mother! Mother, when we get together in the evenings I always think of those brightly descriptive lines of Cowper, beginning thus:

"Let fall the curtains, wheel the sofa round,
And while the bubbling and loud hissing urn
Throws a steamy column, and the cups
That cheer, but do not inebriate, wait on each,
So let us welcome peaceful evening in."

Mother—Brightly descriptive indeed, and now throwing away the "steaming column" and "tea" cups, let *us* welcome peaceful evening in.

Adelaide—Will you be so good mother, as to show us that beautiful topaz breastpin of yours?

Mother—Certainly, my dear, but why do you wish to look at it—you have seen it many times.

Adelaide—Because, mother, our teacher told us to-day in our lesson on minerals, that topaz belongs to the quartz family, and that it is one of the precious stones mentioned in the Bible, as forming part of the dress of the High Priest. This made me anxious to look at it again.

Mother—I am glad you have so laudable motive for your curiosity, daughter. Take this key Caroline and unlock my writing desk, and you will find a small box, bring it to me.

Caroline—Here it is, mother.—*(Caroline brings the box)*

Mother—Before I open the box, tell me Adelaide, where in the Bible I can find the account of the precious stones that were set in the breast plate of the Priest.

Adelaide—In the 28th chapter of Exodus.

Mother—Yes. Repeat the passage, Caroline.

Caroline—And thou shalt set in it settings of stones, even four rows of stones, the first row shall be a sardius , a topaz, and a carbuncle; this shall be the first row. And the second row shall be an emerald, a sapphire and a diamond. And the third row a ligure and agate and amethyst. And the fourth row a beryl, and an onyx, and a jasper; they shall be set in gold in their inclosings.

Mother—Well remembered, Caroline, a few of these stones I have in my possession, and will now show you. I regret that I have not more. At some future time I hope to show them *all* to you.

Mother unlocks the box and spreads out a variety of precious stones, with breast-pins, finger rings, seals, buckles, &c., &c.

Adelaide—Beautiful, splendid, brilliant! Oh, mother, when sisters and I are women, shall we not wear some of these?

Mother—I hope, dear girls, that when you are women you will have no taste for these baubles. 'Tis my wish so to cultivate your hearts and heads that you will care little for the mere adorning of the body. Here is the topaz you wished to look at.

Mary—What a beautiful pale yellow color it is, and how it sparkles.

Anne—Oh, mother, is not this pretty violet colored stone amethyst?

Mother—Yes, Anne, it is. I am glad you have remembered the name.

Ellen—Why my dear mother do you not *wear* these beautiful finger rings and ear rings?

Mother—I have several reasons for not wearing them. First, they are very costly and entirely useless. Second. If I wore them, many persons not so well able to purchase them as I, would be anxious to have them merely because they saw me so ornamented. I think we should be careful to influence those around us for good only. I have no doubt that many of the degraded females of our city owe their ruin to a love of dress and vain ornaments. Third. I cannot bear to deck me in costly apparel, and to wear jewels, when so many thousands of my country women are miserably clad and in bondage. To be neat and clean in plain clothes, is all that seems to me necessary.

Anne—Oh, mother, I never thought of the poor before, when I wished to have pretty and costly clothes to wear. I will remember it now, I *will always* remember it.

Mother—That is right, my little Anne, be willing to deny yourself that you may have the *privilege* of helping God's poor.

Mary—O, mother, let me look at this seal. What a delicate color and how beautiful its shape.

Caroline—What kind of a stone is it, mother?

Mother—It is agate, another member of the quartz family. Its name is derived from the river Achatis in Sicily, near which these stones were found by the ancients, in great abundance. Look at it closely Ellen, and read the inscription.

Ellen—It is "Truth." How beautiful the motto.

Mother—Beautiful indeed, and characteristic of my honored Father to whom it belonged. Oh, children, *ever love the truth,* it will beautify and dignify, and make you honorable in the sight of God, and of man.

Adelaide—Mother, our Teacher says that truthful scholars are a great comfort to her. I will try to be truthful always, so that my Teacher may love and trust me.

Mother—I hope you will be obedient to your kind Teacher, and very attentive to her instructions.

Ellen—Yes, mother, I intend to be very attentive. If our Teacher had not instructed us, we should know but little of minerals and shells.

Caroline—Mother, last week Mr. Kindly was at our school, and he asked Anna Stevenson if she thought girls should learn as much as boys.—Anna said No. Mr. Kindly told her he thought they should learn more, for this reason, girls become mothers and mistresses of families, and that boys and girls too are committed to their care. He said children resembled their mothers most, and therefore she should be well informed, that she might know how to instruct her children. He said he never knew the son of a silly ignorant mother grow up to be a good and great man.

Mother—I hope you will remember Mr. Kindly's just remarks. Look at this cornelian, children, and tell me its form.

Children—It is a perfect ellipse.

Mother—Yes, it is. Describe an ellipse, Anne.

Anne—An ellipse is an oval figure having two diameters or axis, the longer of which is called the transverse, and the shorter the conjugate diameter.

Mother—That is right, Anne. I will have a seal made of this.

Children—Do mother, that will be useful as well as beautiful, and we can all seal our letters with it.

Mother—I wish to have a motto seal, you children are to choose the word. Let it be one that will remind *me* of the friend who gave it to me, and at the same time express *your* regard for your excellent teacher and friend. What shall it be?

Children—(with animation.)—Gratitude, mother!

Mother—That will do well; pleasant associations will cluster round your seal. Go, now, my daughters to your chambers, but before you sleep, kneel down and ask God to give you the garment of humility, time will not dim its lustre, nor wear it threadbare. Let your only ornament, my beloved girls, be a meek and quiet spirit, which is of great price in the Heavenly Father's sight. Farewell for to-night.

Children—Good night, mother.

1859

THE VOICE OF THE RICH PUDDING

Gertrude D[orsey] Browne

The door bell rang furiously, and Mr. Willis, who was in the act of blowing out the light, hastily retraced his steps down the hall, and stopped at the front door.

"Who's there?"

"Father's dead," came the answer, in an excited, childish voice.

Mr. Willis lost no time in drawing the bolts and unlocking the door, but the messenger had vanished and further questioning was impossible.

"Who the deuce was that kid, and why did he come to tell me about it at eleven o'clock?" and as he walked slowly back to his bed chamber he reviewed his limited list of acquaintances and wondered who could possibly consider his friendship and sympathy of sufficient moment that he should be notified at this hour of their loss.

"Now, let's see, there's Tyler, I've known him longer than any one else here, but since when did he become a father? and O—pshaw! I might as well dress and get myself collected. Jones has a family and is tolerably fond of me, but it's a long walk for one of his kids at this time of night. Guess I'll call up and find out the particulars. Yes, I'm afraid it is Jones. Poor old fellow, of course they'd send for me to look after things until his folks can be communicated with. I'll go right down and call up. These telephones are a great thing. Thank God! he didn't say Estella is dead."

Mr. and Mrs. Sarter were roaming about in the sweet land of Nod when they were recalled to things present and terrestrial by loud knocking at their door.

"Go down Jim, for mercy's sake, and find out what's the matter," Mrs. Sarter advised.

The sleepy man very ungraciously stumbled down the stairs, through the sitting room into the parlor and peered through the window at a small white figure on the porch.

"Hey, sonny, what's the row?" he yelled through the window.

"Mother's dead!"

"Whose mother? Mine or Annie's?" screamed Mr. Sarter as he dashed to the door and threw it open.

No one answered him for the porch was empty. In the sitting room, as he returned, he found his wife seated on the floor rocking to and fro moaning and groaning in a most distressing manner.

"Did you hear him Annie? It's so sudden and we're so unprepared for it."

"Oh, Jim, is it my mother?"

"I don't know, but its somebody's mother."

"There now, don't be foolish. If it ain't my mother why would any one come and wake us up in the middle of the night?" responded Mrs. Jim.

"There's just a possibility that should my own mother die, the folks would remember to notify her only son," sarcastically from Jim.

"We won't quarrel Jim, dear, don't be a bear, but if it should be poor, dear, devoted Mama, O—" and the crying began afresh.

"Now, see here, Annie, you might as well calm yourself, for we don't know whether it's proper to laugh or cry."

"We don't, hey? Well maybe you don't. If it's your mother you'll know it's proper to cry, and if it's mine, you'll laugh—O, you beast," wailed Mrs. Sarter.

"I'm going out to Hunters' to see if there's anything wrong, and on the way back I'll stop at your mother's," with which announcement Mr. Sarter slammed the front door.

"He needn't been so grumpy, I guess I stumped my toe against that old rocker hard enough to make a stone image cry," and Mrs. Sarter limped painfully to the switch and turned on the light.

At eleven P.M. Miss Stella Warner had left her sister Alice and brother-in-law Horace and retired to her room, not to sleep, but to "think it all out."

"I don't see why we can't. I'm no infant, and I don't care a snap whether he's high church or low church or any church at all, he suits me, so there! Calls us sinners, just as if he is accusing angel of the judgment." Thus ran the tearful meditations of Stella.

"Horace, I think it is perfectly ridiculous to stand in their way just on account of the slight difference in their church service. For the love of goodness let them alone, and let us get back home. I know little Marie wants to see us. I shouldn't wonder if, because of the stand you take in this matter, something should happen to Marie in our absence, which will always cause us to associate the two affairs."

Pretty Alice Thordeau was half angry with her resolute husband, but far from allowing her indignation to get the better of her prudence, she diplomatically brought into the subject the name and possible welfare of their three-year-old daughter Marie.

"Alice, I am resolved to do my duty by my ward. If Mr. Willis cannot consent to conform with the requirements of the high church, I can not consider his proposal for the hand of Estella. If they are so unwise as to do this thing without my consent, Estella loses a fortune and need expect nothing from me." Mr. Thordeau spoke with the earnest decision of a conscientious man.

"Of course, Horace, you have the say so, but just suppose Marie should ever be left to the care of a guardian and that guardian was a—was a—a Mormon or a—a—"

"Impossible!" impatiently replied Horace. "Utterly impossible, why do you suppose I would ever commit Marie into the hands of any person of whose character I was not certain? Really, Alice, you flatter my judgment by conceiving of such impossible conditions."

"Well, at any rate, father didn't make our church and mode of worship a handicap for Estella, and I'm sure he would hardly appreciate the wisdom of keeping them apart on that issue. If I thought that Marie would be compelled to eat fish on Friday or burn incense to an ebony god, why I should cry my eyes out, I know."

"Very likely," was the dry return. Then with kindness, "Alice, don't confuse our personal affairs with the question we are considering, Marie is not an orphan and God knows—What was that?"

Some one tapping on the window. A faint, but persistent tap. As Mr. Thordeau opened the hall door a voice in the darkness greeted him with the words:

"Baby is dead."

"What is it, Horace?" asked Alice, coming into the hall.

"Baby is dead," he answered in a hoarse whisper. "Come—let us go—If we hurry we can catch the midnight express. Why, in the name of all that is holy, are we here, anyhow?"

But Alice, the emotional, the hysterical, was running out after the messenger.

"Here, stop! whose baby is dead? My Marie isn't dead, stop," she cried as she ran and stumbled over the shrubbery, down the avenue and out upon the street.

"Absurd—simply impossible. Oh, it must have been one of Myrtle's children—the baby—why of course—little Elizabeth. What a pity, but then the Lord knows best." She stopped at the end of the street and considered whether it was best to go on or to return to Mr. Thordeau, who by this time was thoroughly excited. Finally deciding upon the latter course, she hurried back to the house.

"Listen, Horace, have some reason. That was a child who spoke to you, and it couldn't be our Marie, she is with mother in Dayton, and telegrams don't yell at a man in the dark. They are always written or typewritten on paper. Why, it must be one of your cousin's children, the baby—little Elizabeth, no doubt. We might go over there and see what we can do, for Myrtle is utterly prostrated, I know." All the time she was talking, Alice had been making hurried preparations to visit the stricken home, and, as they entered the hall, they were joined by Stella, who insisted upon accompanying them.

"I don't know why that call should upset me as it did, I might have known it wasn't Marie, but all the same I—well—I want to get back home. I'm convinced that converting sinners from the errors of their ways isn't my forte, but mind, Miss Estella, I'm exempt from all reproach if it doesn't result harmoniously," remarked Mr. Thordeau.

Alice and Estella were both unprepared for such a concession from such a stubborn source, and the remainder of the walk was made in complete silence.

When they reached the Smith residence they found it enveloped in darkness. In response to a light rap Otis Smith's head appeared at an upstairs window and his sleepy voice inquired:

"Who's there?"

"Why, it's us," inelegantly replied Horace. "We thought we'd come over and see—and I mean ask—that, is—Say how's your baby? She ain't dead or nothing, is she?"

"For God's sake! hold on a minute and I'll be down."

The head was withdrawn and a few minutes later Otis walked out on the veranda.

"Say, what's the fun? I don't seem to understand this death notice racket. About ten minutes ago Myrt went over to her mother's to see if Helen is dead. Some one came here and made noise enough to wake up the kids, and that's going some—and when Myrt asked what was the trouble, he said her sister or my sister or some sister was dead, and Myrt just threw her rain coat over her shoulders and ran, and left me to look after Elizabeth."

The quartet sank on the steps, overcome by the mystery, and compared notes as they were able.

"Listen, there comes some one now, maybe its the bird of evil omen," cautioned Stella. But when the solitary figure of a man was about to pass them by she called after it, "O, Mr. Willis is that you?"

"It certainly is I, but why this select gathering at the witching hour of night?" he asked as he greeted the other occupants of the veranda steps.

"Who's dead?" abruptly asked Horace. "Have you heard of any deaths tonight, Mr. Willis?"

"Quite a number, I should say, but I can't tell you who."

"For instance," persisted the imaginative Horace.

"Well, for instance, I am informed that father is dead, and I just met Jim Sarter and he is trying to locate a dead mother, having satisfactorily accounted for his own and his wife's mother," was the good natured reply of Willis.

While he was talking, the telephone in the hall began to ring, and Otis answered it.

"That you, Myrt? Come on home, get one of the boys to come with you. Yes—yes—I know. Whose sister? O, is that so? No! Who! Me? You bet I ain't dead. O, rot. It's a shame—why it's the rumest game I ever heard or saw played. Yes. Good-bye."

When he rejoined the company on the steps Otis mopped his perspiring brow.

"O, Lord, my mother is on her way over here to put pennies on my waxen eyelids, and I'm afraid I don't make a very successful corpse just now. At least I can't be one of the silent kind."

"Say, let's all go home and go to bed," advised Alice, to whom each new development was a separate and distinct shock.

"Kind a reminds a fellow of the passover or the ten virgins or the Johnstown flood or something—don't it?" asked Otis as he bade his guests good night and soothed the fretful crying of little Elizabeth.

· · · · ·

The supper bell had rung the second time and the tea was in danger of cooling, before the Rev. Harvey Reynolds and wife entered the dining room. Their son Max—a lad of thirteen—was impatiently awaiting them, and amusing himself in the meantime by deftly balancing a dessert spoon on the edge of a cut glass candlestick.

Rev. Reynolds led his wife to the head of the table, placed her chair, and rang the bell, requesting the maid to serve.

"That was a singular experience I must say—very singular, but quite a pretty little ceremony, Willa, did you not think so?"

"Very pretty, indeed, dear, and O, wasn't she happy?"

"The gentleman, Mr. Thordeau, rather impressed me as being a somewhat zealous person. He didn't seem to hesitate about giving her away, like they sometimes do," remarked the minister.

"After all, the dream of life is happiness and if the reality is more than the dream how very happy they ought to be," Mrs. Reynolds responded.

"Dream? What dream, Mama?" Max inquired.

"Why, dear, the dream that we are speaking of is the dream of two happy hearts made one," laughed his mother.

"O, shucks, I wouldn't give my dream for a dozen old hearts as happy as a bunch of tops."

"Well son, if you've had such a pleasant dream relate it to us. I'm sure we always find pleasure in your dreams."

"I think they supply the lack of printed fiction to which I am not a generous subscriber," added his father.

"Well, sir, last night I dremp—"

"Dreamed, you mean, dear," corrected Rev. Reynolds.

"Well, then, I dreamed that Mr. Morehead took me into the Western Union, where I've always wanted to be, and he made a messenger boy out of me.

"O, shucks, if you could have seen me hustling.

"The telegrams, it seems, were written out on a blackboard and I had to learn ten or more at a time. They was all about people dying. Mr. Morehead would let me study 'em for a while and then he'd say, 'Run to So and So's and tell 'em their father's dead or sister's dead, and stop at What's his Name on your way back and tell 'em the baby's dead.' O, shucks, I almost ran myself to death. When I got up this morning I was so sore and tired I could hardly dress."

"Please excuse me," weakly interposed Mrs. Reynolds.

She left the room, but was gone only a few minutes—with horror she gasped:

"Look, Harvey! see this boy's gown, it's muddy and grass stained and the sheets of his bed—there, there, father, don't give him another bit of that rich pudding."

1907

Letters

FROM JOHN H. RAPIER TO HIS SON JOHN

Florence, Alabama, March 17, 1857

My Son:

Your letter dated St. Paul, February 22 was received. We are all well and was glad to hear from you. I hope you are better of your frostbite.

James will quit school soon and will come out to you to try his luck. I hope you and him will be like brothers towards each other, for it is very unpleasant to hear that my children are disagreeing with each other.

John, you should settle down and not have a wish to ramble so much. I hope your uncle James will come to the same conclusion. You and your uncle have the capacity of doing well in any country.

Your counsel with regard to me, I felt every word of. I hope I shall carry out your wish, my son, with regard of moving out to some free state. As soon as you and your uncle have found the place that will suit you both, you can calculate on me being your neighbor. The time has come for me to act. My eyes are getting so I cannot see how to shave and to tell the truth I hate the name of barber. A farmer I look on as a superior occupation.

I think you and James—I mean your brother—ought to make sure of some land. It do not require more than fifty dollars to do that. You can save that very soon. I am willing to help if you take one piece of a hundred and sixty acres between you. You should encourage James all you can, my son, as you are calculated to advise him.

John H. Rapier

Rapier Family Papers, Moorland Spingarn Research Center, Howard University

FROM PARKER T. SMITH TO "MY DEAR SIR"

Dresden, Canada West, November 1861

My Dear Sir:

Everyone was extremely glad to hear from Philadelphia, especially Margaret who is always glad to hear from what she calls home. I must confess that I am *homesick already myself.* I have never lived in a place where I felt so free. We have a smokehouse well filled with meat, both beef and pork, a plenty of flour, some fifteen or sixteen bushels of wheat ready to grind for winter, a plenty of peas for coffee and wood at hand to keep a good fire.

But you may yet see me in Philadelphia. *I am so lonesome that I cannot content myself here.* These things I say in confidence. I make money and could soon accumulate property, but unless a person is satisfied there is no use of talking about staying in a place.

Give my love to everybody and consider yourself as entitled to the largest share.

Parker T. Smith

Jacob C. White Collection, Moorland Spingarn Research Center, Howard University

Royal Oak, Talbot Co., Md.
Feb. 8, 1867
Fri. 11 A.M.

My Dear Parents & Sister,

Today we are having a cold rain-storm, or as is a more common expression here,—"we're having failing weather," and in consequence of which I am at home today,—privilege of which I am highly glad to avail myself, for the reason that I did not retire till about two this morning, and I am feeling very dull & rather sleepy[. . . .]

Mr. Thomas & I attended the wedding last eve'g., the ceremony took place at 6½ o'ck., the bride wore a Delaine skirt—brown and figured—with a white waist, and her head was decorated with flowers, artificial, as were also the heads of the two bridesmaids, who were likewise attired in delaines. The groom wore a full suit of black his vest being velvet I think, and his attendants wore the same; all looked plain, neat and well. Rev'd. Trantum married them, afterwards congratulated them and eating a small piece of cake very soon retired. The man with whom the bride lives was present with two other white men, they all came & went with the minister, 'twas a relief too, to have them gone, immediately following which the entire company a large number of whom had assembled relapsed or collapsed I don't know which would be the most applicable term here,—into a long and painful silence. I was glad to have some refreshments passed for a relief & a change of scene. The refreshments at this time was iced cake in thin slices, cookies & lemonade, after an interval of an hour or two the tables were arranged for supper, upon which was placed two large Turkies, Cold Boiled Chickens with drawn Butter turned over them, Shad Ham or Bacon & Sausages, Bread Biscuit & Butter, Tea & Coffee, & Scallop Oysters or something similar—they were very nice. I tasted them ate part of a Turkey leg & two flat biscuit cakes, I suppose they're called here, and drank two cups—very small—of tea. At supper a different spirit pervaded the guests which continued till we left which was about 1½ o'ck. After supper & the tables had been removed, played upon; which created much amusement. I did not participate in any of them however, but remained a silent & interested spectator. Mrs. Thomas did not go. We were the first to make a movement to go home although 'twas so late. I can't tell at what hour the rest separated.

While we were at supper a number of men both married and single, came to the house surrounding it making the most horrid noises with cow and sleigh bells, horns etc. added to their yells & songs, firing of pistols & guns, that you ever heard, and I judged they kept it up full an hour, to the discomfiture of all present.

This is a custom here upon such occasions among both black and white, and is considered very annoying, still it has to be endured though now & then I'm told, at the expense of law, for they go too far in their demonstrations sometimes. Just before we came away the bride's loaf which had occupied the center of the table during supper, was cut & passed around with confectionery. Everything seemed to be nice & was enjoyed the meats here decorated with evergreens, also three of the side walls of the room which was quite large & nearly square & warmed by a fire in the fireplace, the floor was uncarpeted but white and very clean.

I think I've now given you a full and fair description of the wedding, and you'll probably infer that 'twas a very pleasant affair upon a whole, which is quite true[. . . .]

Remember one & all accept the best portion to yourselves.

From Rebecca

Courtesy of Farah Jasmine Griffin

FROM DAVE WALDRO TO COUSIN

Milton Fla June the 18th 1867.

Dear Cousin I received word last week that you wer not doing very well in Montgomery and that times there wer very hard there   Now Sarah if you will come down here to me I will take care of you and your children and you and children shall never want for any thing as long as I have any thing to help you with   Come down and I will have a place for you and your three children for I Know that it is hard enough for a woman to get along that has a husband to help her and one that has not I do not Know how they do to get living these times   Cousin I want you to be shure and come down if you posibly can and stay here as long as you want to if it is three or four year it will not make a bit of differance to me   Sarah you must excuse this paper and ill writen letter and bad composition for I am in a great hurry and have not much time to write for I have to go to away   But I shall look for you down here   Please come down and make your home here with my famly   Kate and the children send you there love and best Respects and are wanting you to come down as they want to see you very bad   your friends sends there Respects to you

I shall bring this to a close hoping this will find you well in health if not doing well   And I want to see you as soon as I can

No more at this time   Farewell from your Cousin

Dave Waldro

INFORMATION WANTED

from the Christian Recorder, *1864–1893*

Information is wanted of Charles Brisco, who left Virginia, some four or five years ago, to wait upon Lieutenant Fairfax, on a steamer for San Francisco, at the outbreak of this war. Lieutenant Fairfax returned, leaving my husband behind. I am informed that Charles Brisco left San Francisco for Aspinwall, New Grenada, as a cook, or waiter on a family. Any information concerning him may be left at the Book and Christian Recorder office, No. 619 Pine Street, Philadelphia.

(Signed) ELIZABETH BRISCO, his Wife.

N.B.—Charles has a mother and sister in Georgetown, D.C., by the names of Cynthia Brisco and Mrs. Mary A. Dove.

March 26, 1864

Of the whereabouts of Margaret Steward, wife of Otway M. Steward, better known in South Carolina as "O. M. Steward." When last heard from she was in Charleston, S.C., on the 8th of last January. She was then expecting to go to Abbeville, C.H. She was formerly owned by Wm. L. Venning, of St. Thomas Parish, S.C. Her maiden name is Margaret McClane. Any information of her whereabouts will be most thankfully received by her husband and may be addressed to

O. M. STEWARD,
Richmond, Va.

October 28, 1865

Information wanted of the whereabouts of my husband, Richard Jones, and my two sons, John and Thomas. We were separated in the woods, near a place called alley white, in November, 1862. I was carried back to Suffolk by the Union troops. I have heard nothing of them since.

We were owned by Birven Jones, of Smithfield, Suffolk County, Virginia. I am the grand daughter of Old Tom Pete Wilson. I am much in want at this time. Ministers will please read this notice in the churches.

MATILDA JONES.

Direct to ANTHONY BOWEN,
Agent Christian Recorder,
No. 85 E. St. between 9th & 10th (Island,)
Washington, D.C.
Sept 22—1t.

September 22, 1866

Information wanted of Melissa Walker, who belonged to Richard Christian and was sold to Dr. Boothe. Also of Waverly Johnson, Alexander Johnson, William Woodson, Chloe Woodson, and Archie Woodson, sold to Richmond, VA.

Any information of the above named children of Malinda Smith, formerly of Amelia County, Virginia, will be gratefully acknowledged by

MALINDA SMITH,
(Care of Whitall, Tatum & Co.)
Millville, New Jersey.

November 30, 1867

Of the following persons: Benjamin Harper, my husband; Malinda Turmond, my daughter; Amy A. Cox, my husband's mother; Rily Harper, Augusta and Willis Normond, Sarah Normond, Lucinda Freeman, Gracie A. Cox, Polly Mitchell, and Lizzie Harper, relatives of my husband. Any information addressed to me will be thankfully received.

MARY TURMIN,
(Care of Mrs. Adelaide Townsend)
New Richmond, Ohio.
Nov. 7—1mo.

November 7, 1868

Of my mother, Parthenia Chism, of my brothers Jackson, Green, Willis, and Smith Chism. Also of my sisters Mary and Phillis Chism; all living when last heard from with John Chism, near Versailles, Morgan County, Missouri.

I heard from them about twelve years ago. Any person knowing their whereabouts will confer a favor upon their son and brother Mingo Chism, who was sold to John Gibson about eighteen years ago. Address

THOMAS H. BENTON,
Washington, Iowa.
P.O. Box 315.
P.S.—Ministers will please read this in their congregations.

May 8, 1869

Of Joseph Gidding aged 16 years. He left Philadelphia in Oct 1868, since which time nothing has been heard from him. Address his anxious mother, Mary C. Gidding, 400 Ratcliffe Avenue, Philadelphia, Pa.

March 26, 1870

INFORMATION WANTED

from the Christian Recorder, *January 6, 1893*

Of my mother Fannie Scott; and my brother Edward Scott. All of these belonged to old Sam Scott who lived near Lynchburg, Va., close to Maze's Gro-
cery. My name was Eloise Scott; my name now is E. T. Hill. Any information
concerning them will be thankfully received by

ELOISE T. HILL

808 Jefferson St., Oakland, Cal.

Of my brother James Madison Martin. He left South Carolina in 1872. When
last heard of, he was in Gloss County Seat, Arkansas. Any information concerning his whereabouts will be handsomely rewarded by the undersigned.

GEORGE W. MARTIN,

Pastor A. M. E. Church,

Jovann, Darlington Co., S. C

Of Edward Click who was sold down South to a man by the name of Shumae.
He was a mullato man, very large eyes, bushy hair, about 5 ft. 6 in. high, a carpenter and black-smith by trade. His wife was named Amy Click; his children,
Charles, Henry, Mary, Elizabeth, and Jenny. Any information concerning him
will be liberally rewarded.

MRS. JENNY PICKET.

Humwell, Mo.

Of my son, William Branan, and my daughter, Mary Branan, who, sometime
before the war was sold to Ben Branan in Texas who thereafter moved to Tennessee and my son and daughter with them. Nothing has been heard of them
since. We all, before the separation in Texas, belonged to Jonathan Fine, hence
the change of their names from Fine to Branan after the selling took place.

Address Sallie Fine, Mound City, Kansas.

Of my brother Trussy David who was given to a man by the name of Dr.
David who lived at Bennettsville, S. C. Phillip, Nero, and myself were given
away by Him Speers to his sons-in-law at the same time; Philips to Elijah Pipkin, Nero to Duncan Moore, Trussey to Dr. David and Moses to Isaac Pipkin.
Mother is still living in the same old place. I sign my name,

Your Brother,

MOSES MCCLOUD

No. 1520 E. Mason St., Springfield, Ill.

Of Moses Timstol, who was born in Essex county, Va., and who was sold to Mr. Harden, in Nashville, Tenn., by Mrs. Kittie McCoo. Direct your letters to : Mrs. Elizabeth Fauntroy, 1031 Winton St., Philadelphia, Pa.

Of Charlott Lee formerly Mrs. Charlott Allen. The last time she was heard from she was a widow going by the name of Charlott Lee in Brooklyn, N.Y. Her sister is named Caudes Allen. The inquirer is her brother. If found address: Horace Graves, Mt. Vernon, Ind.

Of Vergel Johnson, the son of Margaret Smith, last heard of was in Camden, South Carolina. Anything of his whereabouts will be gladly received by his mother, in care of: P. J. Jordan, Pastor, A.M.E. Church, Box 29 Hillsboro, N. C.

Nonfiction

THE DYING BED OF A MOTHER
from Colored American

Of all the relations on earth, none are more sacred than that of a mother. If any person this side of heaven, has claims to superior attention, it is an affectionate, pious, aged, helpless, suffering, dying mother. Sixteen days my mother had been suffering keen distress of body. With the exception of one short interview, I had been absent; but now called to gaze upon her dying features. I had ever thought that I could command my feelings on any emergency whatever, but their gushing tide now overwhelmed me. Others told me that she was triumphantly waiting for the chariot to take her home; but I wished to hear the sweet testimony from her own lips. Again and again I went to her bedside, took her hand in mine, with a full resolution to inquire concerning her faith and hope; but as often did the swelling tide stop my utterance—the scenes of infancy all came up in review, and they seemed as it were but yesterday. Her sprightly step, her once blooming features, her soothing voice seemed present before me, renewed in youthfulness and vigor. The hand so often outstretched to save me in the years of childhood, was now growing cold—the eye that once sparkled with rapture at my infantile sports, already half closed—the lips that first told me who made me, and taught me to say "Our Father, who art in heaven;" were about to be sealed forever in death— these impressed upon the feelings in a measure, which I shall not attempt to describe. Once more I stood by her bed-side and with fluttering voice, inquiring: "Mother, have you still unshaken faith in God?" But the thrilling name of mother vibrated no longer upon her ear: she answered no more words or signs. Alas, I kissed the clay cold hand, and exclaimed, "Farewell, mother, my much beloved mother!" It was no less affecting to see a venerable old man, whose hairs were bleached by the frost of nearly seventy winters, after he had done all that love could suggest, weeping over his dying partner, with whom he had lived almost half a century, and still inquiring, "Do you want anything, my dear? What more can we do for you? If you cannot speak, give me a sign."

But she no longer responds to the most endearing names. Alas, we had followed her to the brink of Jordan, and could go no farther. She had already plunged amidst its cold waves, and must go alone. We gazed upon this solemn scene till Faith whispered, "There is a friend that sticketh closer than a brother." Hope sprung up, and with a firm voice, exclaimed, "If we believe that Jesus died and rose again, even so them also, which sleep in Jesus, will God bring with him." Love expanded her wings, and triumphantly shouted, "Blessed be God, who giveth us the victory through our Lord Jesus Christ."

1837

THE USE OF GRANDMOTHERS
from the Christian Recorder

A little boy who had spilled a pitcher of milk, stood crying, in view of a whipping, over the wreck. A little playmate stepped up to him and said, condolingly, "Why, Bobby, haven't you got a grandmother?" If there's not a sermon in that text, where shall one find it? Who of us cannot remember this family mediator, always ready with an excuse for broken china, or torn clothes, or tardy lessons?

1864

AUNT JENNIE THE OLD MAID

from the Christian Recorder

Clara and Lizzie were neighborly girls. Perhaps we had better tell our little readers what we mean by "neighborly;" for they don't like "beg" words. We do not mean that they lived close together, neighborhood, is the word. O; for Clara and Lizzie lived in opposite portions of a very large city. And then it is not to be forgotten that many little girls do live close at hand, and yet are not neighborly. That is, we do not say that such little girls of themselves, would not be neighborly, if allowed by their parents. But how often is it that Parents forbid their children having a neighborly spirit toward those who may live even next door. We once knew a poor man to be the neighbor of a rich one, that is, he lived in the same neighborhood; but between the children of the two families there was no neighborly spirit. Pride forbade it. Again we knew a "colored" man to be the next door neighbor of a 'white' one; but between the children of the two there was no neighborly spirit. Prejudice forbade it. By this time, it is doubtless understood that we mean by a neighborly spirit, one that is, friendly, our Anglo-Saxon fathers taking it for granted that they who *dwell near* each other, would at least be friendly.

Clara and Lizzie, then, were exceedingly neighborly. Neither of them was happier, than when in the other's company. This did not often happen owing to the distance they lived apart. But upon every opportunity they were glad to meet.

To Aunt Jennie, was Clara indebted for the joy of visiting her dear friend Lizzie as often as she did. Aunt Jennie was oldest sister to Clara's mother. She had never been married, and instead of having a home of her own to look after while she never left the old homestead where she was raised, she spent a goodly portion of her time with her married sister. Indeed it may be said, that she took an active part in attending to the numerous children with which her sister had been blessed. She it was that principally saw them to Church, to Sabbath School, and when they went abroad generally. As we have said it was Aunt Jennie, that always saw Clara up to her friend Lizzie Gates'.

It would have pleased you, one day, to have heard Clara tell her youthful playmate about this wonderful aunt. "You wouldn't believe it," said she, "how kind she is. Why if it wasn't for her, we'd never get out." and she gave a kind of a long thankful sigh.

"Why," said Lizzie, "would not your Mamma take you out sometimes. My Mamma, takes me?"

"Yes, but your Mamma has only got you to dress and fix," said Clara. "My Mamma has got so many."

"But don't your aunt Jennie help her?" asked Lizzie.

"Of course, she does, that's what I'm telling you," exclaimed Clara, "she just comes and fixes us for Church, and then takes us home with her to dinner to see Grand-Ma, and then back to Sunday School. Indeed she is awful kind. All the picnics and things she takes us to; and when our Sunday School had its exhibition, if it had not been for her, Mamma never could have got us all ready. But Aunt Jennie just came and learnt us our pieces; and when the time came, she dressed us, and then helped Mamma to get ready, and we all went. I tell you Lizzie," and Clara's eyes fairly danced, "we don't know what we'd do with out her."

"What's her name?" asked Lizzie, in a kind of surprise.

"Why Aunt Jennie, Jennie. Mamma calls her an old maid; and I believe she is, for she takes us out so. Indeed, Lizzie I wish all ladies were old maids, for then we children would have a fine time."

1873

Autobiographical Accounts

SAMUEL RINGGOLD WARD

from Autobiography of a Fugitive Negro

CHAPTER I. FAMILY HISTORY

I was born on the 17th October, 1817, in that part of the State of Maryland, U.S., commonly called the Eastern Shore. I regret that I can give no accurate account of the precise location of my birthplace. I may as well state now the reason of my ignorance of this matter. My parents were slaves. I was born a slave. They escaped, and took their then only child with them. I was not then old enough to know anything about my native place; and as I grew up, in the State of New Jersey, where my parents lived till I was nine years old, and in the State of New York subsequently, where we lived for many years, my parents were always in danger of being arrested and re-enslaved. To avoid this, they took every possible caution: among their measures of caution was the keeping of the children quite ignorant of their birthplace, and of their condition, whether free or slave, when born; because children might, by the dropping of a single word, lead to the betrayal of their parents. My brother, however, was born in New Jersey; and my parents, supposing (as is the general presumption) that to be born in a free State is to be born free, readily allowed us to tell where my brother was born; but *my* birthplace I was neither permitted to tell nor to know. Hence, while the secresy and mystery thrown about the matter led me, most naturally, to suspect that I was born a slave, I never received direct evidence of it, from either of my parents, until I was four-and-twenty years of age; and then my mother informed my wife, in my absence. Generous reader, will you therefore kindly forgive my inability to say exactly where I was born; what gentle stream arose near the humble cottage where I first breathed—how that stream sparkled in the sunlight, as it meandered through green meadows and forests of stately oaks, till it gave its increased self as a contribution to the Chesapeake Bay—if I do not tell you the name of my native town and county, and some interesting details of their geographical, agricultural, geological, and revolutionary history—if I am silent as to just how many miles I was born from Baltimore the metropolis, or Annapolis the capital, of my native State? Fain would I satisfy you in all this; but I cannot, from sheer ignorance. I was born a slave—where? Wherever it was, it was where I dare not be seen or known, lest those who held my parents and ancestors in slavery should make a claim, hereditary or legal, in some form, to the ownership of my body and soul.

My father, from what I can gather, was descended from an African prince. I ask no particular attention to this, as it comes to me simply from tradition— such tradition as poor slaves may maintain. Like the sources of the Nile, my ancestry, I am free to admit, is rather difficult of tracing. My father was a pure-blooded Negro, perfectly black, with wooly hair; but, as is frequently true of the purest Negroes, of small, handsome features. He was about 5 feet 10 inches in height, of good figure, cheerful disposition, bland manners, slow in deciding, firm when once decided, generous and unselfish to a fault; and one of the most consistent, simple-hearted, straightforward Christians, I ever knew. What I have grouped together here concerning him you would see in your first acquaintance with him, and you would see the same throughout his entire life. Had he been educated, free, and admitted to the social privileges in early life for which nature fitted him, and for which even slavery could not, did not, altogether *unfit* him, my poor crushed, outraged people would never have had nor needed a better representation of themselves—a better specimen of the black gentleman. Yes: among the heaviest of my maledictions against slavery is that which it deserves for keeping my poor father—and many like him—in the midnight and dungeon of the grossest ignorance. Cowardly system as it is, it does not dare to allow the slave access to the commonest sources of light and learning.

After his escape, my father learned to read, so that he could enjoy the priceless privilege of searching the Scriptures. Supporting himself by his trade as a house painter, or whatever else offered (as he was a man of untiring industry), he lived in Cumberland County, New Jersey, from 1820 until 1826; in New York city from that year until 1838; and in the city of Newark, New Jersey, from 1838 until May 1851, when he died, at the age of 68.

In April I was summoned to his bedside, where I found him the victim of paralysis. After spending some few days with him, and leaving him very much better, I went to Pennsylvania on business, and returned in about ten days, when he appeared still very comfortable; I then, for a few days, left him. My mother and I knew that another attack was to be feared—another, we knew too well, would prove fatal; but when it would occur was of course beyond our knowledge; but we hoped for the best. My father and I talked very freely of his death. He had always maintained that a Christian ought to have his preparation for his departure made, and completed in Christ, before death, so as when death should come he should have nothing to do BUT TO DIE. "That," said my father, "is enough to do at once: let repenting, believing, everything else, be sought at a proper time; let dying alone be done at the dying time." In my last conversation with him he not only maintained, but he *felt*, the same. Then, he seemed as if he might live a twelve-month; but eight-and-forty hours from that time, as I sat in the Rev. A. G. Beeman's pulpit, in New Haven, after the opening services, while singing the hymn which immediately preceded the sermon, a telegraphic despatch was handed me, announcing my father's death. I begged Mr. Beeman to preach; his own feelings were such, that he could not, and I was obliged to make the effort. No effort ever cost me so much. Have I trespassed upon your time too much by these details? Forgive the fondness of the filial, the bereaved, the fatherless.

My mother was a widow at the time of her marriage with my father, and was ten years his senior. I know little or nothing of her early life: I think she was not a mother by her first marriage. To my father she bore three children, all boys, of whom I am the second. Tradition is my only authority for my maternal ancestry: that authority saith, that on the paternal side my mother descended from Africa. Her mother, however, was a woman of light complexion; her grandmother, a mulattress; her great-grandmother, the daughter of an Irishman, named Martin, one of the largest slaveholders in Maryland—a man whose slaves were so numerous, that he did not know the number of them. My mother was of dark complexion, but straight silklike hair; she was a person of large frame, as tall as my father, of quick discernment, ready decision, great firmness, strong will, ardent temperament, and of deep, devoted, religious character. Though a woman, she was not of so pleasing a countenance as my father, and I am thought strongly to resemble her. Like my father, she was converted in early life, and was a member of the Methodist denomination (though a lover of all Christian denominations) until her death. This event, one of the afflictive of my life, occurred on the first day of September, 1853, at New York. Since my father's demise I had not seen her for nearly a year; when, being about to sail for England, at the risk of being apprehended by the United States' authorities for a breach of their execrable republican Fugitive Slave Law, I sought my mother, found her, and told her I was about to sail at three P.M., that day (April 20th, 1853), for England. With a calmness and composure which she could always command when emergencies required it, she simply said, in a quiet tone, "To England, my son!" embraced me, commended me to God, and suffered me to depart without a murmur. It was our last meeting. May it be our last parting! For the kind sympathy shown me, upon my reception of the melancholy news of my mother's decease, by many English friends, I shall ever be grateful: the recollection of that event, and the kindness of which it was the occasion, will dwell together in my heart while reason and memory shall endure.

In the midst of that peculiarly bereaved feeling inseparable from realizing the thought that one is both fatherless and motherless, it was a sort of melancholy satisfaction to know that my dear parents were gone beyond the reach of slavery and the Fugitive Law. Endangered as their liberty always was, in the *free* Northern States of New York and New Jersey—doubly so after the law of 1851—I could but feel a great deal of anxiety concerning them. I knew that there was no living claimant of my parents' bodies and souls; I knew, too, that neither of them would tamely submit to re-enslavement: but I also knew that it was quite possible there should be creditors, or heirs at law; and that there is no State in the American Union wherein there were not free and independent democratic republicans, and *soi-disant* Christians, "ready, aye ready" to aid in overpowering and capturing a runaway, *for pay.* But when God was pleased to take my father in 1851, and my mother in 1853, I felt relief from my greatest earthly anxiety. Slavery had denied them education, property, caste, rights, liberty; but it could not deny them the application of Christ's blood, nor an admittance to the rest prepared for the righteous. They could not be buried in the same part of a common graveyard, with whites, in their native country; but they can rise at the sound of the first trump, in the day of resurrection. Yes, reader: we who are slaveborn derive a comfort and solace from the death of those dearest to us, if they have the sad misfortune to be BLACKS and AMERICANS, that you know not. God forbid that you or yours should ever have occasion to know it!

My eldest brother died before my birth: my youngest brother, Isaiah Harper Ward, was born April 5th, 1822, in Cumberland County, New Jersey; and died at New York, April 16th 1838, in the triumphs of faith. He was a lad partaking largely of my father's qualities, resembling him exceedingly. Being the youngest of the family, we all sought to fit him for usefulness, and to shield him from the thousand snares and the ten thousand forms of cruelty and injustice which the unspeakably cruel prejudice of the whites visits upon the head and the heart of every black young man, in New York. To that end, we secured to him the advantages of the Free School, for coloured youth, in that city—advantages which, I am happy to say, were neither lost upon him nor unappreciated by him. Upon leaving school he commenced learning the trade of a printer, in the office of Mr. Henry R. Piercy, of New York—a gentleman who, braving the prejudices of his craft and of the community, took the lad upon the same terms as those upon which he took white lads: a fact all the more creditable to Mr. Piercy, as it was in the very teeth of the abominably debased public sentiment of that city (and of the whole country, in fact) on this subject. But ere Isaiah had finished his trade, he suddenly took a severe cold, which resulted in pneumonia, and—in death.

I expressed a doubt, in a preceding page, as to the legal validity of my brother's freedom. True, he was born in the nominally Free State of New Jersey; true, the inhabitants born in Free States are *generally* free. But according to slave law, "the child follows the condition of the mother, during life." My mother being born of a slave woman, and not being legally freed, those who had a legal claim to her had also a legal claim to her offspring, wherever born, of whatever paternity. Besides, at that time New Jersey had not entirely ceased to be a Slave State. Had my mother been legally freed before his birth, then my brother would have been born free, because born of a free woman. As it was, we were all liable at any time to be captured, enslaved, and re-enslaved—first, because we had been robbed of our liberty; then, because our ancestors had been robbed in like manner; and, thirdly and conclusively, in law, because we were black Americans.

I confess I never felt any personal fear of being retaken—primarily because, as I said before, I knew of no legal claimants; but chiefly because I knew it would be extremely difficult to identify me. I was less than three years old when brought away: to identify me as a man would be no easy matter. Certainly, slaveholders and their more wicked Northern parasites are not very particularly scrupulous about such matters; but still, I never had much fear. My private opinion is, that he who would have enslaved me would have "caught a Tartar": for my peace principles never extended so far as to *either seek or accept peace at the expense of liberty*—if, indeed, a state of slavery can by any possibility be a state of peace.

I beg to conclude this chapter on my family history by adding, that my father had a cousin, in New Jersey, who had escaped from slavery. In the spring of 1826 he was cutting down a tree, which accidentally fell upon him, breaking both thighs. While suffering from this accident his master came and took him back into Maryland. He continued *lame* a very great while, without any *apparent* signs of amendment, until one fine morning he was gone! They never took him again.

Two of my father's nephews, who had escaped to New York, were taken back in the most summary manner, in 1828. I never saw a family thrown into such deep distress by the death of any two of its members, as were our family by the re-enslavement of these two young men. Seven-and-twenty years have past, but we have none of us heard a word concerning them, since their consignment to the living death, the temporal hell, of American slavery.

Some kind persons who may read these pages will accuse me of bitterness towards Americans generally, and slaveholders particularly: indeed, there are many *professed* abolitionists, on both sides of the Atlantic, who have no idea that a black man should feel towards and speak of his tormenters as a white man would concerning his. But suppose the blacks had treated *your* family in the manner the Americans have treated *mine,* for five generations: how would you write about these blacks, and their system of bondage? You would agree with me, that the 109th Psalm, for the 5th to the 21st verses inclusive, was written almost purposely for them.

CHAPTER II. PERSONAL HISTORY

I have narrated when and where I was born, as far as I know. It seems that when young I was a very weakly child, whose life for the first two years and a half appeared suspended upon the most fragile fibre of the most delicate cord. It is not probable that any organic or constitutional disease was afflicting me, but a general debility, the more remarkable as both my parents were robust, healthy persons. Happily for me, my mother was permitted to "hire her time," as it is called in the South—i.e., she was permitted to do what she pleased, and go where she pleased, provided she paid to the estate a certain sum annually. This she found ample means of doing, by her energy, ingenuity, and economy. My mother was a good financier. (O that her mantle had fallen on me!) She paid the yearly hire, and pocketed a *surplus,* wherewith she did much to add to the comforts of her husband and her sickly child. So long and so hopeless was my illness, that the parties owning us feared I could not be reared for the market—the only use for which according to their enlightened ideas, a young negro could possibly be born or reared; their only hope was in my mother's tenderness. Yes: the tenderness of a mother, in that *intensely* FREE country, is a matter of trade, and my poor mother's tender regard for her offspring had its value in dollars and cents.

When I was about two years old (so my mother told my wife), my father, for some trifling mistake or fault, was stabbed in the fleshy part of his arm, with a penknife: the wound was the entire length of the knife blade. On another occasion he received a severe flogging, which left his back in so wretched a state that my mother was obliged to take peculiar precaution against mortification. This sort of treatment of her husband not being relished by my mother, who felt about the maltreatment of her husband as any Christian woman ought to feel, she put forth her sentiments, in pretty strong language. This was insolent. Insolence in a negress could not be endured—it would breed more and greater mischief of a like kind; then what would become of wholesome discipline? Besides, if so trifling a thing as the *mere marriage relation* were to interfere with the supreme proprietor's right of a master over his slave, next we should hear that slavery must give way before marriage! Moreover, if a negress may be allowed free speech, touching the flogging of a negro, simply because that negro happened to be her husband, how long would it be before some such claim would be urged in behalf of some other member of a negro family, in unpleasant circumstances? Would this be endurable, in a republican civilized community, A. D. 1819? By no means. It would sap the very foundation of slavery—it would be like "letting out of water": for let the principle be once established that the negress Anne Ward may speak as she pleases about the flagellation of her husband, the Negro William Ward, as a matter of right, and like some alarming and death-dealing infection it would spread from plantation to plantation, until property in husband and wives would not be worth the having. No, no: marriage must succumb to slavery, slavery must reign supreme over every right and every institution, however venerable or sacred; *ergo,* this free-speaking Anne Ward must be made to feel the greater rigours of the domestic institution. Should she be flogged? that was questionable. She never had been whipped, except, perhaps, by her parents; she was now three-and-thirty years old—rather late for the commencement of training; she weighed 184 lbs. avoirdupoise; she was strong enough to whip an ordinary-sized man; she had as much strength of *will* as of mind; and what did not diminish the awkwardness of the case was, she gave most unmistakable evidences of "rather tall resistance," in case of an attack. Well, then, it were not wise to risk this; but one most convenient course was left to them, and that course they could take with perfect safety to themselves, without yielding one hair's breadth of the rights and powers of slavery, but establishing them—they could sell her, and sell her they would: she was their property, and like any other stock she *could* be sold, and like any other unruly stock she *should* be brought to market.

However, this sickly boy, if practicable, must be raised for the auction mart. Now, to sell his mother *immediately,* depriving him of her tender care, might endanger his life, and, what was all-important in his life, his saleability. Were it not better to risk a little from the freedom of this woman's tongue, than to jeopardize the sale of this *article?* Who knows but, judging from the pedigree, it may prove to be a prime lot—rising six feet in length, and weighing two hundred and twenty pounds, more or less, some day? To ask these questions was to answer them; there was no resisting the force of such valuable and logical considerations. Therefore the sale was delayed; the young animal was to run awhile longer with his—(I accommodate myself to the ideas and facts of slavery, and use a corresponding nomenclature) — dam. Thus my illness prevented the separation of my father and my mother from each other, and from their only child. How God sometimes makes the affliction of His poor, and the very wickedness of their oppressors, the means of blessing them! But how slender the thread that bound my poor parents together! The convalescence of their child, or his death, would in all seeming probability snap it asunder. What depths of anxiety must my mother have endured! How must the reality of his condition have weighed down the fond heart of my father, concerning their child! Could they pray for his continued illness? No; they were parents. Could they petition God for his health? Then they must soon be parted for ever from each other and from him, were that prayer answered. Ye whose children are born free, because you were so born, know but little of what this enslaved pair endured, for weeks and months, at the time to which I allude.

At length a crisis began to appear: the boy grew better. God's blessing upon a mother's tender nursing prevailed over habitual weakness and sickness. The child slept better; he had less fever; his appetite returned; he began to walk without tottering, and seemed to give signs of the cheerfulness he inherited from his father, and the strength of frame (and, to tell truth, of will also) imparted by his mother. Were not the owners right in their "calculations"? Had they not decided and acted wisely, in a business point of view? The dismal prospect before them, connected with the returning health of their child, damped by the joy which my parents, in other circumstances, and in a more desirable country, would have felt in seeing their child's improved state. But the more certain these poor slaves became that their child would soon be well, the nearer approached the time of my mother's sale. Motherlike, she pondered all manner of schemes and plans to postpone that dreaded day. She could close her child's eyes in death, she could follow her husband to the grave, if God should so order; but to be sold from them to the far-off State of Georgia, the State to which Maryland members of Churches sold their nominal fellow Christians — sometimes their own children, and other poor relations — *that* was more than she could bear. Submission to the will of God was one thing, she was prepared for that, but submission to the machinations of Satan was quite another thing; neither her womanhood nor her theology could be reconciled to the latter. Sometimes pacing the floor half the night with her child in her arms — sometimes kneeling for hours in secret prayer to God for deliverance — sometimes in long earnest consultation with my father as to what must be done in this dreaded emergency — my mother passed days, nights, and weeks of anguish which wellnigh drove her to desperation. But a thought flashed upon her mind: she indulged in it. It was full of danger; it demanded high resolution, great courage, unfailing energy, strong determination; it might fail. But it was only a thought, at most only an indulged thought, perhaps the fruit of her very excited state, and it was not yet a plan; but, for the life of her, she could not shake it off. She kept saying to herself, "supposing I should"——Should what? She scarcely dare say to herself, what. But that thought became familiar, and welcome, and more welcome; it began to take another, a more definite form. Yes; almost ere she knew, it had incorporated itself with her will, and become a resolution, a determination. "William," said she to my father, "we must take this child and run away." She said it with energy; my father felt it. He hesitated; he was not a mother. She was decided; and when decided, *she was decided* with all consequences, conditions, and contingencies accepted. As is the case in other families where the wife leads, my father followed my mother in her decision, and accompanied her in—I almost said, her *hegira*.

1855

WILLIAM GRIMES

from Life of William Grimes

I am now an old man—"Old Grimes"—being more than seventy years of age, and the father of eighteen lovely and beautiful children, or whom only twelve, I believe, are living. The youngest child, now eight years old, a smart and active lad, is the only one now with me. The other children that are living are scattered all over the world, one son being now in Australia, digging for gold.

My wife, who at the time we were married, was called in the papers, "the lovely and all-accomplished Miss Clarissa Cæsar," has also grown old, since I introduced her to the reader, as may well be supposed; but she is yet very smart, for so fruitful a vine, and I don't think there are many to be compared to her. Like her noble son, she too is seeking for gold, having been for some time in California.

1855

THOMAS JONES

from Narrative of a Refugee Slave

I was born a slave. My recollections of early life are associated with poverty, suffering and shame. I was made to feel, in my boyhood's first experience, that I was inferior and degraded, and that I must pass through life in a dependent and suffering condition. The experience of forty-three years, which were passed by me in slavery, was one of dark fears and darker realities. John Hawes was my first master. He lived in Hanover County, N.C., between the Black and South Rivers, and was the owner of a large plantation, called Hawes' Plantation. He had over fifty slaves. I remained with my parents nine years. They were both slaves, owned by John Hawes. They had six children, Richard, Alexander, Charles, Sarah, myself, and John. I remember well that dear old cabin, with its clay floor and mud chimney, in which, for nine years, I enjoyed the presence and love of my wretched parents.

Father and mother tried to make it a happy place for their dear children. *They* worked late into the night many and many a time to get a little simple furniture for their home and the home of their children; and they spent many hours of willing toil to stop up the chinks between the logs of their poor hut, that they and their children might be protected from the storm and the cold. I can testify, from my own painful experience, to the deep and fond affection which the slave cherishes in his heart for his home and its dear ones. We have no other tie to link us to the human family, but our fervent love for those who are *with* us and of us in relations of sympathy and devotedness, in wrongs and wretchedness. My dear parents were conscious of the desperate and in-curable woe of their position and destiny; and of the lot of inevitable suffer-ing in store for their beloved children. They talked about our coming misery, and they lifted up their voices and wept aloud, as they spoke of our being torn from them and sold off to the dreaded slave-trader, perhaps never again to see them or hear from them a word of fond love. I have heard them speak of their willingness to bear their own sorrows without complaint, if only we, their dear children, could be safe from the wretchedness before us. And I remem-ber, and *now* fully understand, as I did not *then*, the sad and tearful look they would fix upon us when we were gathered round them and running on with our foolish prattle. I am a father, and I have had the same feelings of unspeak-able anguish, as I have looked upon my precious babes, and have thought of the ignorance, degradation and woe which they must endure as slaves. The great God, who knoweth all the secrets of the heart, and He only, knows the bitter sorrow I now feel when I think of my four dear children who are slaves, torn from me and consigned to hopeless servitude by the iron hand of ruthless wrong. I love those children with all a father's fondness. God gave them to me; but my brother took them from me, in utter scorn of a father's earnest pleadings; and I never shall look upon them again, till I meet them and my oppressors at the final gathering. Will not the Great Father and God make them and me reparation in the final award of mercy to the victim, and of Justice to the cruel desolator?

These nine years of wretchedness passed, and a change came for me. My master sold me to Mr. Jones, of Wilmington, N.C., distant forty-five miles from Hawes' plantation. Mr. Jones sent his slave driver, a colored man named Abraham, to conduct me to my new home in Wilmington. I was at home with my mother when he came. He looked in at the door, and called to me, "Tom, you must go with me." His looks were ugly and his voice was savage. I was very much afraid, and began to cry, holding on to my mother's clothes, and begging her to protect me, and not let the man take me away. Mother wept bitterly, and in the midst of her loud sobbings, cried out in broken words, "I can't save you Tommy; master has sold you, you must go." She threw her arms around me, and while the hot tears fell on my face, she strained me to her heart. There she held me, sobbing and mourning, till the brutal Abraham came in, snatched me away, hurried me out of the house where I was born, my only home, and tore me away from the dear mother who loved me as no other friend could do. She followed him, imploring a moment's delay, and weeping aloud, to the road, where he turned around, and striking at her with his heavy cowhide, fiercely ordered her to stop bawling, and go back into the house.

Thus was I snatched from the presence of my loving parents, and from the true affection of the dear ones of home. For thirteen weary years did my heart turn in its yearnings for that precious home. And then at the age of twenty-two, was I permitted to revisit my early home. I found it all desolate; the family all broken up; father was sold and gone; Richard, Alexander, Charles, Sarah, and John were sold and gone. Mother prematurely old, heartbroken, utterly desolate, weak and dying, alone remained. I saw her, and wept once more on her bosom. I went back to my chains with a deeper woe in my heart than I had ever felt before. There was but one thought of joy in my wretched consciousness, and that was, that my kind and precious mother would soon be at rest in the grave. And then, too, I remember, I mused with deep earnestness on death, as the only friend the poor slave had. And I wished that I too might lie down by my mother's side, and die with her in her loving embrace.

1857

JAMES WILLIAMS

from Life and Adventures of James Williams

I then went to Russelville, and asked for Sammy Glasgow, and a noble old gentleman came to the door, and I asked him if he could tell me the way to Somerset, and he pointed out the way. I asked him if he knew any colored families there. He said, "Yes." He told me of one William Jourden, the first house that I came to, on my left hand. This Jourden was my stepfather; he married my mother, who had run away years before, and the way that I knew where she lived was through a man by the name of Jim Ham, who was driving a team in Lancaster City, whose home was in Elkton. He came home on a visit, and was talking to one of the slave women one night; he sat with his arm around her, I, a little boy, sitting in the chimney-corner, asleep, as they thought, but with one eye open, and a listening. He whispered to her, saying, "I saw that boy's mother." She said, "Did you? Where?" He said, "In Somerset; she is married and doing well; she married a man by the name of William Jourden." When I arrived at my mother's house, I met my stepfather in the yard, cutting wood, and I asked him if Mrs. Jourden was at home. He said, "Yes," and asked me in. I went in and sat down by the door. My mother asked me my name. I answered, "James Williams." She said, "Come to the fire and warm yourself!" I said, "No, that I was not cold." After sitting there awhile, I asked her if she had any children. She said, "Yes," and named one boy that belonged to William Hollingsworth, in Elkton. I asked if she had any more. She named my sister, that belonged to Thomas Moore, of Elkton, Vic, that had run away and was betrayed by a colored man, for the sum of one hundred dollars. I had a brother that went with my mother when she run away from Maryland. She did not say anything about him, but spoke of John Thomas. I asked her if she would know him if she saw him. She said, "Yes." I said, "Are you sure that you would know him?" She answered, "Yes; don't you think I would know my own child?" And becoming somewhat excited, she told me that I had a great deal of impudence, and her loud tone brought her husband in, and he suspicioned me of being a spy for the kidnappers. He came with a stick and stood by the door, when an old lady, by the name of Hannah Brown, exclaimed, "Aunt Abby, don't you know your own child? Bless God, that is him." Then my mother came and greeted me, and my father also. My mother cried, "My God, my son, what are you doing here?" I said that "I had given leg-bail for security."

1893

MY MOTHER AS I RECALL HER

Rosetta Douglass Sprague

Looking backward over a space of fifty years or more, I have in remembrance two travelers whose lives were real in their activity; two lives that have indelibly impressed themselves upon my memory; two lives whose energy and best ability was exerted to make my life what it should be, and who gave me a home where wisdom and industry went hand in hand; where instruction was given that a cultivated brain and an industrious hand were the twin conditions that lead to a well balanced and useful life. These two lives were embodied in the personalities of Frederick Douglass and Anna Murray his wife.

They met at the base of a mountain of wrong and oppression, victims of the slave power as it existed over sixty years ago, one smarting under the manifold hardships as a slave, the other in many ways suffering from the effects of such a system.

The story of Frederick Douglass' hopes and aspirations and longing desire for freedom has been told—you all know it. It was a story made possible by the unswerving loyalty of Anna Murray, to whose memory this paper is written.

Anna Murray was born in Denton, Caroline County, Maryland, an adjoining county to that in which my father was born. The exact date of her birth is not known. Her parents, Bambarra Murray and Mary, his wife, were slaves, their family consisting of twelve children, seven of whom were born in slavery and five born in freedom. My mother, the eighth child, escaped by the short period of one month, the fate of her older brothers and sisters, and was the first free child.

Remaining with her parents until she was seventeen, she felt it time that she should be entirely self-supporting and with that idea she left her country home and went to Baltimore, sought employment in a French family by the name of Montell whom she served two years. Doubtless it was while with them she gained her first idea as to household management which served her so well in after years and which gained for her the reputation of a thorough and competent housekeeper.

On leaving the Montells', she served in a family by the name of Wells living on S. Caroline Street. Wells was Post-master at the time of my father's escape from slavery. It interested me very much in one of my recent visits to Baltimore, to go to that house accompanied by an old friend of my parents of those early days, who as a free woman was enabled with others to make my father's life easier while he was a slave in that city. This house is owned now by a colored man. In going through the house I endeavored to remember its appointments, so frequently spoken of by my mother, for she had lived with this family seven years and an attachment sprang up between her and the members of that household, the memory of which gave her pleasure to recall.

The free people of Baltimore had their own circles from which the slaves were excluded. The ruling of them out of their society resulted more from the desire of the slaveholder than from any great wish of the free people themselves. If a slave would dare to hazard all danger and enter among the free people he would be received. To such a little circle of free people—a circle a little more exclusive than others, Frederick Baily was welcomed. Anna Murray, to whom he had given his heart, sympathized with him and she devoted all her energies to assist him. The three weeks prior to the escape were busy and anxious weeks for Anna Murray. She had lived with the Wells family so long and having been able to save the greater part of her earnings was willing to share with the man she loved that he might gain the freedom he yearned to possess. Her courage, her sympathy at the start was the mainspring that supported the career of Frederick Douglass. As is the condition of most wives her identity became so merged with that of her husband, that few of their earlier friends in the North really knew and appreciated the full value of the woman who presided over the Douglass home for forty-four years. When the escaped slave and future husband of Anna Murray had reached New York in safety, his first act was to write her of his arrival and as they had previously arranged she was to come on immediately. Reaching New York a week later, they were married and immediately took their wedding trip to New Bedford. In "My Bondage of Freedom," by Frederick Douglass, a graphic account of that trip is given.

The little that they possessed was the outcome of the industrial and economical habits that were characteristic of my mother. She had brought with her sufficient goods and chattel to fit up comfortably two rooms in her New Bedford home—a feather bed with pillows, bed linen, dishes, knives, forks, and spoons, besides a well filled trunk of wearing apparel for herself. A new plum colored silk dress was her wedding gown. To my child eyes that dress was very fine. She had previously sold one of her feather beds to assist in defraying the expenses of the flight from bondage.

The early days in New Bedford were spent in daily toil, the wife at the wash board, the husband with saw, buck and axe. I have frequently listened to the rehearsal of those early days of endeavor, looking around me at the well appointed home built up from the labor of the father and mother under so much difficulty, and found it hard to realize that it was a fact. After the day of toil they would seek their little home of two rooms and the meal of the day that was most enjoyable was the supper nicely prepared by mother.

Father frequently spoke of the neatly set table with its snowy white cloth—coarse tho' it was.

In 1890 I was taken by my father to these rooms on Elm Street, New Bedford, Mass., overlooking Buzzards Bay. This was my birth place. Every detail as to the early housekeeping was gone over, it was splendidly impressed upon my mind, even to the hanging of a towel on a particular nail. Many of the dishes used by my mother at that time were in our Rochester home and kept as souvenirs of those first days of housekeeping. The fire that destroyed that home in 1872, also destroyed them.

Three of the family had their birthplace in New Bedford. When after having written his first narrative, father built himself a nice little cottage in Lynn, Mass., and moved his family there, previously to making his first trip to Europe. He was absent during the years '45 and '46. It was then that mother with four children, the eldest in her sixth year, struggled to maintain the family amid much that would dampen the courage of many a young woman of to-day. I had previously been taken to Albany by my father as a means of lightening the burden for mother. Abigail and Lydia Mott, cousins of Lucretia Mott, desired to have the care of me.

During the absence of my father, mother sustained her little family by binding shoes. Mother had many friends in the anti-slavery circle of Lynn and Boston who recognized her sterling qualities, and who encouraged her during the long absence of her husband. Those were days of anxious worry. The narrative of Frederick Douglass with its bold utterances of truth, with the names of the parties with whom he had been associated in slave life, so incensed the slaveholders that it was doubtful if ever he would return to this country and also there was danger for mother and those who had aided in his escape, being pursued. It was with hesitancy father consented to leave the country, and not until he was assured by the many friends that mother and the children would be carefully guarded, would he go.

There were among the Anti-Slavery people of Massachusetts a fraternal spirit born of the noble purpose near their heart that served as an uplift and encouraged the best energies in each individual, and mother from the contact with the great and noble workers grew and improved even more than ever before. She was a recognized co-worker in the A. S. Societies of Lynn and Boston, and no circle was felt to be complete without her presence. There was a weekly gathering of the women to prepare articles for the Annual A. S. Fair held in Faneuil Hall, Boston. At that time mother would spend the week in attendance having charge, in company of a committee of ladies of which she was one, over the refreshments. The New England women were all workers and there was no shirking of responsibility—all worked. It became the custom of the ladies of the Lynn society for each to take their turn in assisting mother in her household duties on the morning of the day that the sewing circle met so as to be sure of her meeting with them. It was mother's custom to put aside the earnings from a certain number of shoes she had bound as her donation to the A. S. cause. Bring frugal and economic she was able to put by a portion of her earnings for a rainy day.

I have often heard my father speak in admiration of mother's executive ability. During his absence abroad, he sent, as he could, support for his family, and on his coming home he supposed there would be some bills to settle. One day while talking over their affairs, mother arose and quietly going to the bureau drawer produced a Bank book with the sums deposited just in the proportion father had sent, the book also containing deposits of her own earnings—and not a debt had been contracted during his absence.

The greatest trial, perhaps, that mother was called upon to endure, after parting from her Baltimore friends several years before, was the leaving her Massachusetts home for the Rochester home where father established the "North Star." She never forgot her old friends and delighted to speak of them up to her last illness.

Wendell Phillips, Wm. Lloyd Garrison, Sydney Howard Gay and many more with their wives were particularly kind to her. At one of the Anti-Slavery conventions held in Syracuse, father and mother were guests of Rev. Samuel J. May, a Unitarian minister and an ardent Anti-Slavery friend. The spacious parlors of the May mansion were thrown open for a reception to their honor and where she could meet her old Boston friends. The refreshments were served on trays, one of which placed upon an improvised table made by the sitting close together of Wendell Phillips, Wm. Lloyd Garrison and Sydney Howard Gay, mother was invited to sit, the four making an interesting tableaux.

Mother occasionally traveled with father on his short trips, but not as often as he would have liked as she was a housekeeper who felt that her presence was necessary in the home, as she was wont to say "to keep things straight." Her life in Rochester was not less active in the cause of the slave, if anything she was more self-sacrificing, and it was a long time after her residence there that she was understood. The atmosphere in which she was placed lacked the genial cordiality that greeted her in her Massachusetts home. There were only the few that learned to know her, for, she drew around herself a certain reserve, after meeting her new acquaintances that forbade any very near approach to her. Prejudice in the early 40's in Rochester ran rampant and mother became more distrustful. There were a few loyal co-workers and she set herself assiduously to work. In the home, with the aid of a laundress only, she managed her household. She watched with a great deal of interest and no little pride the growth in public life of my father, and in every possible way that she was capable aided him by relieving him of all the management of the home as it increased in size and in its appointments. It was her pleasure to know that when he stood up before an audience that his linen was immaculate and that she had made it so, for, no matter how well the laundry was done for the family, she must with her own hands smooth the tucks in father's linen and when he was on a long journey she would forward at a given point a fresh supply.

Being herself one of the first agents of the Underground Railroad she was an untiring worker along that line. To be able to accommodate in a comfortable manner the fugitives that passed our way, father enlarged his home where a suite of rooms could be made ready for those fleeing to Canada. It was no unusual occurrence for mother to be called up at all hours of the night, cold or hot as the case may be, to prepare supper for a hungry lot of fleeing humanity.

She was greatly interested in the publication of the "North Star" or Frederick Douglass' paper as it was called later on, and publication day was always a day for extra rejoicing as each weekly paper was felt to be another arrow sent on its way to do the work of puncturing the veil that shrouded a whole race in gloom. Mother felt it her duty to have her table well supplied with extra provisions that day, a custom that we, childlike, fully appreciated. Our home was two miles from the center of the city, where our office was situated, and many times did we trudge through snow knee deep, as street cars were unknown.

During one of the summer vacations the question arose in father's mind as to how his sons should be employed, for them to run wild through the streets was out of the question. There was much hostile feeling against the colored boys and as he would be from home most of the time, he felt anxious about them. Mother came to the rescue with the suggestion that they be taken into the office and taught the case. They were little fellows and the thought had not occurred to father. He acted upon the suggestion and at the ages of eleven and nine they were perched upon blocks and given their first lesson in printer's ink, besides being employed to carry papers and mailing them.

Father was mother's honored guest. He was from home so often that his home comings were events that she thought worthy of extra notice, and caused renewed activity. Every thing was done that could be to add to his comfort. She also found time to care for four other boys at different times. As they became members of our home circle, the care of their clothing was as carefully seen to as her own children's and they delighted in calling her Mother.

In her early life she was a member of the Methodist Church, as was father, but in our home there was no family alter. [*sic*] Our custom was to read a chapter in the Bible around the table, each reading a verse in turn until the chapter was completed. She was a person who strived to live a Christian life instead of talking it. She was a woman strong in her likes and dislikes, and had a large discernment as to the character of those who came around her. Her gift in that direction being very fortunate in the protection of father's interest especially in the early days of his public life, when there was great apprehension for his safety. She was a woman firm in her opposition to alcoholic drinks, a strict disciplinarian—her *no* meant *no* and *yes, yes,* but more frequently the *no*'s had it, especially when I was the petitioner. So far as I was concerned, I found my father more yielding than my mother, altho' both were rigid as to the matter of obedience.

There was a certain amount of grim humor about mother and perhaps such exhibitions as they occurred were a little startling to those who were unacquainted with her. The reserve in which she held herself made whatever she might attempt of a jocose nature somewhat acrid. She could not be known all at once, she had to be studied. She abhorred shames. In the early 70's she came to Washington and found a large number of people from whom the shackles had recently fallen. She fully realized their condition and considered the gaieties that were then indulged in as frivolous in the extreme.

On one occasion several young women called upon her and commenting on her spacious parlors and the approaching holiday season, thought it a favorable opportunity to suggest the keeping of an open house. Mother replied: "I have been keeping open house for several weeks. I have it closed now and I expect to keep it closed." The young women thinking mother's understanding was at fault, endeavored to explain. They were assured, however, that they were fully understood. Father, who was present, laughingly pointed to the New Bay Window, which had been completed only a few days previous to their call.

Perhaps no other home received under its roof a more varied class of people than did our home. From the highest dignitaries to the lowliest person, bond or free, white or black, were welcomed, and mother was equally gracious to all. There were a few who presumed on the hospitality of the home and officiously insinuated themselves and their advice in a manner that was particularly disagreeable to her. This unwelcome attention on the part of the visitor would be grievously repelled, in a manner more forceful than the said party would deem her capable of, and from such a person an erroneous impression of her temper and qualifications would be given, and criticisms sharp and unjust would be made; so that altho she had her triumphs, they were trials, and only those who knew her intimately could fully understand and appreciate the enduring patience of the wife and mother.

During her wedded life of forty-four years, whether in adversity or prosperity, she was the same faithful ally, guarding as best she could every interest connected with my father, his lifework and the home. Unfortunately an opportunity for a knowledge of books had been denied her, the lack of which she greatly deplored. Her increasing family and household duties prevented any great advancement, altho' she was able to read a little. By contact with people of culture and education, and they were her real friends, her improvement was marked. She took a lively interest in every phase of the Anti-Slavery movement, an interest that father took full pains to foster and to keep her intelligently informed. I was instructed to read to her. She was a good listener, making comments on passing events, which were well worth consideration, altho' the manner of the presentation of them might provoke a smile. Her value was fully appreciated by my father, and in one of his letters to Thomas Auld (his former master,) he says, "Instead of finding my companion a burden she is truly a helpmeet."

In 1882, this remarkable woman, for in many ways she was remarkable, was stricken with paralysis and for four weeks was a great sufferer. Altho' perfectly helpless, she insisted from her sick bed to direct her home affairs. The orders were given with precision and they were obeyed with alacrity. Her fortitude and patience up to within ten days of her death were very great. She helped us to bear her burden. Many letters of condolence from those who had met her and upon whom pleasant impressions had been made, were received. Hon. J. M. Dalzell of Ohio, wrote thus:

"You know I never met your good wife but once and then her welcome was so warm and sincere and unaffected, her manner altogether so motherly, and her goodby so full of genuine kindness and hospitality, as to impress me tenderly and fill my eyes with tears as I now recall it."

Prof. Peter H. Clark of Cincinnati, Ohio, wrote: "The kind treatment given to us and our little one so many years ago won for her a place in our hearts from which no lapse of time could move her. To us she was ever kind and good and our mourning because of her death, is heartfelt."

There is much room for reflection in the review in the life of such a woman as Anna Murray Douglass. Unlettered tho' she was, there was a strength of character and of purpose that won for her the respect of the noblest and best. She was a woman who strove to inculcate in the minds of her children the highest principles of morality and virtue both by precept and example. She was not well versed in the polite etiquette of the drawing room, the rules for the same being found in the many treatises devoted to that branch of literature. She was possessed of a much broader culture, and with discernment born of intelligent observation, and wise discrimination she welcomed all with the hearty manner of a noble soul.

I have thus striven to give you a glimpse of my mother. In so doing I am conscious of having made frequent mention of my father. It is difficult to say any thing of mother without the mention of father, her life was so enveloped in his. Together they rest side by side, and most befittingly, within sight of the dear old home of hallowed memories and from which the panting fugitive, the weary traveler, the lonely emigrant of every clime, received food and shelter.

1900

OF THE PASSING OF THE FIRST-BORN

W. E. B. DuBois, from The Souls of Black Folk

> *O sister, sister, thy first-begotten,*
> *The hands that cling and the feet that follow,*
> *The voice of the child's blood crying yet,*
> Who hath remembered me? who hath forgotten?
> *Thou hast forgotten, O summer swallow,*
> *But the world shall end when I forget.*
> —Swinburne

"Unto you a child is born," sang the bit of yellow paper that fluttered into my room one brown October morning. Then the fear of fatherhood mingled wildly with the joy of creation; I wondered how it looked and how it felt,— what were its eyes, and how its hair curled and crumpled itself. And I thought in awe of her,—she who had slept with Death to tear a man-child from underneath her heart, while I was unconsciously wandering. I fled to my wife and child, repeating the while to myself half wonderingly, "Wife and child? Wife and child?"—fled fast and faster than boat and steamcar, and yet must ever impatiently await them; away from the hard-voiced city, away from the flickering sea into my own Berkshire Hills that sit all sadly guarding the gates of Massachusetts.

Up the stairs I ran to the wan mother and whimpering babe, to the sanctuary on whose altar a life at my bidding had offered itself to win a life, and won. What is this tiny formless thing, this new-born wail from an unknown world,—all head and voice? I handle it curiously, and watch perplexed its winking, breathing, and sneezing. I did not love it then; it seemed a ludicrous thing to love; but her I loved, my girl-mother, she whom now I saw unfolding like the glory of the morning—the transfigured woman.

Through her I came to love the wee thing, as it grew and waxed strong; as its little soul unfolded itself in twitter and cry and half-formed word, and as its eyes caught the gleam and flash of life. How beautiful he was, with his olive-tinted flesh and dark gold ringlets, his eyes of mingled blue and brown, his perfect little limbs, and the soft voluptuous roll which the blood of Africa had moulded into his features! I held him in my arms, after we had sped far away to our Southern home,—held him, and glanced at the hot red soil of Georgia and the breathless city of a hundred hills, and felt a vague unrest. Why was his hair tinted with gold? An evil omen was golden hair in my life. Why had not the brown of his eyes crushed out and killed the blue?—for brown were his father's eyes, and his father's father's. And thus in the Land of the Color-line I saw, as it fell across my baby, the shadow of the Veil.

Within the Veil was he born, said I: and there within shall he live,—a Negro and a Negro's son. Holding in that little head—ah, bitterly!—the unbowed pride of a hunted race, clinging with that tiny dimpled hand—ah, wearily!—to a hope not hopeless but unhopeful, and seeing with those bright wondering eyes that peer into my soul a land whose freedom is to us a mockery and whose liberty a lie. I saw the shadow of the Veil as it passed over my baby, I saw the cold city towering above the blood-red land. I held my face beside his little cheek, showed him the star-children and the twinkling lights as they began to flash, and stilled with an even-song the unvoiced terror of my life.

So sturdy and masterful he grew, so filled with bubbling life so tremulous with the unspoken wisdom of a life but eighteen months distant from the All-life,—we were not far from worshiping this revelation of the divine, my wife and I. Her own life builded and moulded itself upon the child; he tinged her every dream and idealized her every effort. No hands but hers must touch and garnish those little limbs; no dress or frill must touch them that had not wearied her fingers; no voice but hers could coax him off to Dreamland, and she and he together spoke some soft and unknown tongue and in it held communion. I too mused above his little white bed; saw the strength of my own arm stretched onward through the ages through the newer strength of his; saw the dream of my black fathers stagger a step onward in the wild phantasm of the world; heard in his baby voice of the Prophet that was to rise within the Veil.

And so we dreamed and loved and planned by fall and winter, and the full flush of the long Southern spring, till the hot winds rolled from the fetid Gulf, till the roses shivered and the still stern sun quivered its awful light over the hills of Atlanta. And then one night the little feet pattered wearily to the wee white bed, and the tiny hands trembled; and a warm flushed face tossed on the pillow, and we knew baby was sick. Ten days he lay there,—a swift week and three endless days, wasting, wasting away. Cheerily the mother nursed him the first days, and laughed into the little eyes that smiled again. Tenderly then she hovered round him, till the smile fled away and Fear crouched beside the little bed.

Then the day ended not, and night was a dreamless terror, and joy and sleep slipped away. I hear now that Voice at midnight calling me from dull and dreamless trance,—crying, "The Shadow of Death! The Shadow of Death!" Out into the starlight I crept, to rouse the gray physician,—the Shadow of Death, the Shadow of Death. The hours trembled on; the night listened; the ghastly dawn glided like a tired thing across the lamplight. Then we two alone looked upon the child as he turned toward us with great eyes, and stretched his string-like hands,—the Shadow of Death! And we spoke no word, and turned away.

He died at eventide, when the sun lay like a brooding sorrow above the western hills, veiling its face; when the winds spoke not, and the trees, the great green trees he loved, stood motionless. I saw his breath beat quicker and quicker, pause, and then his little soul leapt like a star that travels in the night and left a world of darkness in its train. The day changed not; the same tall trees peeped in at the windows, the same green grass glinted in the setting sun. Only in the chamber of death writhed the world's most piteous thing—a childless mother.

I shirk not. I long for work. I pant for a life full of striving. I am no coward, to shrink before the rugged rush of the storm, nor even quail before the awful shadow of the Veil. But hearken, O Death! Is not this my life hard enough,—is not that dull land that stretches its sneering web about me cold enough,—is not all the world beyond these four little walls pitiless enough, but that thou must needs enter here,—thou, O Death? About my head the thundering storm beat like a heartless voice, and the crazy forest pulsed with the curses of the weak; but what cared I, within my home beside my wife and baby boy? Wast thou so jealous of one little coign of happiness that thou must needs enter there,—thou, O Death?

A perfect life was his, all joy and love, with tears to make it brighter,—sweet as a summer's day beside the Housatonic. The world loved him; the women kissed his curls, the men looked gravely into his wonderful eyes, and the children hovered and fluttered about him. I can see him now, changing like the sky from sparkling laughter to darkening frowns, and then to wondering thoughtfulness as he watched the world. He knew no color-line, poor dear,—and the Veil, though it shadowed him, had not yet darkened half his sun. He loved the white matron, he loved his black nurse; and in his little world walked souls alone, uncolored and unclothed. I—yea, all men—are larger and purer by the infinite breadth of that one little life. She who in simple clearness of vision sees beyond the stars said when he had flown, "He will be happy There; he ever loved beautiful things." And I, far more ignorant, and blind by the web of mine own weaving, sit alone winding words and muttering, "If still he be, and he be There, and there be a There, let him be happy, O Fate!"

Blithe was the morning of his burial, with bird and song and sweet-smelling flowers. The trees whispered to the grass, but the children sat with hushed faces. And yet it seemed a ghostly unreal day,—the wraith of Life. We seemed to rumble down an unknown street behind a little white bundle of posies, with the shadow of a song in ours ears. The busy city dinned about us; they did not say much, those pale-faced hurrying men and women; they did not say much,—they only glanced and said, "Niggers!"

We could not lay him in the ground there in Georgia, for the earth there is strangely red; so we bore him away to the northward, with his flowers and his little folded hands. In vain, in vain!—for where, O God! beneath thy broad blue sky shall my dark baby rest in peace,—where Reverence dwells, and Goodness, and a Freedom that is free?

All that day and all that night there sat an awful gladness in my heart,— nay, blame me not if I see the world thus darkly through the Veil—and my soul whispers ever to me, saying, "Not dead, not dead, but escaped; not bond, but free." No bitter meanness now shall sicken his baby heart till it die a living death, no taunt shall madden his happy boyhood. Fool that I was to think or wish that this little soul should grow choked and deformed within the Veil! I might have known that yonder deep unworldly look that ever and anon floated past his eyes was peering far beyond this narrow Now. In the poise of his little curl-crowned head did there not sit all that wild pride of being which his father had hardly crushed in his own heart? For what, forsooth, shall a Negro want with pride amid the studied humiliations of fifty million fellows? Well sped, my boy, before the world had dubbed your ambition insolence, had held your ideals unattainable, and taught you to cringe and bow. Better far this nameless void that stops my life than a sea of sorrow for you.

Idle words; he might have borne his burden more bravely than we,—aye, and found it lighter too, some day; for surely, surely this is not the end. Surely there shall yet dawn some mighty morning to lift the Veil and set the prisoned free. Not for me,—I shall die in my bonds,—but for fresh young souls who have not known the night and waken to the morning; a morning when men ask of the workman, not "Is he white?" but "Can he work?" When men ask artists, not "Are they black?" but "Do they know?" Some morning this may be, long, long years to come. But now there wails, on that dark shore within the Veil, the same deep voice, *Thou shalt forego!* And all have I foregone at that command, and with small complaint,—all save that fair young form that lies so coldly wed with death in the nest I had builded.

If one must have gone, why not I? Why may I not rest me from this restlessness and sleep from this wide waking? Was not the world's alembic, Time, in his young hands, and is not my time waning? Are there so many workers in the vineyard that the fair promise of this little body could lightly be tossed away? The wretched of my race that line the alleys of the nation sit fatherless and unmothered; but Love sat beside his cradle, and in his ear Wisdom waited to speak. Perhaps now he knows the All-love, and needs not to be wise. Sleep, then, child,—sleep till I sleep and waken to a baby voice and the ceaseless patter of little feet—above the Veil.

1901

SUGGESTIONS FOR FURTHER READING

The best place to read more on love, marriage, family values, and other aspects of early African America is in its press. Many college libraries and historical societies have collections of periodicals, such as the *Colored American Magazine*, the *Missionary Record*, the *Pacific Appeal*, and the *Voice of the Negro*, in print or on microform. Increasingly, research libraries are making at least some of their holdings available online. The vast holdings of the New York Public Library's Schomburg Collection for Research in Black Culture can be explored via its web site www.nypl.org/research/sc/digital.html. By accessing the Wisconsin Historical Society online, at www.wisconsinhistory.org/libraryarchives/aanp/freedom, one can read *Freedom's Journal* in its original form. Most college libraries and some public libraries make available early African American documents through databases such as *African American Newspapers: The Nineteenth Century*, *African American Poetry, 1760–1900*, and *American Slave: A Composite Autobiography*. The *Christian Recorder*, the *Colored American*, *Frederick Douglass' Paper*, *Freedom's Journal*, the *National Era*, and the *North Star* are all included in *African American Newspapers*, which can also be read online at www.accessible.com. Some of the autobiographical accounts excepted in this volume may be found in *American Slave: A Composite Autobiography*, which is also available in a series of volumes published under the same title by Greenwood Press. George P. Rawick is the general editor. Most of the autobiographical accounts excerpted in this volume can be read in their entirety on web sites such as *Documenting the American South: North American Slave Narratives, Beginnings to 1920*, www.docsouth.unc.edu.

Links to a plethora of resources about slavery in the United States are found at www.slave-studies.net.

This volume is perhaps the first to focus upon love, marriage and family in early African America; however, the following books can be helpful in understanding the literary tradition and the historical context or in providing additional examples of other early documents on this and other topics.

Andrews, William L., Trudier Harris, and Frances Smith Foster, eds. *The Oxford Companion to African American Literature*. New York: Oxford University Press, 1997.

Berlin, Ira, and Leslie S. Rowland, eds. *Families and Freedom: A Documentary History of African-American Kinship in the Civil War Era*. New York: The New Press, 1997.

Berlin, Ira, Marc Favreau, and Steven F. Miller, eds. *Remembering Slavery: African Americans Talk about their Personal Experiences of Slavery and Emancipation.* New York: The New Press, 1998.

Blassingame, John. *Slave Testimony: Two Centuries of Letters, Speeches, Interviews and Autobiographies.* Baton Rouge: Louisiana State University Press, 1977.

Brewer, J. Mason. *American Negro Folklore.* Chicago: Quadrangle Press, 1968.

Dance, Daryl, ed. *Honey, Hush! An Anthology of African American Women's Humor.* New York: W.W. Norton & Company, 1998.

Gates, Henry Louis, Jr., and Nellie Y. McKay, eds. *The Norton Anthology of African American Literature.* 2nd ed. New York: W.W. Norton & Company, 2004.

Gutman, Herbert G. *The Black Family in Slavery and Freedom, 1750–1925.* New York: Pantheon Press, 1976.

Horton, James Oliver. *Free People of Color: Inside the African American Community.* Washington: Smithsonian Institution Press, 1993.

Sterling, Dorothy, ed. *Speak Out in Thunder Tones: Letters and Other Writings by Black Northerners, 1787–1865.* New York: Da Capo Press, 1998.

Stevenson, Brenda E. *Life in Black and White: Family and Community in the Slave South.* New York: Oxford University Press, 1996.

West, Emily. *Chains of Love: Slave Couples in Antebellum South Carolina.* Urbana: University of Illinois Press, 2004.

Woodson, Carter G. *The Mind of the Negro as Reflected in Letters Written during the Crisis, 1800–1860.* Washington: The Association for the Study of Negro Life and History, Inc., 1926.

Practically every library has books published by African Americans from the eighteenth century to the first part of the twentieth that are of some relevance to love, marriage, and family. Those listed below are among those excerpted in this collection or that give significant attention to the topic.

Bibb, Henry. *The Life and Adventures of Henry Bibb, An American Slave.* 1849. Madison: The University of Wisconsin Press, 2001.

Craft, William, and Ellen Craft. *Running a Thousand Miles for Freedom.* 1860. Athens: University of Georgia Press, 1999.

Davis, Noah. *A Narrative of the Life of Rev. Noah Davis, a Colored Man.* 1859. Philadelphia: Historic Publications, 1969.

Egypt, Ophelia Settle, ed. *Unwritten History of Slavery: Autobiographical Accounts of Negro Ex-Slaves.* Nashville, Tenn.: Fisk University, 1945.

Griffith, Farah Jasmine, ed. *Beloved Sisters and Loving Friends: Letters from Rebecca Primus of Royal Oak, Maryland, and Addie Brown of Hartford, Connecticut, 1854–1868*. New York: Alfred A. Knopf, 1999.

Henson, Josiah. *Father Hensons Story of His Own Life*. 1858. Baltimore, Md.: Black Classic Press, 1998.

Jacobs, Harriet. *Incidents in the Life of a Slave Girl*. 1861. Nellie Y. McKay and Frances Smith Foster, eds. New York: W. W. Norton & Company, 2001.

Lane, Lunsford. *The Narrative of Lunsford Lane*. In *North Carolina Slave Narratives*, William L. Andrews, ed. Chapel Hill: University of North Carolina Press, 2005.

Menard, John Willis. *Lays in Summer Lands*. 1879. Larry Rivers, Richard Matters, and Canter Brown, eds. Tampa: University of Tampa Press, 2002.

Payne, Daniel A. *Repository of Religion and Literature*.

Sherman, Joan R., ed. *The Black Bard of North Carolina: George Moses Horton*. Chapel Hill: University of North Carolina Press, 1997.

Still, William. *The Underground Railroad: A Record of Facts, Authentic Narratives, Letters, &c.* 1871. Mineola, N.Y.: Dover Publications, 2007.

Ward, Samuel Ringgold. *Autobiography of a Fugitive Negro*. 1850. Eugene, Ore.: Wipf & Stock Publishers, 2000.

Williams, James. *Fugitive Slave in the Gold Rush: Life and Adventures of James Williams*. 1893. Lincoln: University of Nebraska Press, 2002.